Larry Becker

JOHN H. MCKAY, Head Football Coach at the University of Southern California since 1960, is widely known for his *Shifty-I* offense. Coach McKay won the Coach of the Year award in 1962 following a successful season that saw his team win ten games without a loss, capped by a victory over Wisconsin in the Rose Bowl. Before coming to USC, he was assistant football coach at the University of Oregon.

FOOTBALL COACHING

John H. McKay
University of Southern California

THE RONALD PRESS COMPANY • NEW YORK

Copyright © 1966 by
THE RONALD PRESS COMPANY

All Rights Reserved

No part of this book may be reproduced
in any form without permission in writing
from the publisher.

6MP

Library of Congress Catalog Card Number: 66-20082
PRINTED IN THE UNITED STATES OF AMERICA

In Memory of the late
JIM AIKEN
my college coach at the University of Oregon

Preface

Coaching football is a way of life. It is a sixteen-hour day during the season, and a ten-hour day in the off-season. It is thousands of hours looking at film. It is tinkering with plays on paper. It is talking to other coaches to find how to better teach a particular skill. It is convincing a young boy that all he needs to be a good player is physical confidence. It is convincing your supporters that you are intelligent, and at times this is very difficult. It is convincing your players that practice is not as bad as it seems. It is great joy when you win, and despair when you meet defeat. It is putting your work out on display and saying, "Here is what I have accomplished this week." It is going into a locker room before a game and finding it so silent that you can cut the tension with a knife, and then following the game to shouts of joy in victory or tears of frustration in defeat. It is many things to many people, but to me it is a way of life, "the only way."

The football philosophy and techniques followed at USC constitute the basis of this book. We believe in teaching each player all that he can possibly learn rather than concentrating on perfecting the specialist. We also believe that physical conditioning and practice are the heart of a successful football program. The plays discussed and diagrammed in the text that follows are those with which we actually experimented and practiced, tried on the playing field, analyzed, revised and used again. As such they, too, reflect the USC philosophy. Ultimately a football coach is judged by the efforts of his men on the field. For this reason the fundamentals of the offensive and defensive game are thoroughly explored. Both the mechanics and the theory of blocking, running, passing, tackling, kicking, and the other playing skills are carefully developed and discussed. Yet we have not neglected those functions and problems of coaching that lie beyond the play of the game itself. These include discipline, post-game and opponent analysis, and the coach's relations with the players, the school and the community at large. It is hoped that the prospective physical education teacher and football coach for whom this book was primarily written will gain from our experiences.

Grateful appreciation is herewith expressed to the following assistant coaches that are serving and have served on my fine staff, who assisted in the preparation of this book: Mike Giddings (now Head Football Coach at the University of Utah), Dave Levy, Jim Stangeland, Mel Hein, Charles Hall, Marv Goux, Craig Fertig, and Ray George.

Los Angeles, California
March, 1966

JOHN H. McKAY

Contents

Part I. OFFENSE

1	Philosophy and Preliminaries	3
2	Blocking	20
3	USC Running Attack	31
4	USC Passing Attack	69
5	Offense Drills	105

Part II. DEFENSE

6	Defensive Fundamentals and Line Play	113
7	Defensive End Play	130
8	Linebacker Play	144
9	Defensive Secondary Play	156

Part III. KICKING

10	The Kicking Game	177

Part IV. ORGANIZATION AND COACHING PROBLEMS

11	Practice and Training	191
12	Scouting and Analysis	204
13	The Coach's Personal and Public Relations	224
	Index	235

Part I

OFFENSE

1

Philosophy and Preliminaries

USC OFFENSIVE PHILOSOPHY

We at the University of Southern California believe in having an offense as complete as we coaches can intelligently teach to our players. We do not adhere to the theory that a simple, well-mastered offense is the best offense. We believe anything is simple to the person or persons who understand it.

We believe in having our offense an option-type offense as much as possible. By that we mean that we work hard on our running plays' breaking to daylight and not forcing the ball carrier to go into a certain designated hole. We design our practice schedule with this in mind.

In our passing game, we give our receivers a lot of leeway in changing their cut according to the way the defensive man is playing them, or the type of pass defense (man-for-man, zone, etc.) being used. We work hard on having our receivers and quarterback read the defense after we have assumed our offensive set. We also read "on the move" after the ball is snapped. To accomplish this, we have our outside men stand up rather than use a three-point stance. When they are set wide, we feel it is easier for them to notice any shifting or changing of secondary men if they are upright.

PERSONNEL

We do not believe we can always be blessed with the ideal player for each position. However, given our choice, this is what we prefer in each individual. I shall also include the basic moves he must master.

Split End (X)

He must have fine hands, good moves, and good running ability after the catch. He is a receiver first, runner second, blocker third. He must be able to make the key catch and must have the faking ability to get clear if covered by one man.

His stance is upright, hands on hips, with one foot staggered to the rear. He watches the ball, as it is sometimes difficult to hear the snap count in crowded stadia. We prefer an upright stance, in which he can best ascertain the defensive pass coverage and can best see the ball and initial defensive moves.

His start on a pass play must be quick and hard off the line. As he drives off the line, he aims at the outside leg of the defensive back.

Tight End (Y)

He must be big enough and strong enough to block tackles and ends, and yet possess the ability to catch when called upon. He is a blocker first, receiver second, and runner third. His is perhaps the toughest line position to fill.

His stance is the initial key to his success. We use a three-point stance with the down arm in front of the rear foot. We do not designate which arm is down. The rear foot is normally staggered with the toe to the heel of the front foot. However, this varies from player to player, depending on height and leg length and also on the block we intend to employ. His feet should be spread shoulder width.

His start is very important. If he is to drive a man back he should stagger his back foot farther to the rear and place more weight on his down hand. If he is to block down, which he does most often, he must even his feet and place his weight on his outside foot, so as to drive down with his inside foot.

He should adjust his split from his tackle according to the play called. If he is to release on a pass he should widen some. But, if he is to block down alone, he should tighten down to prevent penetration by the defender. He should, as a general rule, widen on inside plays, tighten down on outside plays, and vary his split on weakside plays.

Weak Tackle (WT)

He is the quickest of the tackles, as he is called on to cut off a defender by himself. Height and agility can help here. He must

PHILOSOPHY AND PRELIMINARIES

also be strong enough to perform the one-on-one block. If he can catch, we like to throw tackle-eligible passes to him.

His stance and starts are similar to those of the Y-End. He should remember to tighten down when attempting to cut off a defender.

Strong Tackle (ST)

Our strongest blocker. He does not need to be as quick as our weak tackle, but must be able to handle a defender one-on-one. He also makes important blocking calls on the line and so must possess a fair knowledge of the game.

His stance and starts are similar to those of our Y and WT.

Weak Guard (WG)

He should be our fastest interior lineman, as he pulls on many plays. He does not have to be a great one-on-one blocker, as he is seldom called on for this.

His stance varies somewhat, depending on whether he is pulling. We prefer a balanced stance so that he does not "tip" his pulling by leaning back or to one side. He staggers more if he is driving straight ahead.

His start on pulls is very important. He steps laterally (not back) with the foot that is to the side he is pulling to, driving his corresponding elbow back hard and tight to his side. He then crosses over with his trailing foot and sprints down the line, remaining as low as possible. His depth into the backfield depends on the play. On a trap, he must "get up into the hole." If leading through a hole, he must "belly" back slightly to be able to turn up into the hole at an angle where he can pick off the inside pursuit men. If attempting to take an end in, he must get depth immediately on his second step.

Strong Guard (SG)

He should be the stronger of the guards, as he will be called on to block good-sized defenders by himself. He must also be agile enough to pull.

His stance and starts are the same as for our WG.

Center (C)

We prefer a big man to shield our QB. He must be quick enough to cut off a man head-on and to fill for our pulling guards. Quickness is needed before strength.

His stance is with his left arm down, knuckles or fingers touching the ground, grasping the ball in his right hand. He has the ball as far forward as possible, to allow the maximum distance between the defensive linemen and our blockers. This is to improve our chances of blocking down. Our linemen align their heads on our center's shoulders. The laces of the football are to the left, and as the ball is brought up the center twists his wrist so that the laces hit the QB's top hand.

His starts are lateral on many plays; thus we prefer a balanced stance. His right toe is slightly back of his left toe.

R-back (R)

He should be a top runner who has the speed to go outside, the durability to go inside, and the toughness to block. This is a tough position to fill, as we also like this man to be a receiver and a motion man. We will sacrifice speed for durability and toughness.

His stance when aligned as a halfback behind a tackle is a three-point stance with no more than a toe-to-heel stagger. We emphasize weight concentration, with the weight on the foot opposite the direction in which he will start. If aligned as a T-back behind our F-back, he is in a two-point stance, feet parallel, hands on his knees, and as close to F as possible.

His start is with a lead step in the direction he is going. He steps directly at the man or hole he intends to hit. We feel the lead step allows him to adjust more quickly if a defender alters his charge. He has a split-second advantage with the lead step as opposed to the cross-over step.

When going in motion, the T-back always sprints laterally at full speed. His motion is as fast as he can go. The QB must get the ball snapped at the proper instant.

F-back (F)

He must be a blocker of the first rank. He must also be able to pick up key gains in short-yardage situations. We would also like him to have enough speed to be a threat on our option play outside.

His stance and starts are the same as for our R-back. He must be intelligent in varying his depth in order to give himself good blocking angles, yet must not be so obvious that he tips the play. Generally, if he is to block an end out he should go shallow, and if he is to block an end in or run an option, he should deepen.

Z-back (Z)

He can be the swift runner-receiver type who may not be as durable as the R-back. He should be a sprinter if possible, and need not possess the toughness for blocking duties inside. We prefer a good runner who can catch, over a receiver who is a fair runner, as we like to align Z as a T-back some of the time.

His stance when flanked is the same as for X, and when aligned as a T-back, it is the same as for R in the T-back position.

Quarterback (QB)

We prefer a running QB who is first a passer and secondly a runner. We prefer a passer to a runner who is only an adequate passer. Leadership and dedication to the game are essential. In short, he must be able to move our team on the ground or in the air.

His feet are parallel and he is comfortably back from the center, not hunched over him. This enables him to sprint out quickly, and also allows room for our pulling guards.

The exchange between QB and C is vital, of course. We instruct our QB to place his thumbs together then rotate his hands to the left until the middle finger of the right hand splits the buttocks of C. His thumbs must always touch. His elbows are slightly flexed, to allow for C's initial move. As he receives the ball, the QB should place the ball in his "third hand," that is, quickly pull the ball into his stomach, as he pivots or moves along the line. We use both open and reverse pivots, and weight concentration on the foot that remains planted is imperative.

On the handoff exchange to a ball carrier, the QB places the ball in the man's stomach at belt level. The back receives the ball with his hands in the same position as if he were catching a thrown ball at the belt, palms out, thumbs out, fingers pointing down. We feel this is the most natural position for his hands.

On pitch-out plays, the QB tosses a soft underhand lob using both hands. He aims at the waist, leading the ball carrier slightly.

In passing the football, the QB has several key points to remember. First, because we use roll-out passes, the QB must remember that if he and the receiver are moving, he aims at the helmet and does not lead the receiver. He throws with a downward motion of the arm, so that, being aimed at the helmet, the ball should arrive no higher than chest-high on short passes. Second, the QB must endeavor to get his shoulders square to the line of scrimmage on roll-out passes. We want him to face upfield prior to throwing, to insure correct arm motion. Third, when a right-handed passer rolls out to his left, he should throw somewhat sidearm to insure maximum accuracy and velocity. Fourth, when throwing to a deep receiver we want "a lot of air" under the ball and we make the receiver "run under the ball."

FORMATIONS

We use strongside and weakside in our offensive line, and the men flop from side to side depending on our call. We have four calls to put our strongside to the right and four calls to put our strongside to the left. These calls also determine the alignment of the backs.

Strongside to our Right:

1. Star
2. East
3. Right
4. Gee

Strongside to our Left:

1. Port
2. West
3. Left
4. Haw

All other words or letters are for the placement of the backs. A letter added to one of the calls denotes a shift to another backfield alignment. A word added to one of the calls means another backfield alignment as soon as we line up on the ball.

In Gee formation our strongside is to our right, and the weakside to our left (Fig. 1–1). In Haw the opposite is true (Fig. 1–2). Our strongside guard, tackle, and end (Y) always go together.

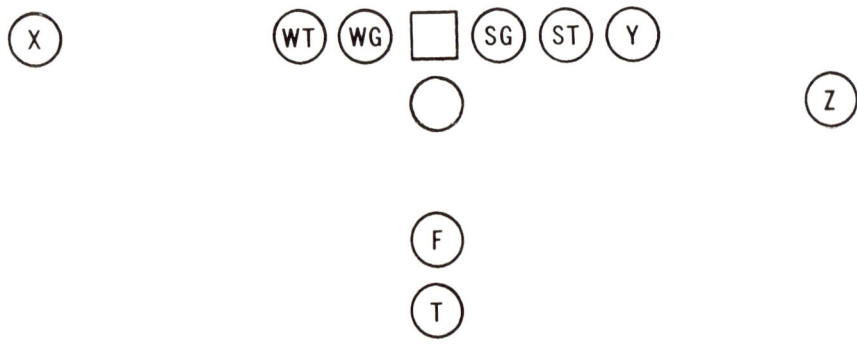

Fig. 1–1. Gee formation. Strongside to the Right.

PHILOSOPHY AND PRELIMINARIES 9

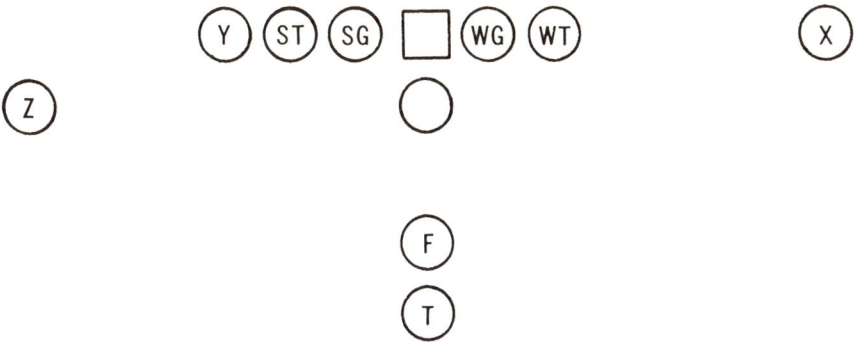

Fig. 1–2. Haw formation. Strongside to the Left.

Our weakside guard and tackle always go together. Our split end (X) usually goes weakside, but at times we align him to our strongside, as we will show later.

Our backfield consists of our quarterback, our remaining halfback (R), our fullback (F), and our flankerback (Z). If R lines up in the I-formation behind F, we then call him the T-back (for tailback). This simplifies our offensive assignments. (See play diagrams to follow.)

If we wish R to align himself as a T-back, we call Gee or Haw. But, if we wish him to align behind one of our tackles in a normal halfback position, we must add a word in front of Gee or Haw. If we wish to align him behind our weak tackle, we call "Pro" Gee (Fig. 1–3). If we wish to align him behind our strong tackle, we call "Strong" Gee (Fig. 1–4).

If we wish to split our backs, we call "Split" Gee (Fig. 1–5).

At times we prefer to line up in Gee or Haw (with a T-back) and then shift to another set. In this case, we give our formations a letter designation instead of a word. Split-Gee becomes A-Gee,

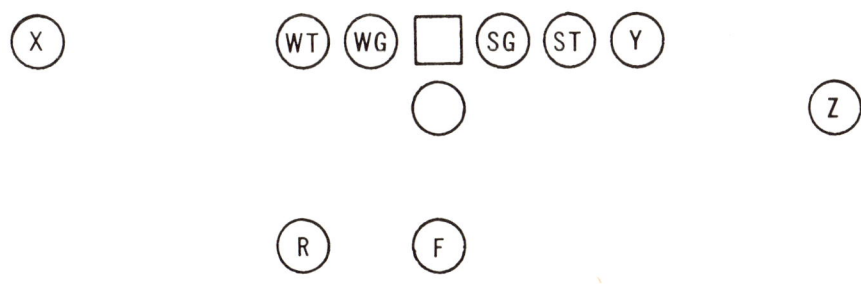

Fig. 1–3. Pro-Gee formation.

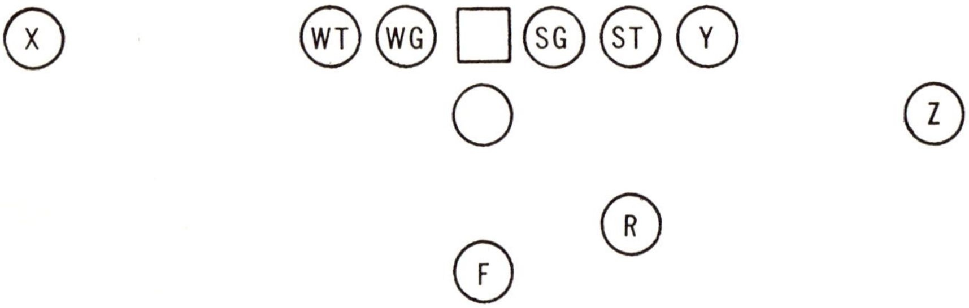

Fig. 1-4. Strong-Gee formation.

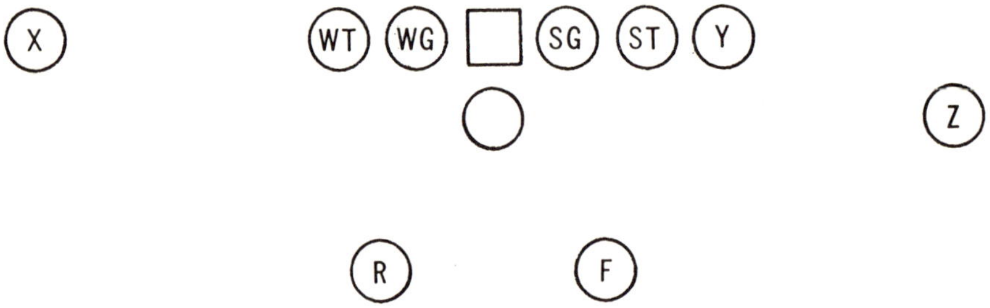

Fig. 1-5. Split-Gee formation.

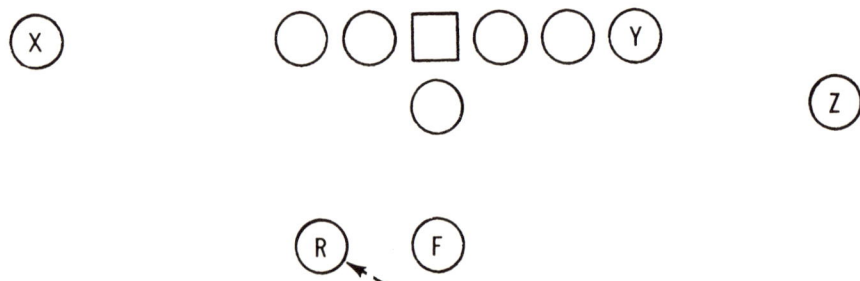

Fig. 1-6. C-Gee formation.

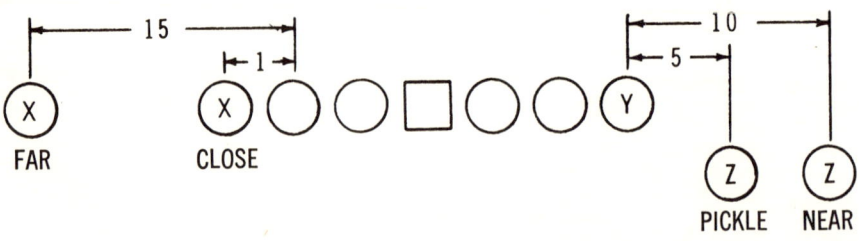

Fig. 1-7. Split positions.

Strong-Gee becomes B-Gee, Pro-Gee becomes C-Gee. Thus, if in the huddle we called Pro-Gee, the R-back would come out of the huddle and immediately align himself weakside. But, if we called C-Gee, the R-back would line up in the T-back position and shift weakside (Fig. 1–6).

In Gee and Haw formations, the Z-back always flanks strongside and our X-end splits weakside. We have four positions for these men. The "Far" position is a split of 15 yards, the "Near" position, 10 yards, the "Pickle" position, 5 yards, and the "Close" position, one yard (Fig. 1–7).

If we wish to align Z in the T-back position, we change the call of our formation and call the formation "Right" or "Left." Our strongside would go to the right if "Right" formation was called. Z aligns himself in the T position, and A aligns himself weakside (Fig. 1–8).

If we wish R strongside, we call "Strong" Right (Fig. 1–9).

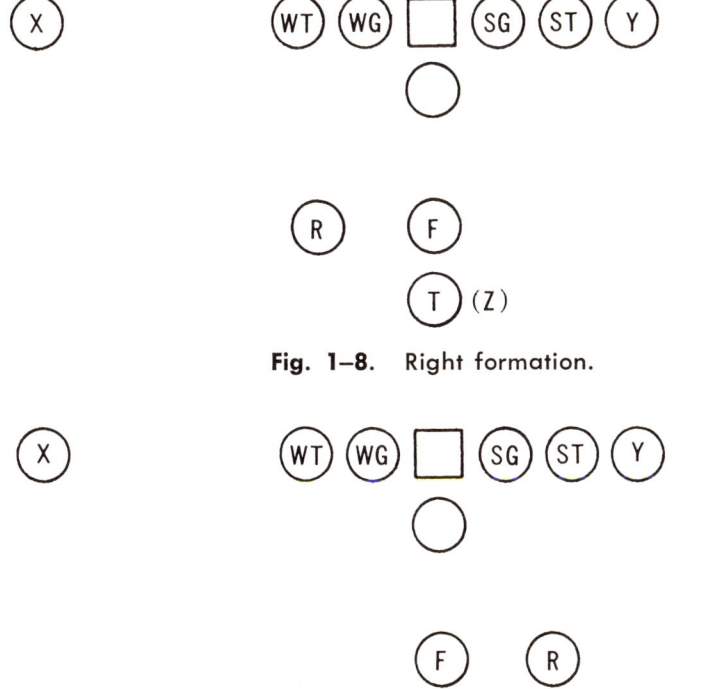

Fig. 1–8. Right formation.

Fig. 1–9. Strong-Right formation.

If we wish to go unbalanced, we call "East," or "West," and X aligns himself strongside (Fig. 1-10).

We have one other formation change, where we align X and Z to the same side, bringing Z over as a slot-back 7 yards from the tackle (Fig. 1-11); we call this "Star" (strongside right), or "Port" (strongside left). Once again, if we wish R to align himself weakside, we call Pro-Star (Fig. 1-12); strongside, we call Strong-Star; split backs we call Split-Star.

If we wished to shift to Strong-Star, we would call "B" Star in the huddle (Fig. 1-13).

Huddle Procedure

Because we have a strongside and a weakside, our procedure for breaking the huddle will vary with the formation called; however, we have basic principles to govern our huddle break.

1. We huddle 5 yds. directly behind the ball and it is the center's responsibility to check our huddle alignment. (Line up is on the center, not the QB.) (Fig. 1-14)

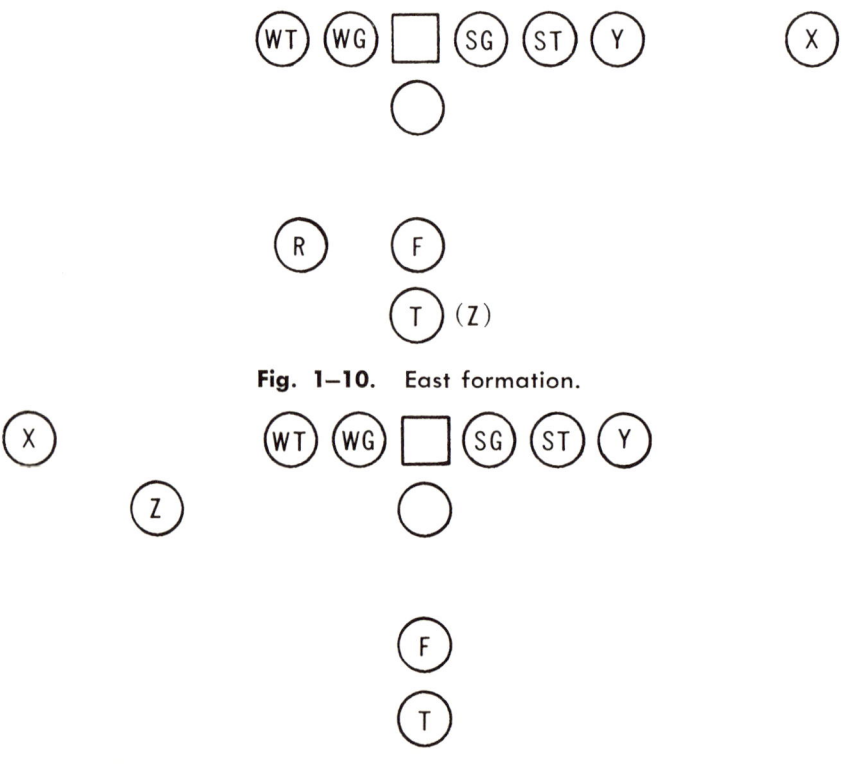

Fig. 1-10. East formation.

Fig. 1-11. Star formation.

PHILOSOPHY AND PRELIMINARIES

2. C and X leave the huddle as soon as the QB calls the play. X goes behind C if X is going to the left.
3. If Z is going to be in a flanked position then he will also leave the huddle early.
4. Whenever it is necessary for a lineman to cross through the huddle, the strongside lineman will cross in front of his respective weakside lineman.
5. F and R will hesitate for linemen who are crossing through the huddle.
6. The QB will break the huddle with the command "Break."
7. Procedure for calling a play is: 1st—formation, 2nd—play, 3rd—snap count.

Example: "Gee—24 Power—on Go."

Cadence

Our cadence is designed to enable us to go quickly without shifting, and to allow us to shift or get motion and go on a later count. We believe the non-rhythm and the rhythm counts both have merit, so have tried to combine the two. Our cadence is: Go—Set—Ready-y-y Hike. If we go on the first count it is non-

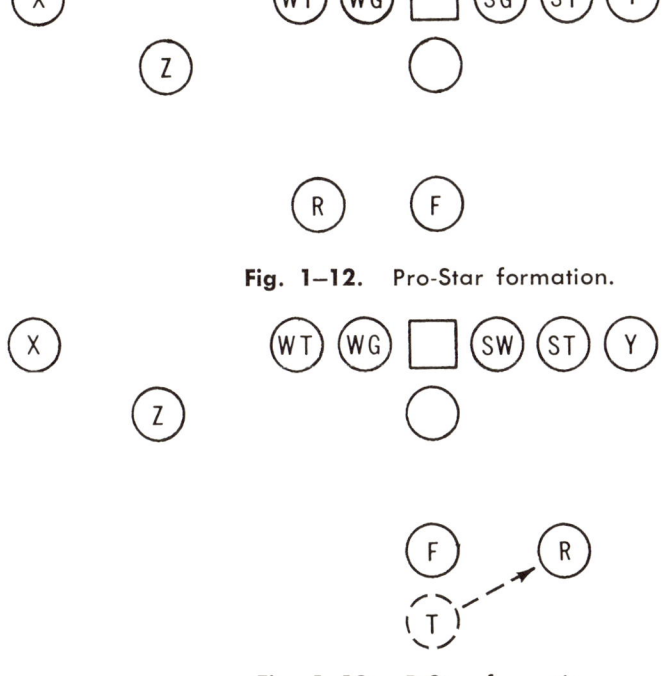

Fig. 1–12. Pro-Star formation.

Fig. 1–13. B-Star formation.

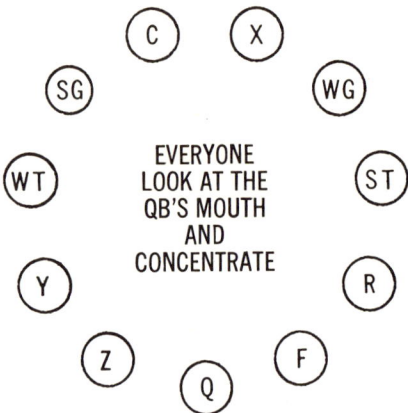

Fig. 1-14. USC huddle.

rhythm, of course. But, if we go on Hike, we obtain some rhythm with the Ready-y-y sound.

If we desire motion we can snap the ball on Go or on Hike, depending on our preference. If a team likes to shift defenses, we like to get off early on Go. But, we also, at times, like to either shift or motion, to cause rotation of a 4' Deep or Monster (Rover) secondary and then prefer to snap the ball on Hike.

The QB controls the snap of the ball when we motion a back. If we want to snap the ball on Hike (probably the easiest and safest for inexperienced teams) our motion man starts his lateral movement on Set. Depending on how wide we wish our motion man to be on the snap, the QB then hesitates for a period before the Ready-Hike.

But, if we wish to snap the ball on Go (first sound), we must coordinate our motion man with the QB. It is illegal, of course, to begin motion until the team has been stationary for one full second. As we align ourselves at the line of scrimmage, each lineman assumes the three-point stance from which he will move on the snap. Our F-back also assumes this stance. Our T-back is in an upright, two-point stance, feet parallel, with his hands on his knees. (X and Z are upright, hands on hips, feet staggered.) The T-back (our motion man) watches the hands of our QB. Our QB allows the team to set at least the full one second time, then places his hands under the center to receive the snap. This is the key for T to motion. The QB allows time for the length of motion we want, then commands Go, and the ball is snapped.

We feel we can align ourselves in a multitude of formations and present varied pictures and problems to the defense without an

PHILOSOPHY AND PRELIMINARIES 15

over-abundance of learning on our part. Our cadence allows us to shift and/or motion to force defensive adjustments that may gain us an advantage at a certain point of the defensive alignment. The next phase for us is our method of calling plays. This, too, must not cause undue learning on our part as we must be able to run each play from several different formations without changing the assignments of our offensive men.

Hole Numbering

Our holes are numbered even to our strongside, and odd to our weakside, and they flop with our offensive linemen (Figs. 1–15 and 1–16). That is, for example, the 4-hole is always between our strong tackle and Y-end no matter where they align themselves.

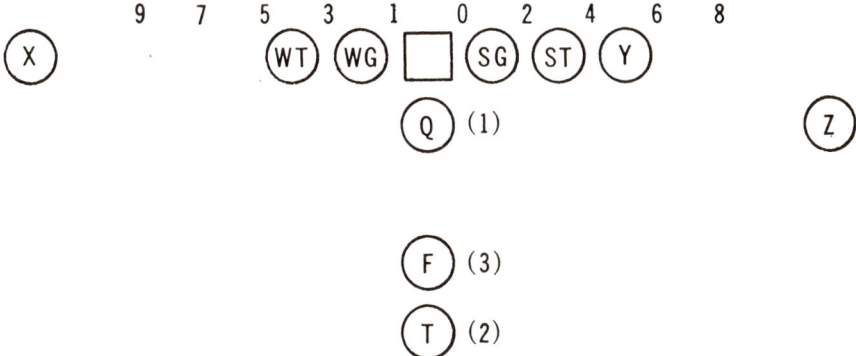

Fig. 1–15. Hole numbering in Gee formation.

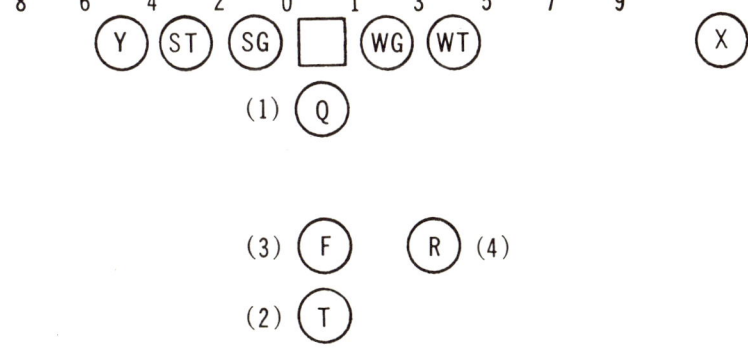

Fig. 1–16. Hole numbering in Left formation.

Our backs are numbered as follows: The QB is one; the F-back, three; the T-back, two; and the R-back, four, if in a halfback position. Certain plays involving the T-back, such as our "24 Power" play can involve either the R-back as the ball carrier (in Gee formation, Fig. 1–17) or the Z-back as the ball carrier (in Right formation, Fig. 1–18).

In addition, we give each play a name, such as sweep, power, trap, etc., to simplify our blocking rules. Our linemen (and backs involved in blocking) learn blocking rules according to the name of the play, not the number. Thus, we have sweep blocking, power blocking, etc., and each blocker has a rule for a sweep, a power, etc.

To take one example of a run from several formations, let us take our power play vs. a 5-man line. We call it "24 Power" (Fig. 1–19), and occasionally "44 Power" (Figs. 1–17 to 1–20).

The blocking rules remain constant, the hole remains the same, but the play takes on a different look from each formation. Other possibilities include: Right 44 Power and Pro-Star 44 Power.

Any time Z is aligned at T-back and he is not the ball carrier (any play beginning with 3 (the F-back) or 4 (the R-back), he motions to the side of the play (Fig. 1–21). If we wish to have him motion opposite the play, we add the word "Fly" (Fig. 1–22).

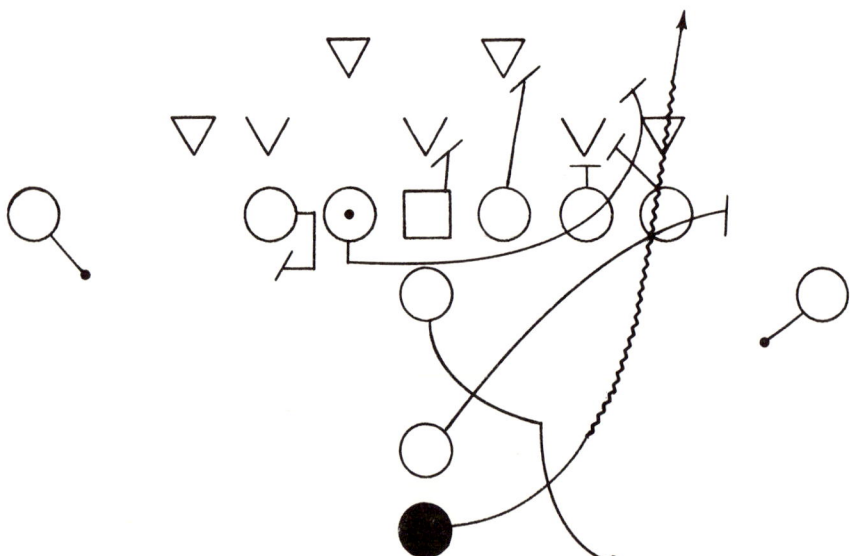

Fig. 1–17. 24 Power from Gee formation.

PHILOSOPHY AND PRELIMINARIES

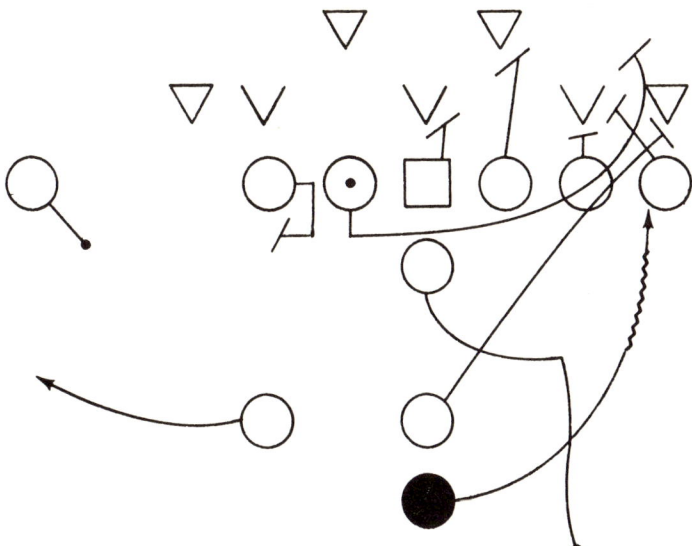

Fig. 1–18. 24 Power from Right formation.

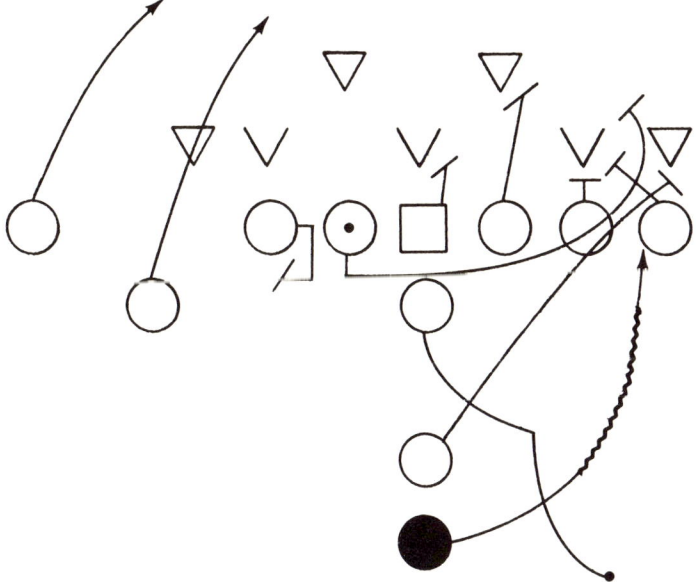

Fig. 1–19. 24 Power from Star formation.

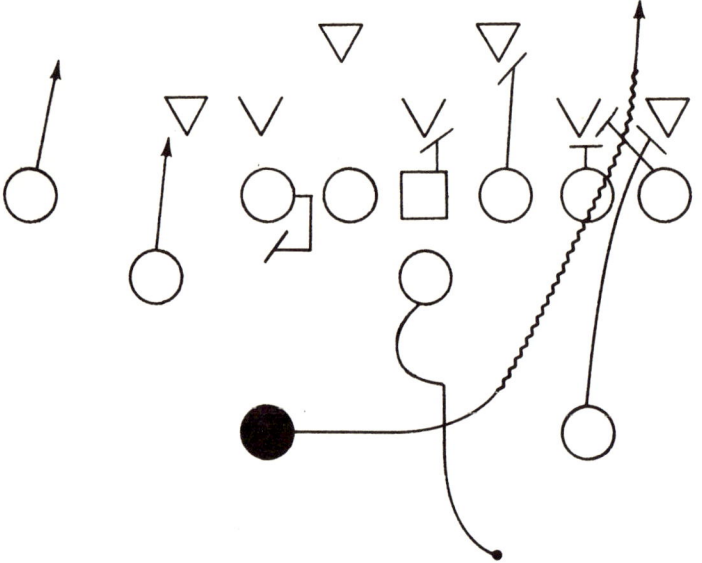

Fig. 1-20. 44 Power from Split-Star formation.

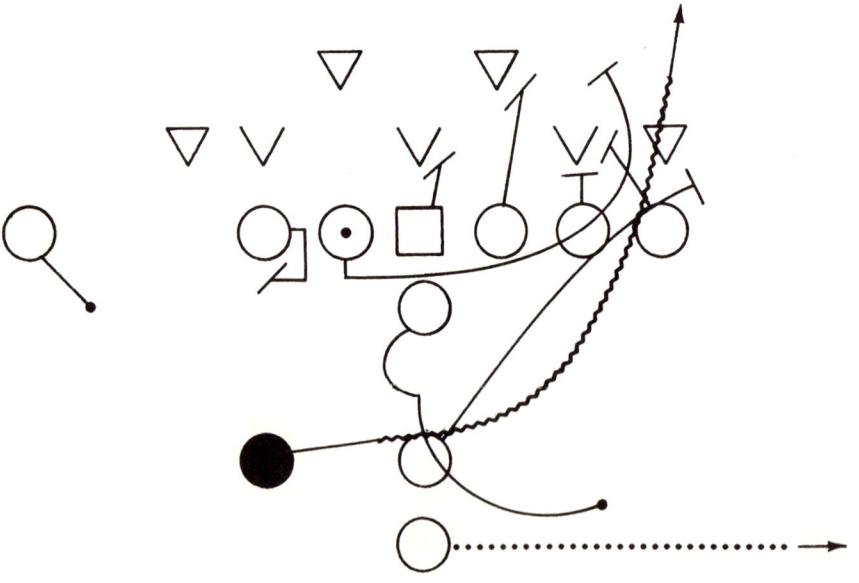

Fig. 1-21. Normal motion by T-back.

PHILOSOPHY AND PRELIMINARIES

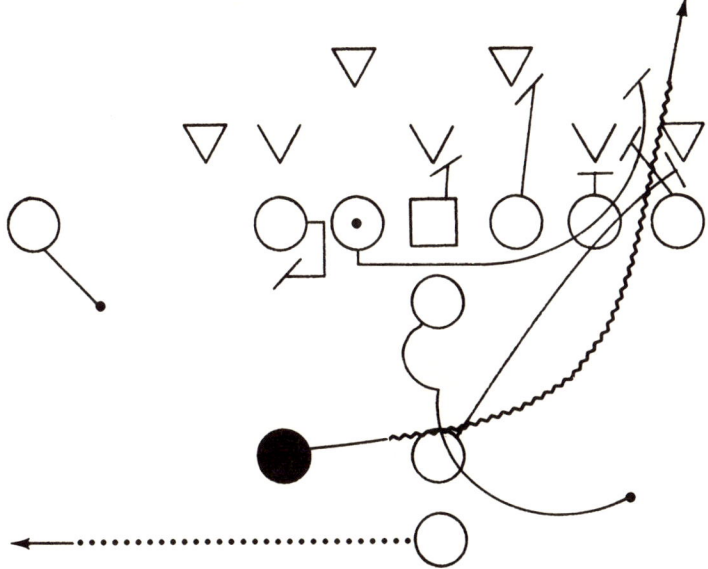

Fig. 1–22. "Fly" motion by T-back.

2

Blocking

ASSIGNMENTS

We have attempted to simplify our blocking assignments and rules by numbering the defensive men and then assigning our blockers a numbered man. We number the defensive men on each side of our Center. Any man on our Center is given the number 0, and we then number outside, and finally into the secondary. (See Figs. 2–1 to 2–4.)

Note that if a linebacker is stacked behind a lineman, we number the lineman first.

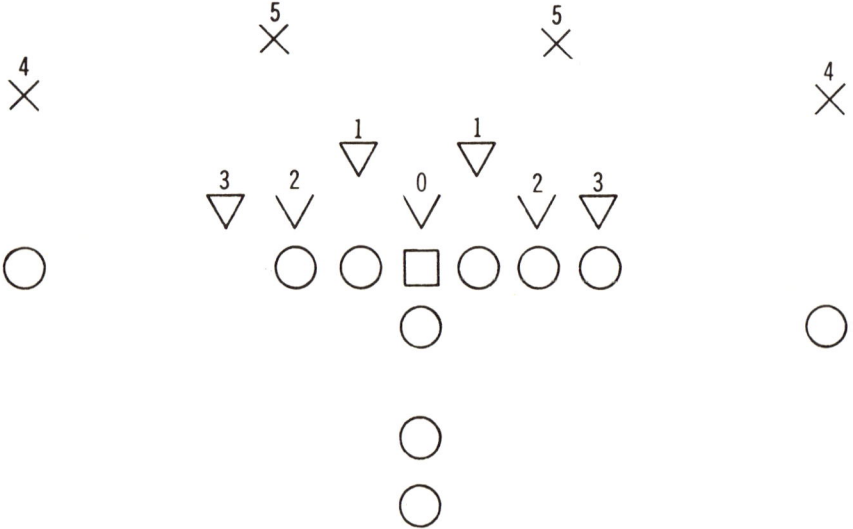

Fig. 2–1. Numbering the 50 defense.

BLOCKING

Our blocking rules become relatively simple as we merely say, "Block one," and our offensive man knows who to block. Another example would be, "Two if on the line, otherwise out." This would mean to block number two if he is aligned on the line; but if two is a linebacker, you block to your outside.

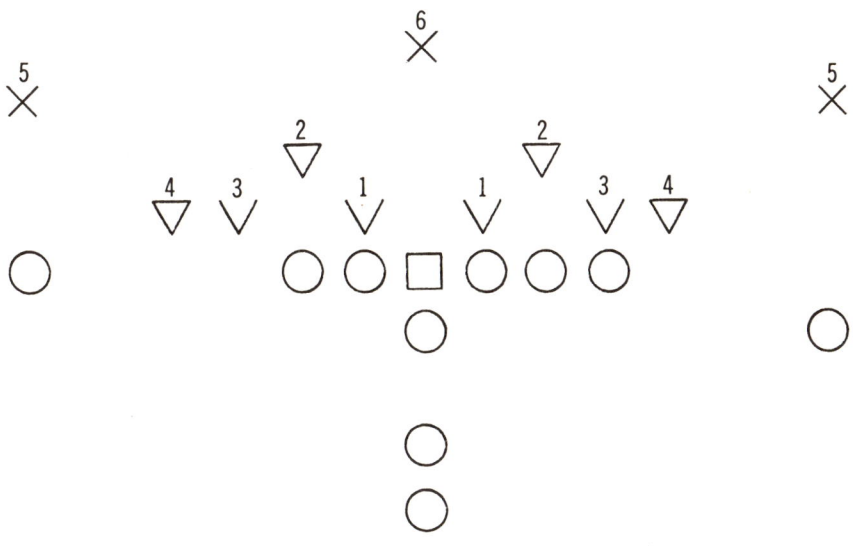

Fig. 2–2. Numbering the 60 defense.

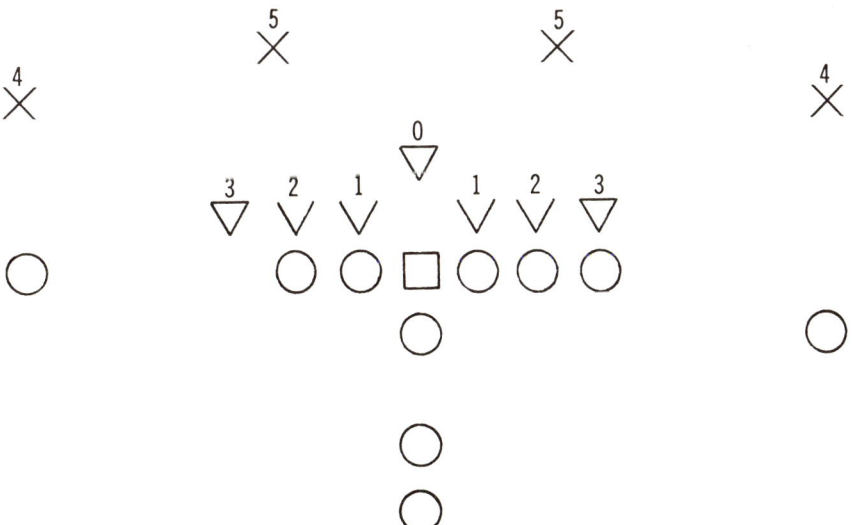

Fig. 2–3. Numbering the 6-1 defense.

TYPES OF BLOCKS

Before getting into the running and passing phases of our offense, I feel an explanation of our blocking techniques is necessary. We employ a variety of blocks, and all have their place in our scheme of offense, depending on the play that is called. We do not believe a blocker can use the same technique on each play as it just will not get the job done. Thus, we spend a great deal of practice time attempting to perfect our various blocking techniques. We feel it is important for our blockers to know the correct technique they are to use as well as their particular assignment. Here is a list of our blocks.

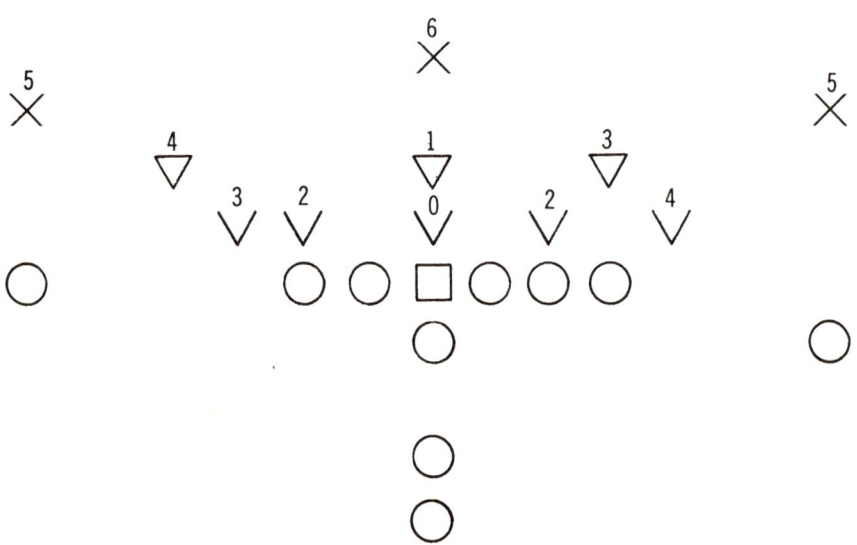

Fig. 2–4. Numbering the 5-3 defense.

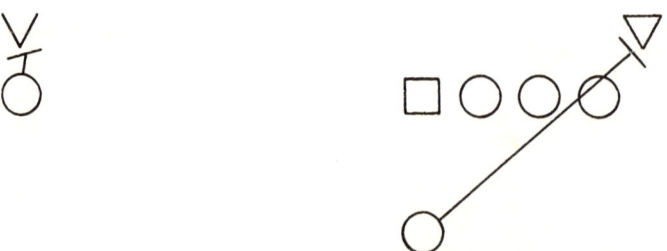

Fig. 2–5. Drive blocks.

BLOCKING

Drive Block

The basic shoulder block used to drive a defender back is the drive block. Most of our blocks involve the technique of this block. We drive our head at the belt of the defender, slide our head by and at the same time deliver a hard jolt with our shoulder and thrust our free arm forward and by the defender. We stress keeping our head up, back arched, feet spread, and short, choppy steps following contact. We feel a blocker must jolt a defender back before he attempts to turn him. (See Fig. 2–5.)

Cut-off Block

This is a difficult block designed to cut a defender off from the direction of the play (Fig. 2–6). If cutting off an opponent who is slightly outside us, we drive off our outside foot, stepping to the outside knee of the defender with our inside foot. We attempt to jolt the defender's outside knee with our inside shoulder. We then scramble upfield on all fours and try at all times to keep outside position on our opponent.

Seal Block

A block similar to the cut-off is one where we seal our inside, such as by a tackle stopping penetration inside when our guard pulls in the opposite direction (Fig. 2–7). The difference is that we step with our near foot to close the gap and we do not need to scramble. Clipping is legal in this case, also.

Fig. 2–6. Cut-off block.

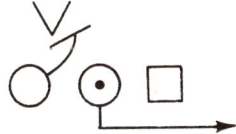

Fig. 2–7. Seal block.

Option Block

We use this block in conjunction with our seal block. We "option" (Fig. 2–8) when there is no man to seal. After stepping down with our inside foot we wheel around in a low football position ready to pin-block an opponent.

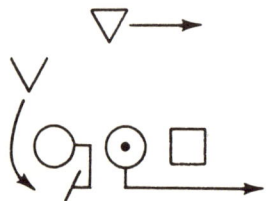 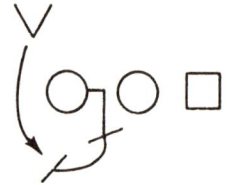

Fig. 2–8. Option block.   Fig. 2–9. Pin block.

Pin Block.

This is a body block used in pass protection where we invite the defender to go outside and then we drive our head across his body and go into a body block (Fig. 2–9).

Far-Shoulder Block

This block is used when we block down to our inside in an attempt to take our opponent to the inside (Figs. 2–10 and 2–11). The most important concern here is to prevent penetration, and that is why we attempt to drive our far (outside) shoulder to the opponent's belt. We step with our inside foot first, aiming down the line. The second step is quite important, as it must also be down the line and not upfield. Once we make contact, the drive-block technique is used, unless the defender tries to escape by backing off. If he does this, we use a "reverse" technique, whipping our tail around so that our head is now facing into our backfield and our legs cut off the defender (Fig. 2–11).

Reverse Block

This block is used to take an opponent to the inside when a cut-off block is impossible to use because the defender reads the head too quickly. Initially, we execute a drive block with our *outside* shoulder, forcing the defender to meet us hard with his inside shoulder. Then we whip our tail in the reverse technique described above (see also Fig. 2–12). This block is more effective if an inside fake is involved.

Close Block

A block similar to the seal block is where we keep going down the line following our step to seal rather than executing the option block (Fig. 2–13).

BLOCKING

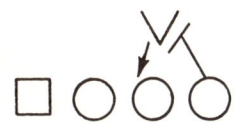

Fig. 2–10. Far-shoulder block.

Fig. 2–11. Far-shoulder block with reverse.

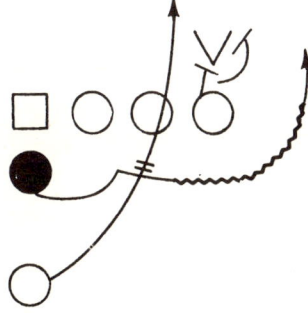

Fig. 2–12. Reverse block.

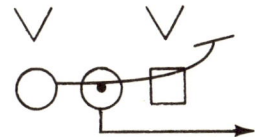

Fig. 2–13. Close block.

Over Block

This is a block initially executed as a drive block where we end up taking the defender to the inside. It is usually executed by a pulling guard. We drive our outside shoulder into our opponent and then slip our head to his outside and drive him back and to the inside. (See Figs. 2–14 and 2–15.)

Wall-off Block

This is used on a far linebacker (Fig. 2–16). We emphasize using a higher block than our normal drive block, and aim at the numbers. Otherwise, the basic techniques of the drive block are used.

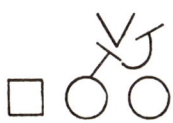

Fig. 2–14. Over block on a drive block.

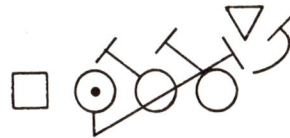

Fig. 2–15. Over block by pulling guard.

Fig. 2–16. Wall-off block on a linebacker.

Fig. 2–17. Influence block by an end.

Influence Block

We fake a drive block with our inside shoulder to set up a trap block by an inside blocker. We attempt to get a quick jolt on the defender. (See Fig. 2–17.)

Bump Block

This block is a high jolt at the numbers used when we are going downfield to block but wish to impede the charge of the defender (Fig. 2–18).

Chop Block

This is our downfield body block (Fig. 2–19). We try to run right up to the defender, jolt him with our far shoulder, and then throw our hip at his numbers. The key point is to get close and not throw too soon.

Fig. 2–18. Bump block before going downfield to chop.

Fig. 2–19. Chop block downfield.

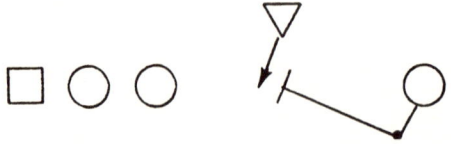

Fig. 2–20. Crackback block.

BLOCKING 27

Crackback Block

This is a block by a flanked blocker to his inside. He steps back with his inside foot, finds the defender, and comes down high and hard with a block similar to the wall-off technique. To prevent penetration, he initially drives his head across and jolts with his outside shoulder. (See Fig. 2–20.)

Area Block

This block is used by a flanked blocker to control his area. We step back and watch our ball carrier, and if he breaks our way we will then use our crackback technique or go downfield and use our chop technique (Fig. 2–21).

Junction Block

The basic block used by our back who is a lead blocker to the outside is the junction block. We use a knee-high body block, and we can take the defender in or out (Figs. 2–22 and 2–23). We aim

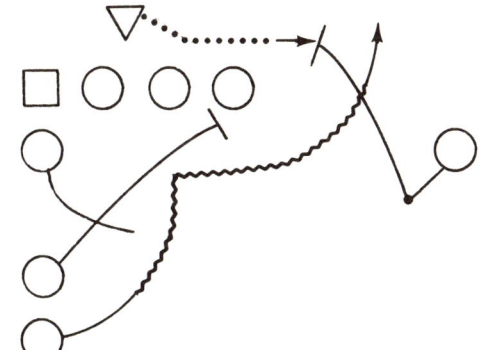

Fig. 2–21. Area block with a crackback.

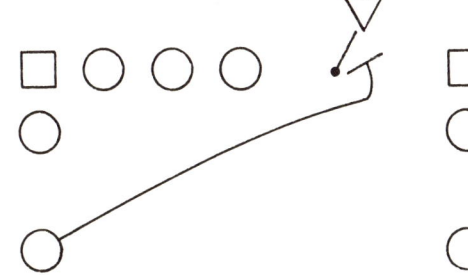

Fig. 2–22. Junction block taking a defender in.

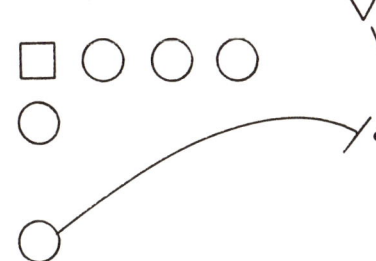

Fig. 2–23. Junction block taking a defender out.

at the opponent's outside knee and attempt a cut-off block, but if the defender flees outside we throw our tail into him with our head pointed back to our goalline.

Fill Block

This is a block used by a back to replace a pulling guard. We use drive block techniques. (See Fig. 2–24.)

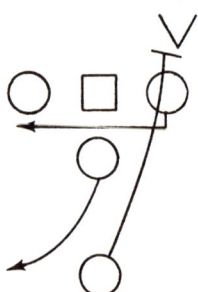

Fig. 2–24. Fill block.

Double-Team Block

Our post man drive-blocks the defender with his outside shoulder, but does not follow through. He is attempting to stop the charge of the defender. Our turn man blocks down with a near shoulder drive block aimed at the rib area. He steps with his inside foot. As soon as the post man feels the turn man he turns his tail into the turn man and together they drive the defender down the line. If the defender slants outside our blockers merely switch assignments with the turn man now posting for our inside blocker. We then drive the defender to the outside. (See Figs. 2–25 and 2–26.)

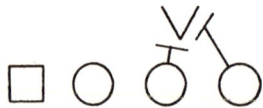 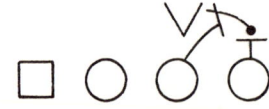

Fig. 2–25. Double-team block taking a defender in.

Fig. 2–26. Double-team block taking a defender out.

BLOCKING CALLS

In addition to the above techniques, we have calls we use to give us better blocking angles against certain defensive sets. On each play our tackles call a block. The strong tackle calls first. The

BLOCKING 29

call may mean nothing, or it may alter the basic rule that has been assigned on this particular play. Our center may also call at times. We feel it is important for our tackles and centers to make false calls quite often and we spend some blackboard time discussing this. Besides the blocking angles it gives us, the calls add an interesting aspect to the game for our linemen.

Eagle Blocking

Tackle and guard exchange assignments, with tackle blocking 1 and guard blocking 2; tackle goes first (Fig. 2–27).

Pigeon Blocking

Guard and tackle exchange assignments, with guard blocking 2 and tackle blocking 1; guard goes first (Fig. 2–28).

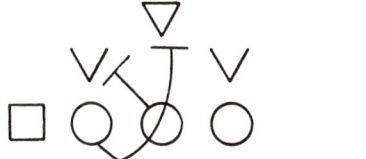

Fig. 2–27. Eagle blocking.

Fig. 2–28. Pigeon blocking.

Trojan Blocking

End and tackle exchange assignments, with end blocking 2 and tackle blocking 3; end goes first (Fig. 2–29).

Roman Blocking

Tackle and end exchange assignments, with tackle blocking 3 and end blocking 2; tackle goes first (Fig. 2–30).

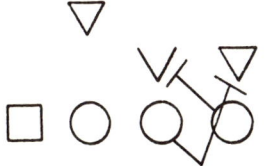

Fig. 2–29. Trojan blocking.

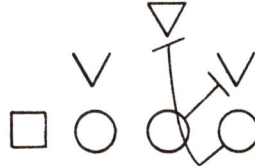

Fig. 2–30. Roman blocking.

George Blocking

Includes SG, ST, SE, with end and tackle blocking first man to inside on or off LOS—SG pulling and blocking first man past his tackle (Fig. 2–31).

Gap Blocking

All strongside linemen block the defensive man on their inside gap (Fig. 2–32).

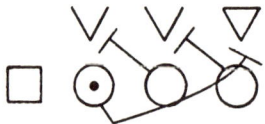 

Fig. 2–31. George blocking.   Fig. 2–32. Gap blocking.

X Blocking

Call is made by the center for exchange block between center and guard—off-side call (Fig. 2–33).

Solid Blocking

Call is made by the center when a trap or blast play has been called and the linebackers are lined up tight and appear to be prepared to penetrate (Fig. 2–34).

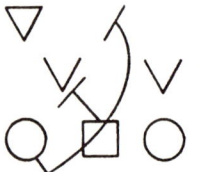 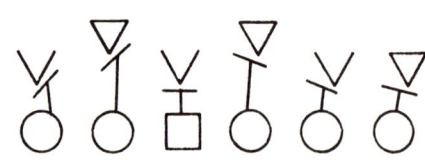

Fig. 2–33. X blocking.   Fig. 2–34. Solid blocking.

3

USC Running Attack

THE RUNNING PLAYS

As stated previously, our running plays are called with two numbers and a descriptive name that signifies the blocking to be used. I shall discuss our running plays in the following categories:

Power Off-tackle play with "option" running by the T-back.

Option Outside option play where the QB either keeps the ball or pitches to the F-back.

Keep Option play where the QB first fakes a belly to the F-back, then either keeps the ball or pitches to the T-back.

Sweep A wide run by the R-back.

Counter An off-tackle play where the F-back fakes away from the play.

Belly An off-tackle play with the F-back carrying.

Drive An inside play with the F-back carrying.

Blast An inside play with the T-back carrying and the F-back (and possibly the R-back) leading.

Trap An inside play carried by the F-back or R-back in which our guard traps the first man past the center.

I shall attempt to indicate the key coaching points we feel are necessary to make a play work, as well as the assignments of each man. I shall also indicate the theory behind the play and the defenses against which we like to use it.

Power Strongside—24 Power

See Figs 3–1 and 3–2.

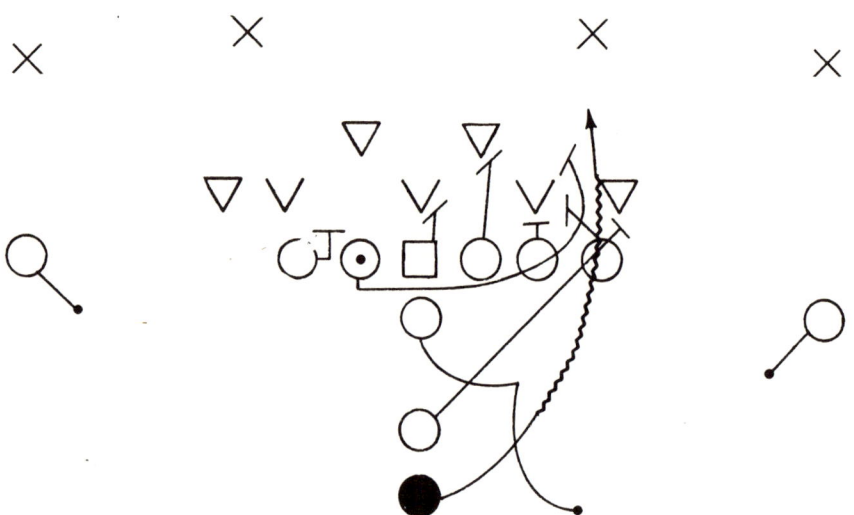

Fig. 3-1. Gee—24 Power vs. a 50 defense.

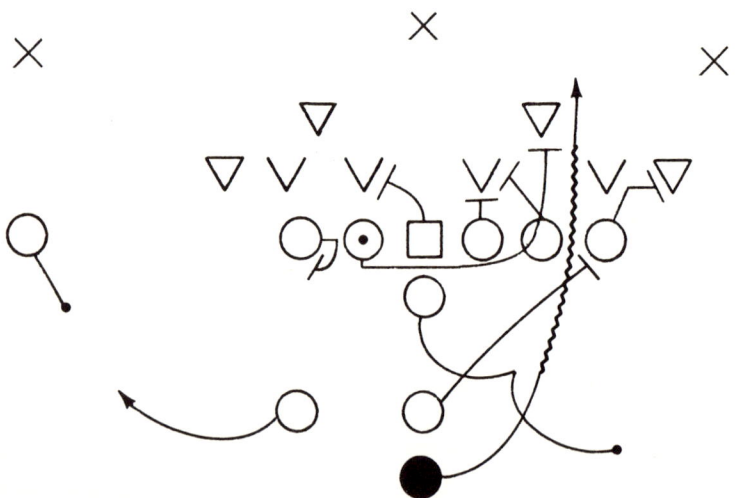

Fig. 3-2. Right—24 Power vs. a 60 defense.

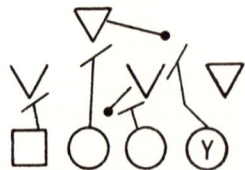

Fig. 3-3. Y picking up a stunting linebacker.

USC RUNNING ATTACK

Assignments

Y—If 2 is on the line, block in. Otherwise, out.
ST—Block 2 on the line. Otherwise, nearest defender inside.
SG—Block 1.
C—On. Offside.
WG—Pull and lead.
WT—Seal. Option.
X—Block area.
QB—Reverse pivot and hand off to T. Fake Green 24. (Pass.)
F—Lead over outside leg of your tackle and block the first defensive man.
R—Swing. (Ball carrier on 44 Power.)
T—Ball carrier. (Motion strong on 44 Power.)
Z—Block area. Away, chop 6.

Coaching Points

Y—If 2 is on the line in a 5-man set, Y's block will be a double-team. He is the turn man. If 2 slants inside, Y must be in position to block the LB (Fig. 3-3).
ST—If 2 is on the line, his block will be a double-team and he will be the post man. If 2 is off the line, he will be the turn man and his guard will post.
SG—If 2 is off the line, he will be the post man on a double-team block. If blocking a LB, fleeing outside, he turns inside and looks for the off LB coming across (Fig. 3-4).

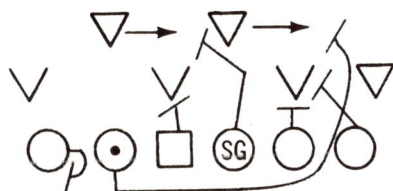

Fig. 3-4. SG picking up the off linebacker.

C—He uses a cut-off block if the man is on.
WG—He pulls tight along the line and cuts up tight into the hole looking to his inside. The hole will be longer vs. a 5-man line; vs. a 6-man line, if the LB shoots, he traps him (Fig. 3-5).
WT—Seal-option technique. He can clip in this area.
X & Z—They watch the ball carrier for a possible break to their area. (We have broken several long gainers because of key blocks by these men.)
QB—He must get the ball to the T-back as deep as possible so as to allow more time for the T-back to see the hole open.

T—He takes one lead step to the outside. Thus his weight must be on the foot to the weakside as he aligns himself. He watches the block of the tackle for the initial hole. He must be aware of down and distance, because although he has an option to hit any hole where daylight shows, we want him to stay up in the hole when going for short yardage.

F—The key is the angle he takes. The first step is very important and must be at his tackle and not too wide. He must drive his head inside the defender and "dig him out."

We prefer 24 Power to 44 Power (R-back carrying from an alignment behind his weak tackle) for several reasons. For one thing, the play hits quicker by a couple of steps; the one difficulty this creates is that the weak guard must be quite quick to beat the T-back to the hole. Secondly, the ball carrier can see daylight easier and sooner from his T-back position. This play has broken well at all holes along the line, especially over the 1-hole, and we feel this would be impossible from the R-back alignment. Thirdly, and in conjunction with the second point, the ball carrier has three directions in which to cut—straight, left, or right—and this is much easier from the T-back position. These factors force the defenders, especially the off-side line and linebackers to "stay at home" longer and thus cuts down pursuit when the play does break at the 4-hole. It also forces wide defenders to stay put for an instant and this makes Green 24 (Pass) much more effective. The power has averaged good yardage in the 4-hole vs. the 60 defense, and has broken back well vs. the 50 (Figs. 3–6 and 3–7).

Power Weakside—25 Power

See Figs. 3–8 and 3–9.

Assignments

Y—Chop 6.
ST—Seal-option.
SG—Pull and lead.
C—On. Offside.
WG—Block 1.
WT—Block 2 if on the line. Otherwise, nearest defender inside.
X—Block area.
QB—Reverse pivot and give the ball to T. Fake Green 25 (Pass).
F—Lead over outside leg of your tackle and block the first defensive man.
R—Swing.
T—Ball carrier.
Z—Block area.

USC RUNNING ATTACK

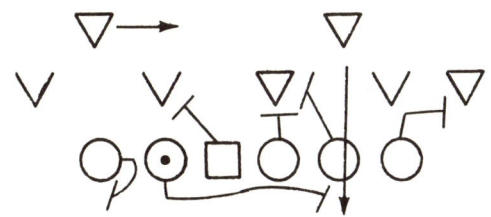

Fig. 3-5. WG picking up a shooting linebacker.

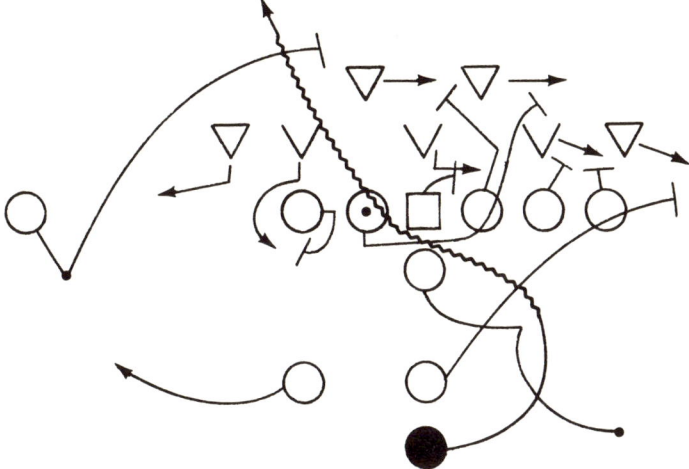

Fig. 3-6. Right—24 Power breaking at the 1-hole vs. a 50.

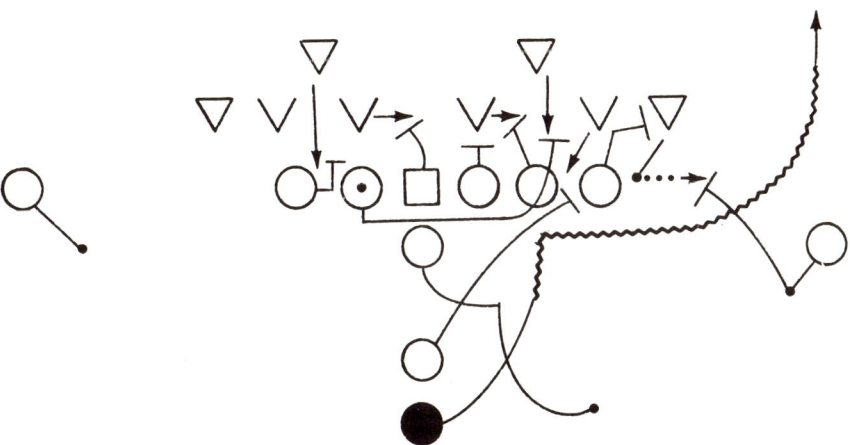

Fig. 3-7. Gee—24 Power breaking outside vs. a 60.

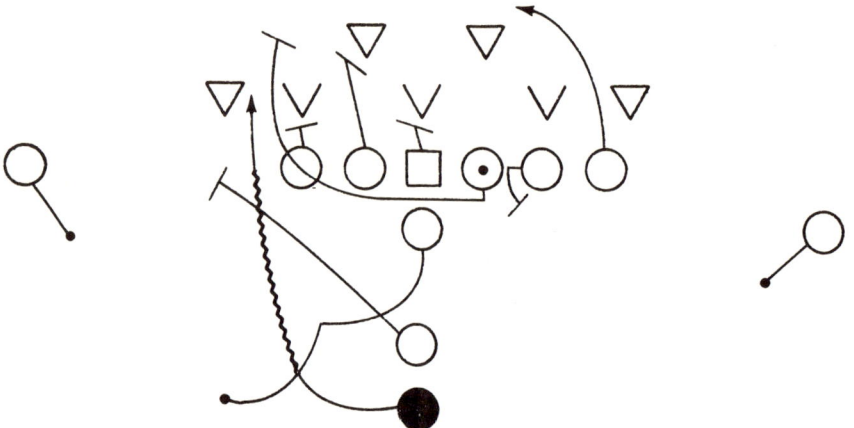

Fig. 3-8. Gee—25 Power vs. a 50.

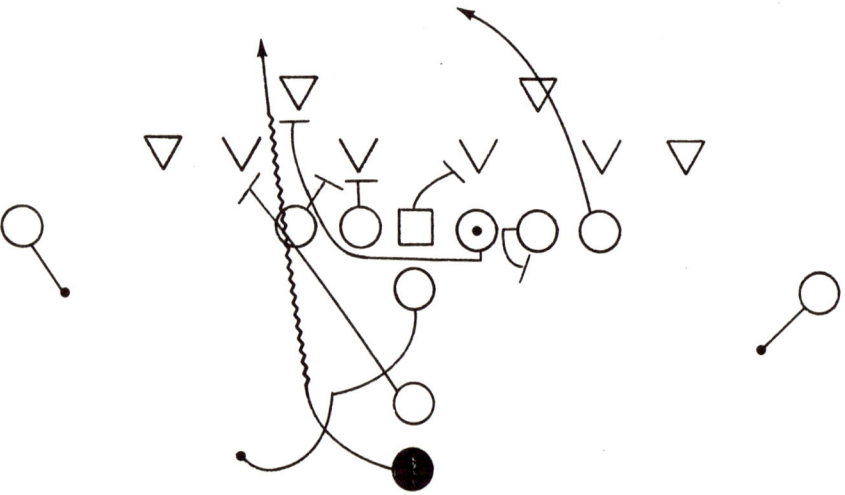

Fig. 3-9. Gee—25 Power vs. a 60.

Coaching Points. As this play is just the opposite of 24 Power, the same coaching points apply. The one man with a different assignment is the weak tackle vs. the 5-man line. His is a one-on-one block, and the key point is to drive-block the man and not worry about taking him in or out. The ball carrier will hit daylight.

This play is especially tough on the defensive end as he is almost forced to play the run, and thus Green 25 becomes effective. Also, we have had some luck breaking outside against ends who close too tough and are susceptible to an over block by our fullback.

USC RUNNING ATTACK

We prefer to run the play vs. a 5-man front and will run it on any down and distance situation.

Option Strongside—16 Option

See Figs. 3–10 and 3–11.

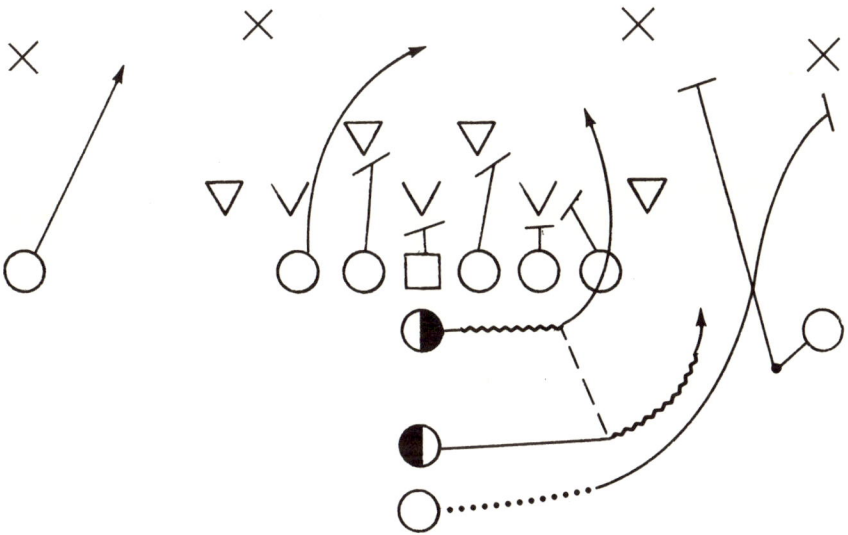

Fig. 3–10. Gee—16 Option vs. a 50.

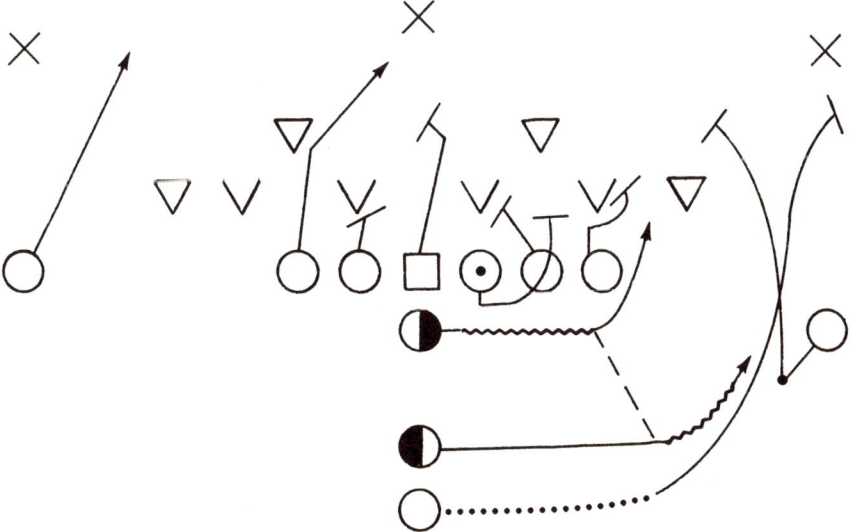

Fig. 3–11. Gee—16 Option vs. a 60.

Assignments

Y—Between, on. (Note: 5–3, block LB.)
ST—Block 2. Or, tackle call.
SG—Block 1. Or, tackle call.
C—Block 0. Off LB.
WG—Cut 1.
WT—Bump 2, chop 6. (Note: Gap 8, block inside gap.)
X—Chop 6.
Q—Open step and execute option technique on first man outside Y.
F—Ball carrier.
R—Swing.
T—Motion strong and block the HB.
Z—3-deep, block 1st defensive man coming out. 4-deep, inside safety. Away, Chop 6.

Coaching Points

Y—"Between" means any man between Y and his strong tackle. If it is 2, then the block will be a double-team, and Y will be the turn man. If it is 3, the reverse technique should be used if possible.
ST—If 2 is on the line, a double-team exists and he is the post man. Vs. a 60 defense, we like an "Eagle" call. He uses a far-shoulder block when blocking down.
SG—Vs. a 50, a good cut-off angle must be taken, as the LB will probably leave quickly. Vs. a 60 an "Eagle" call should arise. He must get up in the hole for the LB who may step up tough if he is keying our tackle.
WT—He must recognize the gap situation and prevent backside chase.
Z—He must recognize 3 deep and 4 deep defenses. If the 50 is a rotated 4 deep, Z must crackback on the rotated man who is up on the line of scrimmage.
QB—As he takes his open step out and slightly back, he immediately looks to the 1st defensive man outside his Y end. This man will be his key. If this man comes, the QB will pitch to the FB. If he floats, the QB will cut up tight off the block of the Y end. This play has on occasion broken tighter, also. The technique on the pitch is a two-handed flip-toss emphasizing wrist action. He allows motion no further than Y.
F—He aligns himself slightly deeper on this play and maintains the proper relationship with the QB at all times. If the QB cuts upfield, the FB must cut with him.
T—We want full speed motion, and he aims for the HB. He uses a junction block.

This play has been effective vs. 5-man lines that employ a 4-deep secondary. We prefer to run it against this type of set, especially if the 4-deep secondary is rotating the outside man (4, or corner-

USC RUNNING ATTACK 39

back) up and the safety deep. If the inside safety is coming up, we still have a good crackback block angle. It is more difficult to run the play if 4 is on the line. We then prefer Green 16 (Pass).

Option Weakside—17 Option

See Figs. 3–12 and 3–13.

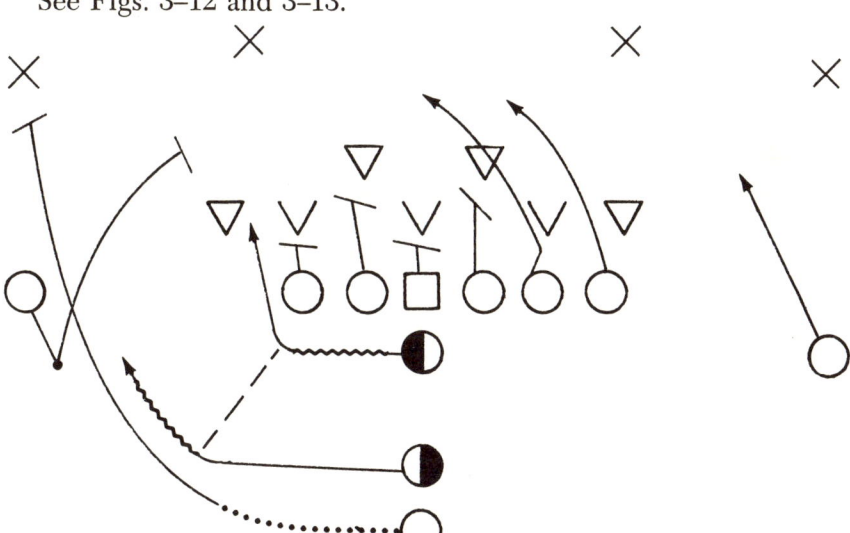

Fig. 3–12.   Gee—17 Option vs. a 50.

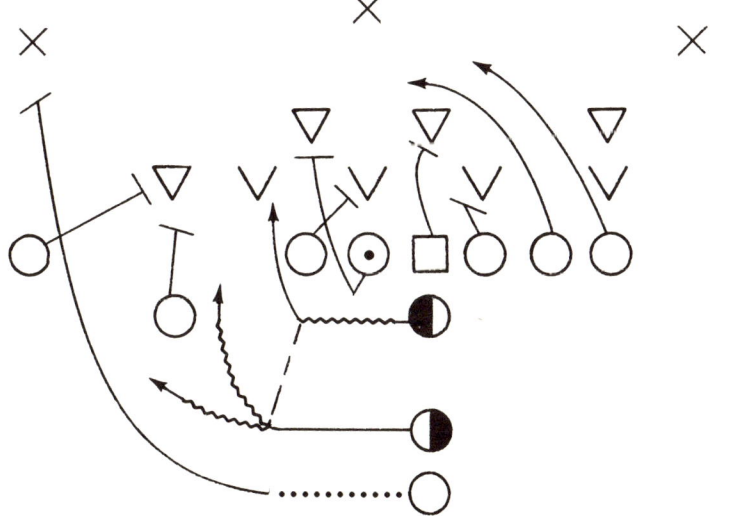

Fig. 3–13.   Star—17 Option vs. a 60.

Assignments

Y—Chop 6.
ST—Bump 2, chop 6.
SG—Cut 1.
C—Block 0. Off LB.
WG—Block 1. Or, tackle call.
WT—Block 2. Or, tackle call.
X—Block 4. (Inside safety vs. 4-deep.)
QB—Open and execute option technique on first man past tackle.
F—Ball carrier.
R—Dive inside third defensive man and block the first defensive man.
T—Motion weak and block the HB.
Z—To. 3-deep, block 4; 4-deep, 1st man coming out. Away, chop 6.

Coaching Points

WT—He executes a cut-off block. Vs. 60, he calls "Eagle."
X—He uses the crackback technique. He must recognize a 3-deep set. If the QB pitches early, X must be ready to crack on the end as he pursues wide.
Z—If in port or star (to weakside in the slot), X will be cracking in on his man. Z should set 4 up with a high post-like block, and then look inside for a defender coming out.
R—If we run 17 option from left or right (R behind weak tackle) vs. a 50, then R will help our weak tackle on 2 unless 2 slants inside. In this case, R picks up the LB. Vs. a 60, R will block the LB.

This play can be an effective gainer inside our weak tackle if the defensive tackle and backer are running off quickly. The one coaching point involves our weak guard, and it is a basic one on all plays: If his backer flees outside, he turns inside to help. If we find a crashing end against us, this play can be very effective as we can get two blockers (X and T) ahead of our FB.

Keep Strongside—34 Belly Keep

See Figs. 3–14 and 3–15.

Assignments

Y—Block 3. Or, tackle call.
ST—Block 2. Or, tackle call.
SG—Block 1. Or, tackle call.
C—Block 0. Or, off LB.
WG—Block 1.
WT—Bump 2, chop 6.
X—Area.

USC RUNNING ATTACK

Z—4-deep, inside safety. 3-deep, halfback.
QB—Reverse pivot and option technique keying 4.
F—Fake over the outside leg of your tackle. Block the LB.
T—Ball carrier.
R—Swing.

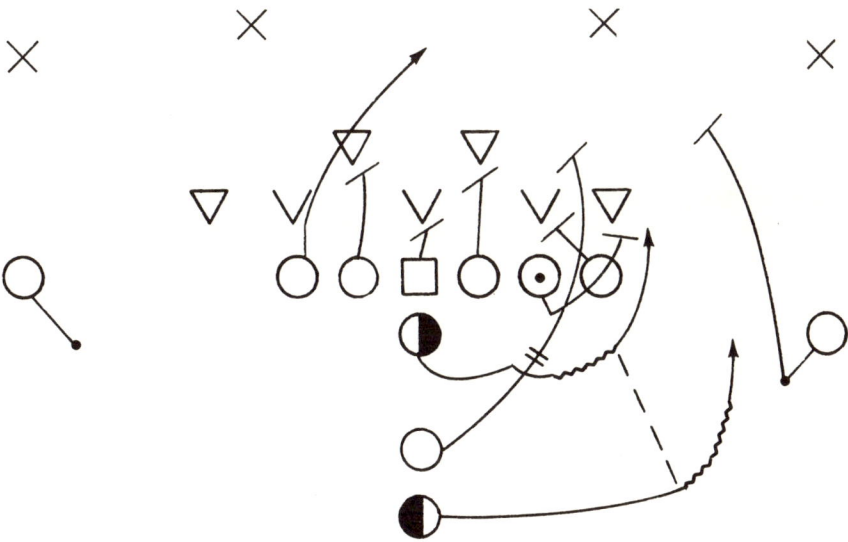

Fig. 3–14. Gee—34 Belly Keep vs. a 50.

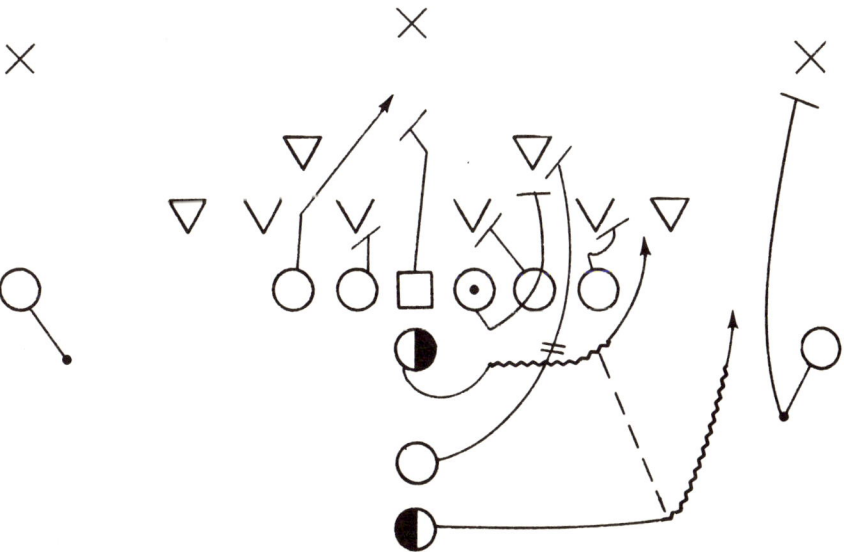

Fig. 3–15. Gee—34 Belly Keep vs. a 60.

Coaching Points

Y—He uses the reverse technique. If "Trojan" is called, he uses a far-shoulder block.

ST—He calls "Eagle" vs. a 60. He uses a far-shoulder block. He calls "Trojan" vs. 50. He does *not* use a cut-off block. He uses a drive block, and then over-blocks if the end closes tough. A "George" call is also a possibility especially vs. a 6–1. He uses a far-shoulder block.

SG—He uses the same technique as on 16 option. If "George" call, he uses a drive block on the end and over-blocks him if he closes tough. He does *not* use a cut-off block on "George" call.

Z—He must recognize 4-deep and 3-deep sets, especially a rotated 4-deep. Same techniques as on 16 option, but he will not crack-back on a rotated man on the line.

QB—As he pivots he looks to the 4th defensive man. This is different from the option where he keys the first man past his Y end. He does not fake the ball to F, but rather gets the ball in the pitch position, waist high, both hands on the ball. (We feel the movement of the F-back provides the fake needed to hold the LB, and that faking the ball just shows the defense where the ball is located.) He then executes his option technique.

F—He must fly into the line on his fake in a ball-carrying position. He should find the LB and cut him off with a cut-off block. This block has sprung our QB for long gains on occasion.

T—He must maintain his position relative to the QB. If the QB cuts upfield, T must do likewise.

This play has been effective vs. the 60 defense, as it puts pressure on the defensive tackle (FB fake) and end (QB or pitch man).

Keep Weakside—35 Belly Keep

See Figs. 3–16 and 3–17.

Assignments

Y—Chop 6.
ST—Bump 2, chop 6.
SG—Cut 1.
C—Block 0. Or, off LB.
WG—Block 1. Or, tackle call.
WT—Block 2. Or, tackle call.
X—4-deep, inside safety. 3-deep, HB.
Z—To, first man coming outside. Away, chop 6.
QB—Reverse pivot and option technique keying 4.
F—Fake over the outside leg of your tackle. Block the LB.
T—Ball carrier.
R—Block 3.

USC RUNNING ATTACK

Coaching Points

X—He must recognize 3-deep and 4-deep. He does not crackback on a man on the line.

WT—He uses a cut off block vs. 50. Vs. 60, he calls "Eagle" and uses a far shoulder block.

F—Same points as 34 Belly Keep. He must get that LB.

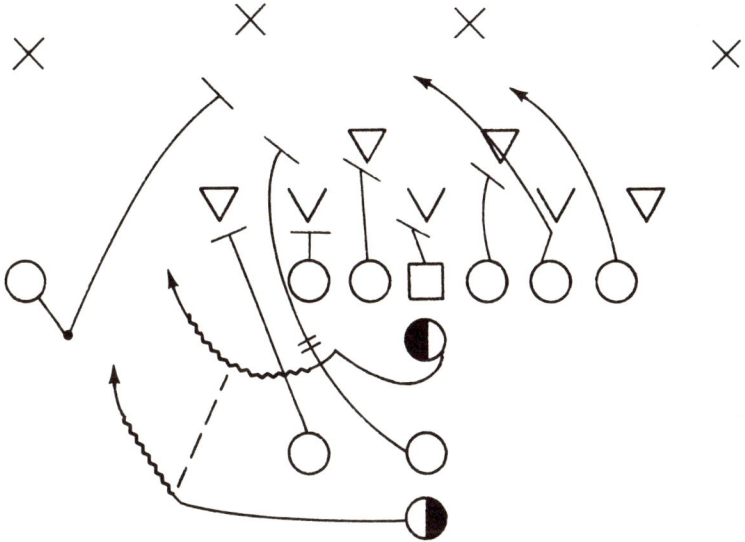

Fig. 3–16. Right—35 Belly Keep vs. a 50.

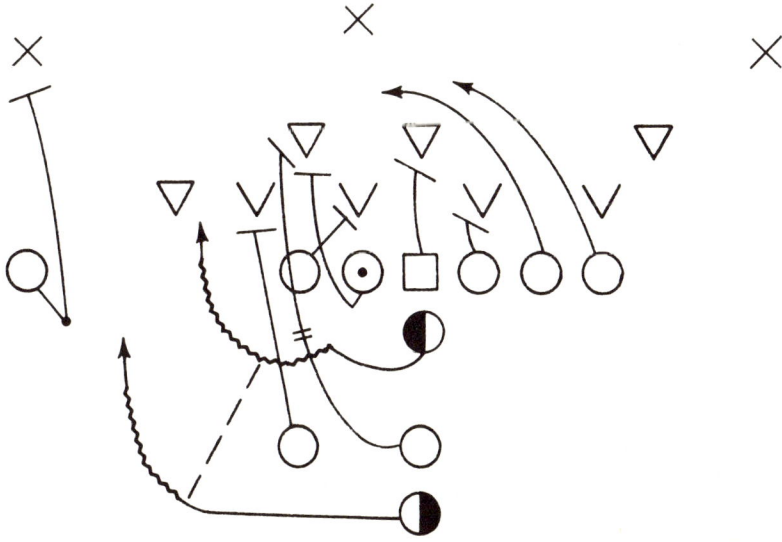

Fig. 3–17. Right—35 Belly Keep vs. a 60.

R—He does *not* use a cut off block on 3. He drive blocks him and if 3 closes, uses an over block.

T—He maintains position with the QB.

We prefer to run this vs. a 60 set for the same reasons listed under 34 Belly Keep.

Sweep Strongside—48 Sweep

See Figs. 3–18 and 3–19.

Assignments

Y—Block 3.
ST—Block 2 if on the line. Otherwise, 1st LB inside.
SG—Pull and lead.
C—Onside. Otherwise, zero.
WG—Pull and lead.
WT—Close.
X—Chop 6.
Z—4-deep, inside safety. 3-deep, halfback.
QB—Reverse pivot, toss ball to R. Lead strongside.
F—Block the man on our tackle. Otherwise, block 1st man inside on the line.
R—Ball carrier.

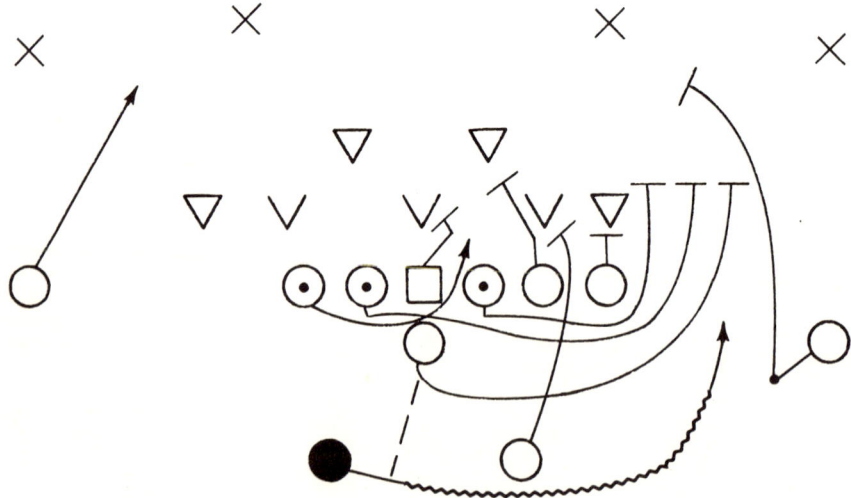

Fig. 3–18. Split-Gee—48 Sweep vs. a 50.

USC RUNNING ATTACK

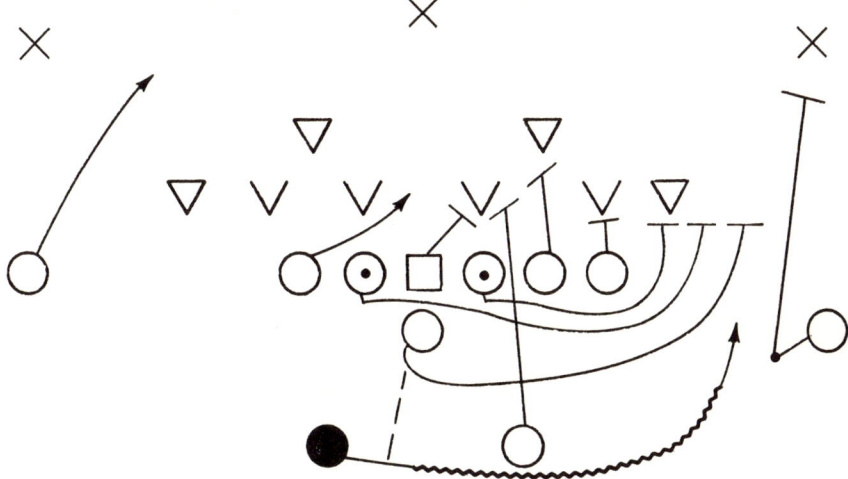

Fig. 3–19. Split-Gee—48 Sweep vs. a 60.

Coaching Points

Y—He uses a "stand-up" block whereby he attempts to stick his nose in the defender's numbers. Y does not jolt, but merely runs and sticks to the defender wherever he goes. The play often breaks inside Y. We like Y to take a two- to four-yard split if 2 is on the line, and no split if 2 is off the line. If 2 is off the line, Y uses a cut-off or reverse block.

ST—He must know that F will block 2 vs. a 50 defense. Thus, he bumps 2 vs. the 50, and looks for 1 (the LB) to shoot. If the LB flees outside, the ST picks up the offside LB. Vs. a 6–1, he bumps 2 and then looks for either the LB or G shooting outside. (See Figs. 3–20 and 3–21.)

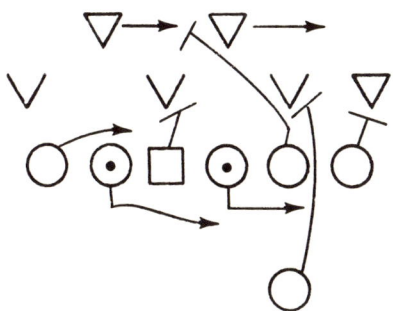

Fig. 3–20. ST picking up the offside linebacker.

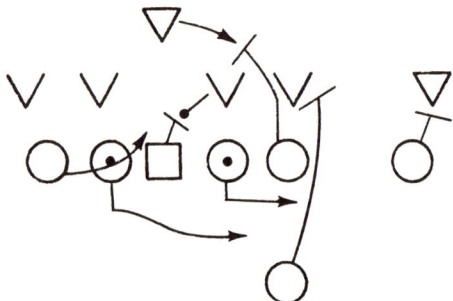

Fig. 3–21. ST picking up a stunting middle linebacker.

SG—He pulls deep when 2 is on the line (50) and shallow when 2 is off (60). On the 50, he looks to the Y-end's block and will cut inside him if Y is taking 3 out. Vs. the 60, he drives 4 out most of the time.

C—He always steps onside as our WT is closing. He can clip in this area.

WG—He keys the block of the SG. He usually cuts inside vs. the 60.

WT—He must close fast and prevent a trailing defender from catching us from the backside. Clipping is legal.

QB—He can be a great help blocking on this. He looks inside and picks up any defender who has escaped his blocker. But, first he must get the ball to R with a soft, two-handed toss.

F—He must widen some if there is a man on our tackle. We employ a low, cut-off block here. Get off is the key to success in this block.

R—He follows his guards and also tries to key the block of his Y-end. If Y's man (3) drifts out, R must cut up and run for daylight. Following our theory of having three ways to cut, R must get wide quickly so as to be in position to cut. The initial steps are vital and he must use great speed.

We prefer this play vs. a 4-deep defense and against a 50 or 6-1 front. It is a full-flow play that attempts to get a maximum fleet of blockers in front of our ball carrier. It has been effective on occasion in short-yardage situations. We do not run the play to our weakside.

Counter Strongside—44 Counter

See Figs. 3–22 and 3–23.

Assignments

Y—2 on the line, block in. Otherwise, out. (Power rule.)
ST—Block 2. Or, tackle call.
SG—Block 1. Or, tackle call.
C—Block 0. Or, offside.

USC RUNNING ATTACK

WG—Pull and block the 1st man past your tackle.
WT—Block 2.
X—Chop 6.
Z—Chop 6.
QB—Open weakside, step back and hand forward to R. Fake 44 counter pass.
F—Fill block on 1st man to the weakside of center.
R—Ball carrier.
T—Block 3. Fake 25 Power.

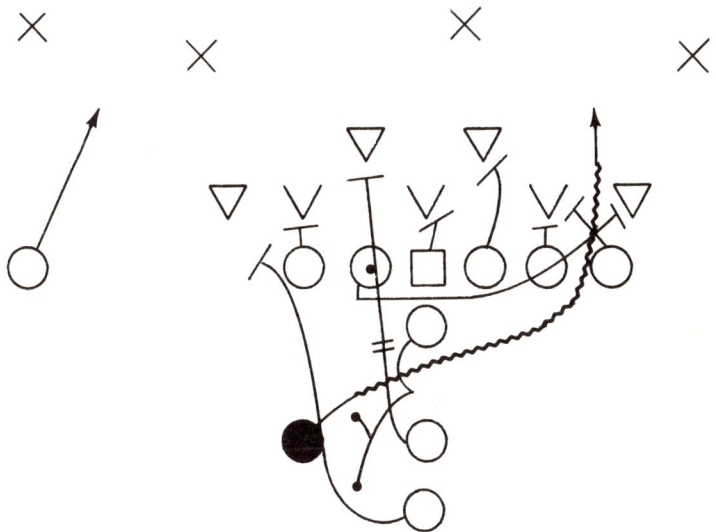

Fig. 3–22. Right—44 Counter vs. a 50.

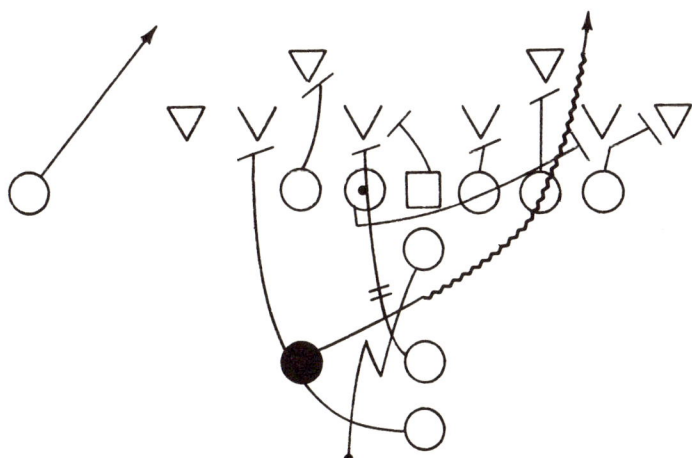

Fig. 3–23. Right—44 Counter vs. a 60.

Coaching Points

Y—Same points as power. Exception: vs. a 5–3 defense, Y must block the LB on him.

ST—If 2 is on the line, the ST will be the post on a double-team block. If, vs. 60, our SG cannot block the defensive guard, "Eagle" should be called.

SG—Vs. 50 the LB should take a weakside fake. Vs. 60, the SG drives his man back. "Eagle" may be called.

C—Note: His rule is to block 0, not on, offside. Vs. a 6–1, C blocks the middle linebacker.

WG—He stays up tight along the line and maintains an inside-out position on the defender. The hole is wider vs. a 50.

QB—His initial step is back with the foot to the weakside. This gives WG room to pull. He keeps the ball in the "third hand," letting F and T drive past, and then hands forward. Following the hand-off he fakes 44 counter pass, dropping behind his weak guard.

F—He uses a fill-block technique. Alignment is closer to ball.

R—He drives for the outside hip of the strong tackle. He should cut inside off his weak guard's trap block.

T—He fill blocks on 3 after faking 25 power.

This play keeps linebackers "honest" and cuts down their pursuit on 25 power. We use it as a surprise element, mainly.

Belly Strongside—34 Belly

See Figs. 3–24 and 3–25.

Assignments

Y—Block 3. Or, tackle call.
ST—Block 2. Or, tackle call.
SG—Block 1. Or, tackle call.
C—Block 0. Or, off LB.
WG—Block 1.
WT—Bump 2, chop 6.
X—Chop 6.
Z—To, area. Away, chop 6.
QB—Reverse pivot and give to F. Fake 34 belly keep.
F—Ball carrier.
R—Swing.
T—Fake 34 belly keep.

Coaching Points

Y—Vs. 60, he must drive the man back and not try to cut him off. If "Trojan" or "George" is called, he uses a far-shoulder block.

ST—He calls George or Trojan vs. 50. He uses a far-shoulder block on George vs. a 6–1. He uses a drive block on Trojan. He calls Eagle vs. 60 and uses a far-shoulder block.

USC RUNNING ATTACK

SG—If Eagle is called, he steps tight up into the hole ready to drive the LB out, or over-blocks if the LB closes down. On George, he stays tight to the line to maintain an inside-out position on the defender.

QB—He gets the ball to F as deep as possible. A good keep-fake can freeze the outside pursuit men.

F—He listens for a tackle call. The hole should be tighter vs. a 60.

The belly is used primarily to set up the belly keep play vs. a 60. It also allows us to use a variety of blocks. We do not prefer it on short yardage.

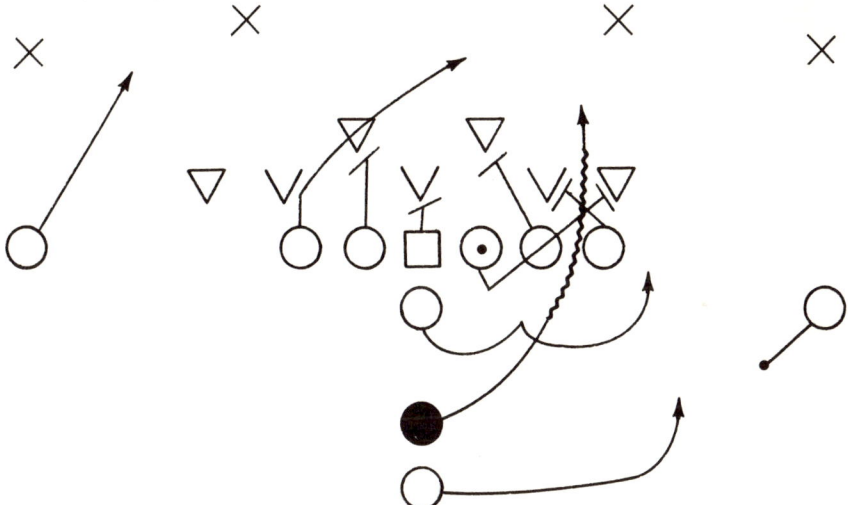

Fig. 3-24. Gee—34 Belly vs. a 50.

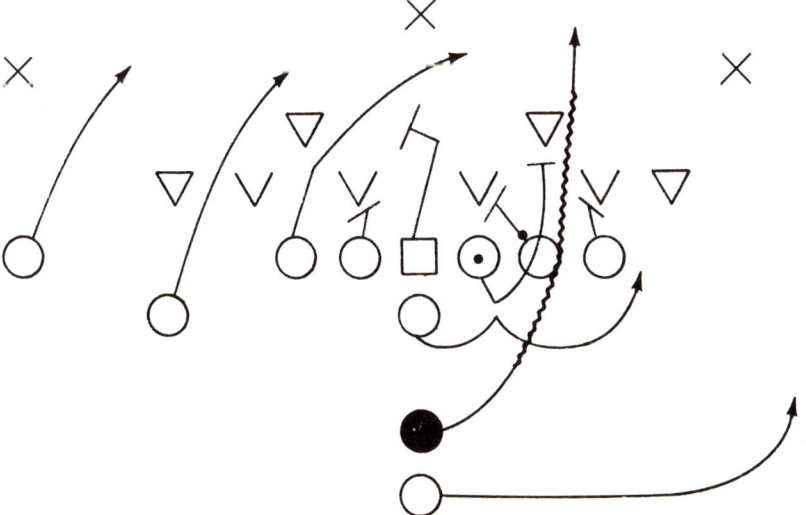

Fig. 3-25. Star—34 Belly vs. a 60.

Belly Weakside—35 Belly

See Figs. 3–26 and 3–27.

Assignments

Y—Chop 6.
ST—Bump 2, chop 6.
SG—Block 1.
C—Block 0. Or, off LB.
WG—Block 1. Or, tackle call.
WT—Block 2. Or, tackle call.
X—Chop 5.
Z—Chop 6.
QB—Reverse pivot and give to F. Fake 35 belly keep.
F—Ball carrier.
R—Block 3.
T—Fake 35 belly keep.

Coaching Points

WT—Vs. 50, he uses a drive block. He does not attempt a cut-off block. F will cut off his block. Vs. 60, he calls Eagle and uses a far shoulder block.

WG—On Eagle call, he must get up tight in the hole ready to drive the LB out, or over-block if the LB closes down.

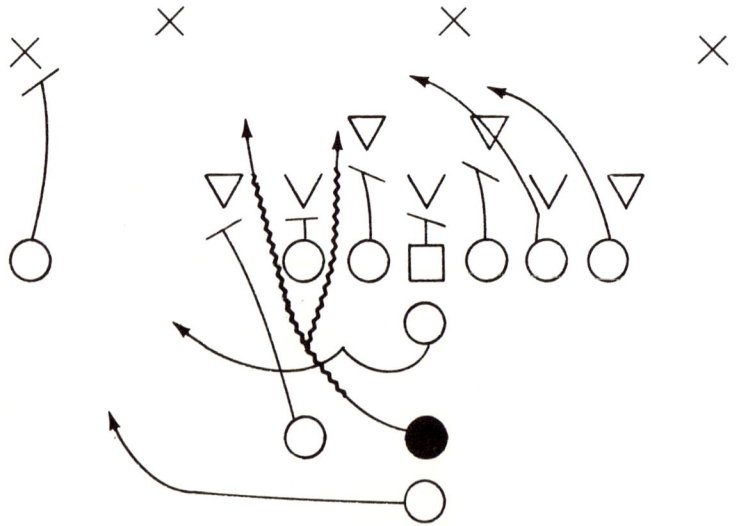

Fig. 3–26. Right—35 Belly vs. a 50.

USC RUNNING ATTACK

R—His lead step must be upfield to prevent 3 from shooting inside. R must get an inside-out position on 3. The keep fake by our QB should help.

This play (combined with the keep) is another play that will cause the defensive end some problems. If our backfield executes quickly, these two plays are difficult to diagnose. We especially like to break the belly inside a tackle who is playing wide to stop our rollouts and options.

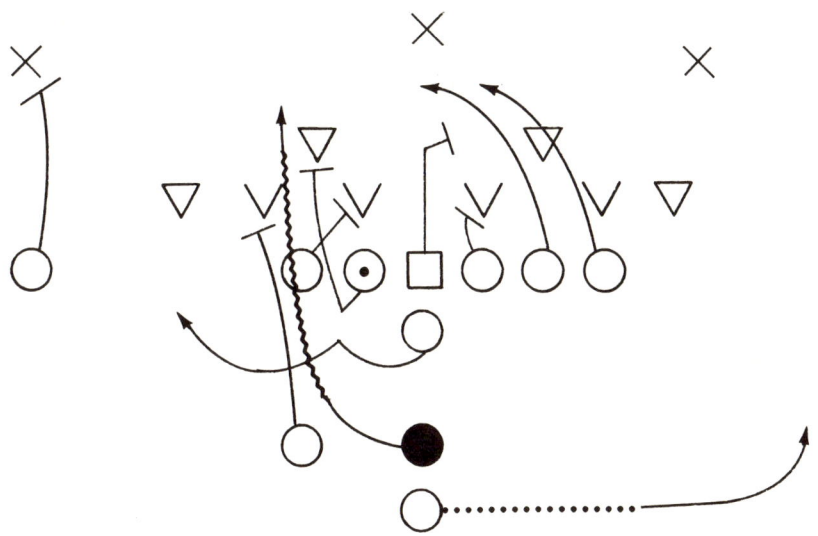

Fig. 3–27. Right–35 Belly "Fly" vs. a 60.

Drive Strongside—32 Drive

See Figs. 3–28 and 3–29.

Assignments

Y—Block 3.
ST—Block 2. Or, tackle call.
SG—Block 1. Or, tackle call.
C—Block 0. Or, offside. Or, "X" call.
WG—Block 1. Or, center call.
WT—Block 2.
X—Chop 6.
Z—Chop 6.
QB—Open and hand ball to F. Set up for pass fake.
F—Ball carrier.
T—Motion strong and block the HB.

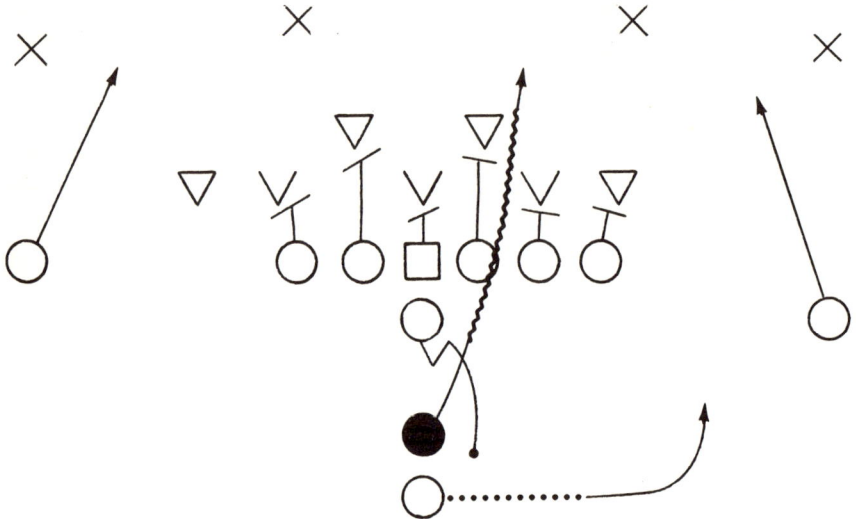

Fig. 3–28. Gee—32 Drive vs. a 50.

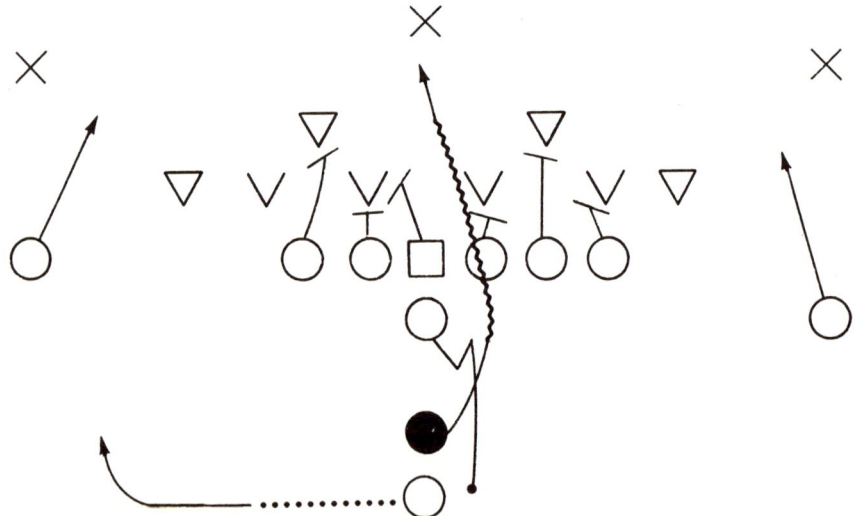

Fig. 3–29. Gee—32 Drive "Fly" vs. a 60.

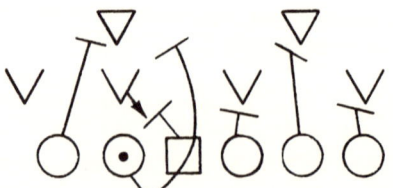

Fig. 3–30. X-Block on 32 Drive.

USC RUNNING ATTACK

Coaching Points

ST—Vs. 50, if the defensive tackle is pinching down he can call pigeon. He steps tight around the guard and drive blocks the LB.

SG—If pigeon is called, he drive blocks out on the tackle.

C—If no zero man, he drive blocks weakside. If his weak guard cannot block his man, or if the defender is in the gap, he calls X (for *exchange*) and drive-blocks the guard's man (Fig. 3–30).

WG—If no zero man, he is the post man for the center. If X is called, he steps around C and looks for the LB in the hole. If the LB shoots, he must be prepared to trap the LB.

F—If no 0 man, this play should break over center. He keys the block of his SG. Vs. 50, he listens for a Pigeon call, which should make the hole wider.

This play is used against backers who loosen up for lateral pursuit and against tackles and guards who play off the ball to slide outside vs. the power play.

Drive Weakside—33 Drive

See Figs. 3–31 and 3–32.

Assignments

Y—Chop 6.
ST—Block 2.
SG—Block 1.
C—Block 0. Or, offside. Or, X.
WG—Block 1. Or, tackle call.
WT—Block 2 if on the line. Otherwise, out. Or, tackle call.
X—Chop 6.
Z Chop 6.
QB—Open and hand ball to F. Set up for pass fake.
F—Ball carrier.
R—Block 2 if not on the LOS. Otherwise, 1st defensive man. Gap 8, Block 3.
T—Motion weak.

Coaching Points

C—Same points as 32 Drive. He can call X to his strong guard.

WG—He listens for a Pigeon call. Note that vs. a slanting middle guard in the 50 defense, we may change the guard's assignment to double-team with C.

WT—He does not block 2, but rather 2 only if he is *on the* line.

F—He listens for Pigeon call and a wider hole. Or, he must recognize a 60 defense and the possible daylight over center.

R—He must align closer to the ball and get off quickly and drive the LB back.

This play has been good vs. loose LB'ers. It can also be effective vs. 6-1 defenses that attempt to send a guard inside (easily taken by our guard) and send the middle backer through the dive hole (Fig. 3–33). If our R-back picks off the LB, this play may break for long yardage. It is also effective vs. tackles who play wide to stop our rollouts and options.

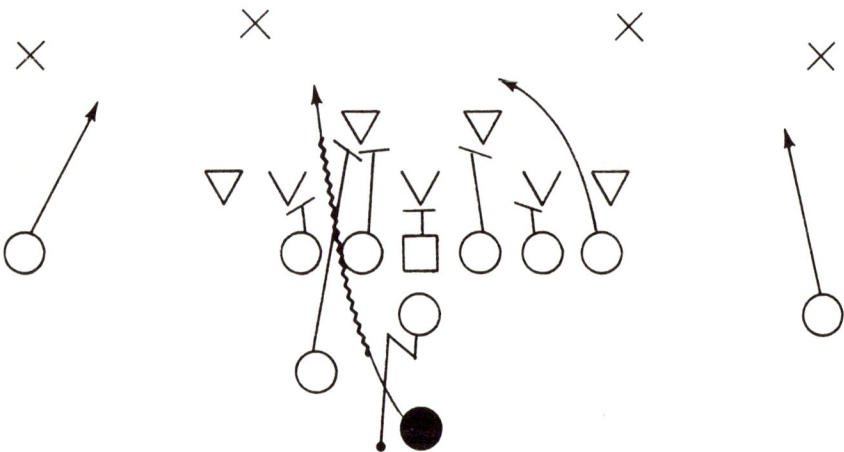

Fig. 3–31. Pro-Gee—33 Drive vs. a 50.

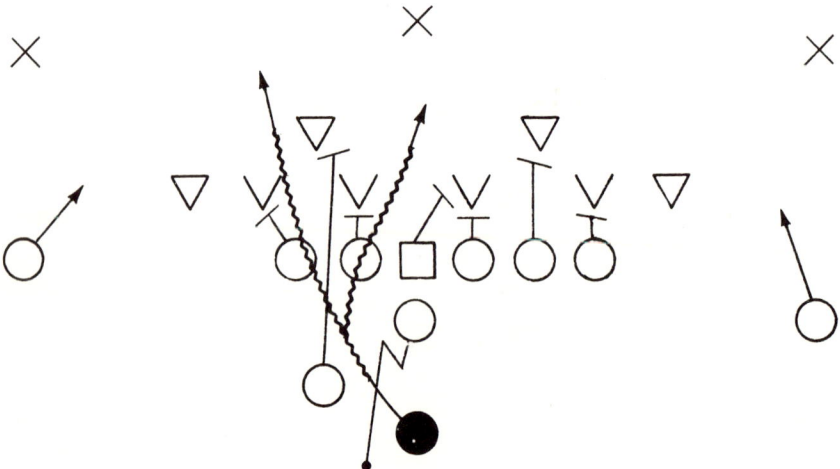

Fig. 3–32. Pro-Gee—33 Drive vs. a 60.

USC RUNNING ATTACK 55

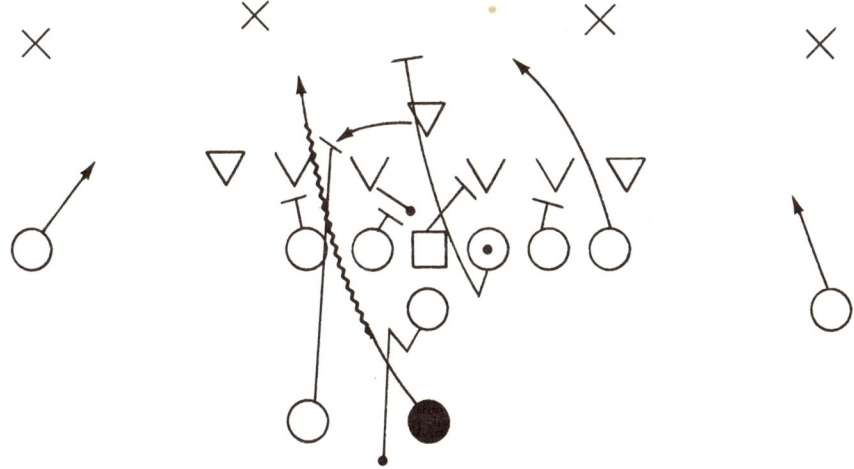

Fig. 3–33. 33 Drive vs. 6-1 Stunt.

Blast Strongside—22 Blast

See Figs. 3–34 and 3–35.

Assignments

Y—Block out.
ST—Block 2 if on the line. Otherwise, out.
SG—Block man on center. Or, one.
C—Block 0. Or, off gap. Or, off LB.
WG—Block 1.
WT—Block 2.
X—Chop 6.
Z—Chop 6.
QB—Reverse pivot and hand ball to T. Set up for pass fake.
F—Block onside LB. Gap 8—Block 3. Lead over tail of the guard.
R—Block onside LB. Lead over outside leg of the guard.
T—Ball carrier.

Coaching Points

ST—He blocks 2 only if 2 is on the line.
SG—If there is a man on the C, our guard is the turn man in a double-team block. If center calls Solid, our guard drives on the LB.
C—We want a Solid call if the LB is tight and might penetrate before

our F can reach him. If Solid is called, C expects help from F (Fig. 3–36).

WG—If no zero man, he will post for our center.

F—He aligns closer to the ball and drive blocks the LB with his outside shoulder. If Solid is called (or if his guard drives on the LB) F should block the defender on our center with his inside shoulder. He must recognize a gap 8 defense.

R—He aligns closer to the ball and drive-blocks the LB with his inside shoulder.

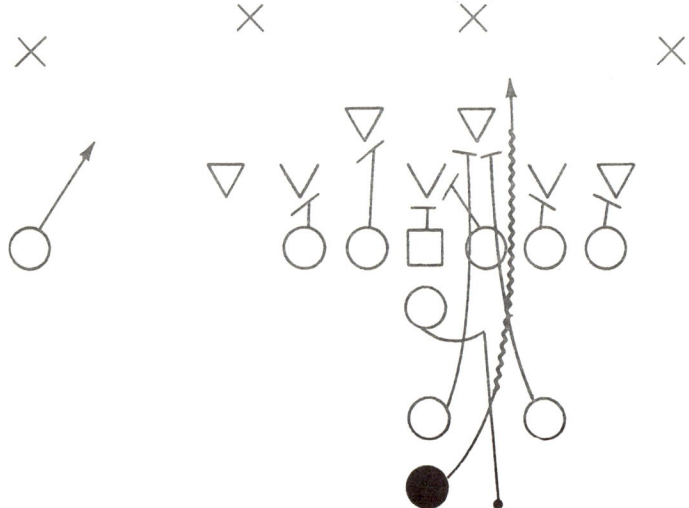

Fig. 3–34. Strong Right—22 Blast vs. a 50.

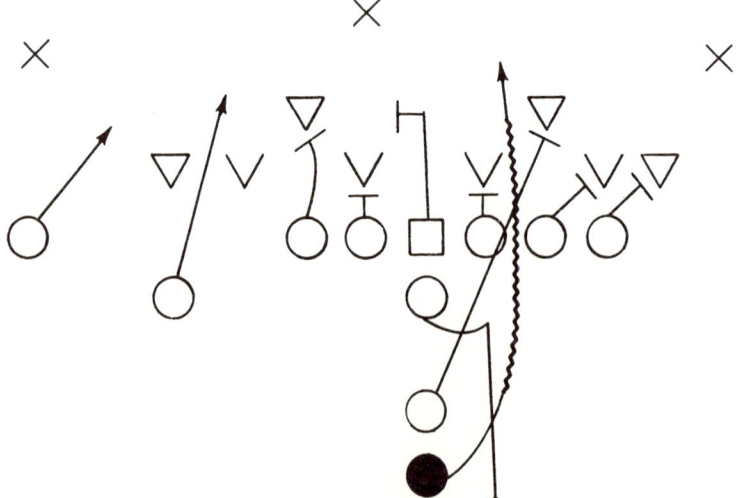

Fig. 3–35. Star—22 Blast vs. a 60.

USC RUNNING ATTACK

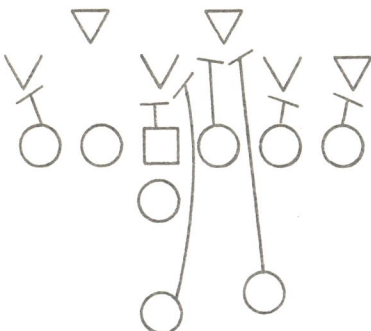

Fig. 3-36. Solid call on 22 Blast.

This play is effective vs. loose LB's and also for short yardage plays. The T-back must realize that we want him to quickly get up into the hole for positive yardage, and that unlike the power there is no Option running here.

Blast Weakside—23 Blast

See Figs. 3-37 and 3-38.

Assignments

Y—Chop 6.
ST—Block 2.
SG—Block 1.

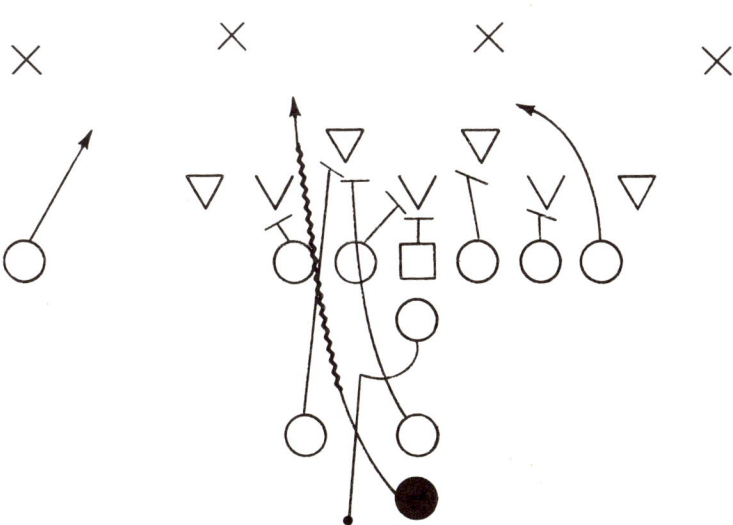

Fig. 3-37. Right—23 Blast vs. a 50.

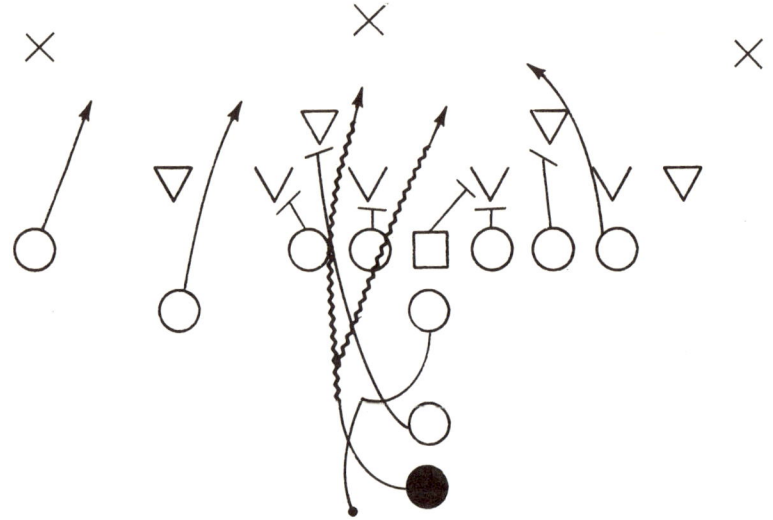

Fig. 3–38. Star—23 Blast vs. a 60.

C—Block 0. Or, offside.
WG—Block man on Center. Otherwise, block 1.
WT—Block 2 if on the line. Otherwise, out.
X—Chop 5.
Z—Chop 6.
QB—Reverse pivot and hand ball to T. Set up for pass fake.
F—Block onside LB. Gap 8—block 3.
R—Block onside LB.
T—Ball carrier.

Coaching Points. The same basic points apply here as for strongside blast.

Traps Strongside—30 and 40 Trap

See Figs. 3–39 and 3–40.

Assignments

Y—Block 1st LB inside.
ST—Block 1st LB inside.
SG—Block 0. Or, 1st man outside.
C—Block on. Or, offside.
WG—Pull and block the 1st man past the Center.
WT—Block inside gap. Or, near LB.
X—Chop 6.

USC RUNNING ATTACK

Z—Chop 6.
QB—Open weakside, hand ball to F (30) or R (40). Fake strongside.
F—Ball carrier (30). Or, block 1st man past man being trapped.
R—Ball carrier. Or, fake 44 counter.
T—Motion strong and block the HB.

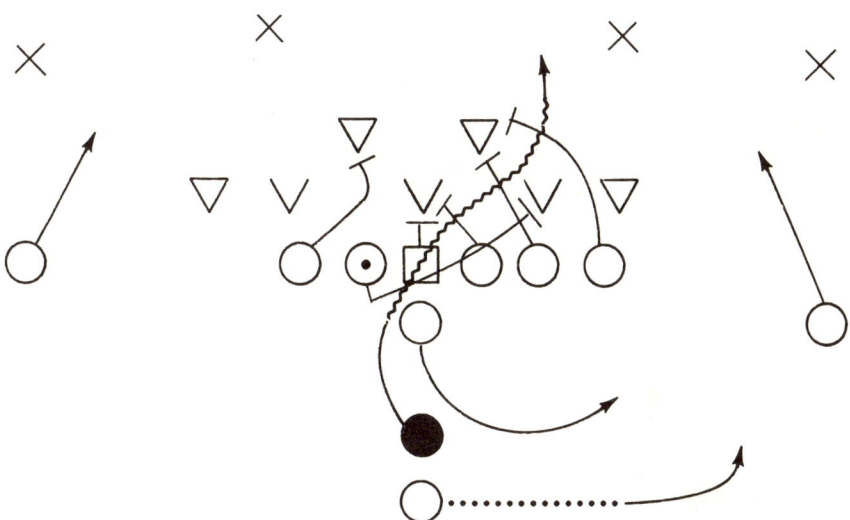

Fig. 3–39. Gee—30 Trap vs. a 50.

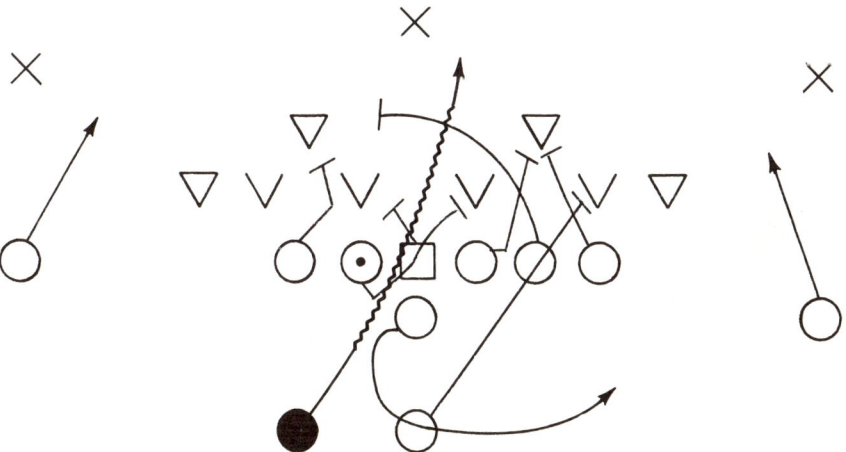

Fig. 3–40. Pro-Gee—40 Trap vs. a 60.

Coaching Points

Y—He should split some to assure getting off the line. If the tackle has the LB blocked, he goes on for the safety.

ST—Vs. a 50, he should split some to try to get the defensive tackle to widen and ease the job of our trapping guard. If the defensive tackle is playing too tight to allow our ST to crack down on the LB, he should influence him and block out (Fig. 3–41). Vs. a 60, the Eagle call (a false call) can help our trapping guard.

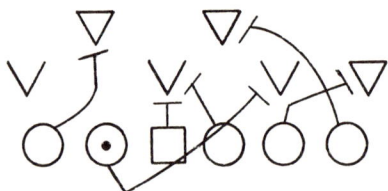

Fig. 3–41. ST influence.

SG—He must recognize defenses. If 0 is on the line, he will be the turn man of a double-team block. But if 0 is a LB (6–1), he will have him alone. If there is no 0 man, he must hesitate an instant to let our ST clear and then go on the LB. He must be awake for a Solid call.

C—In the 50 or 6–1 defenses, if the LB is up tight we want a Solid call to prevent penetration. (See Fig. 3–42.)

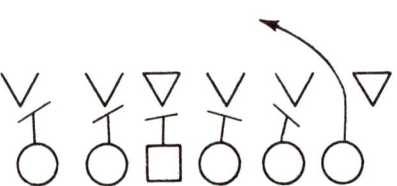

Fig. 3–42. Solid call on a trap.

WG—He must stay tight to the line to maintain an inside-out position on the defender. He must be awake for a "Solid" call. On "Solid" he drives straight out. The man he traps is wider on a 50 defense.

WT—A very important man on a trap as he must prevent a defender from shooting his inside gap. His toughest assignment arises when the opponents align men on our center and our weak guard. He must cut off the man on our weak guard (Fig. 3–43).

Ball Carrier—Must recognize the defensive set. The trap hole is over center vs. an even (60 or 6–1) defense, but is over guard vs. an odd (50 or 5–3) defense.

Fig. 3-43. WT cutting off a man on WG.

The strongside trap has been effective against teams playing their tackles or guards wide, to stop the power. The Eagle false call has caused defensive guards in the 60 to step outside. Vs. the 50, our strong tackle continues for the offensive LB if the onside LB flees outside on motion. This has been effective vs. teams that adjust their LB's to motion.

Trap Weakside—31 Trap

See Figs. 3-44 and 3-45.

Assignments

Y—Chop 6.
ST—Block inside gap. Or, near LB.
SG—Pull and trap 1st man past your center.
C—Block on. Or, offside.
WG—Block 0. Or, 1st man outside.
WT—Block 1st LB inside.
X—Chop 5.
7—Chop 6.
QB—Open strongside and hand ball to F. Fake weakside (79 pass play).
F—Ball carrier.
R—Fake block on the defensive tackle and chop the safety.
T—Motion weakside.

Coaching Points. The same basic techniques and coaching points as used in the strongside trap apply to the weakside trap. One additional point is the fake of the R-back on the defensive tackle. This sets up our 79 pass play, which will be explained later. This play is another that puts pressure on the defensive tackle who wants to stay outside and contain. It is also tough on LB's who slide with motion.

SPECIAL RUNNING PLAYS

We have several plays that we classify as *special*, because they are not a part of a specific classification and are used against certain defenses. Four such plays are the toss, pitch, draw, and weak tackle trap.

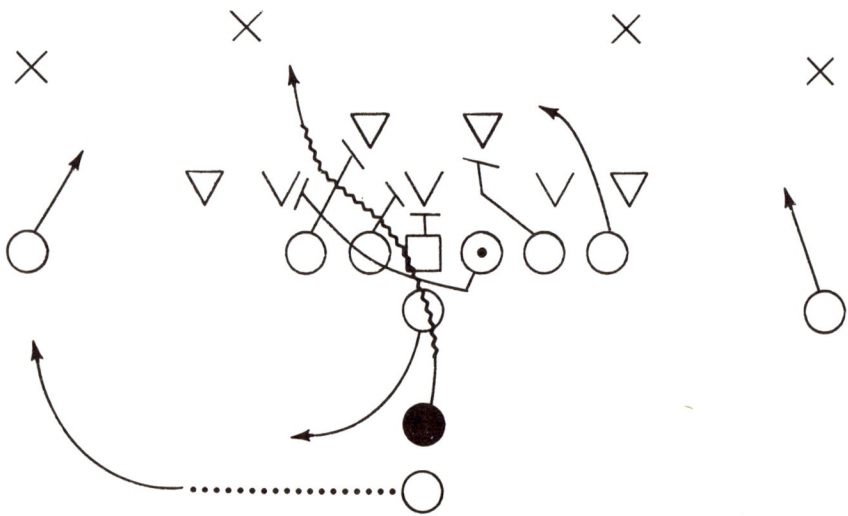

Fig. 3-44. Gee—31 Trap vs. a 50.

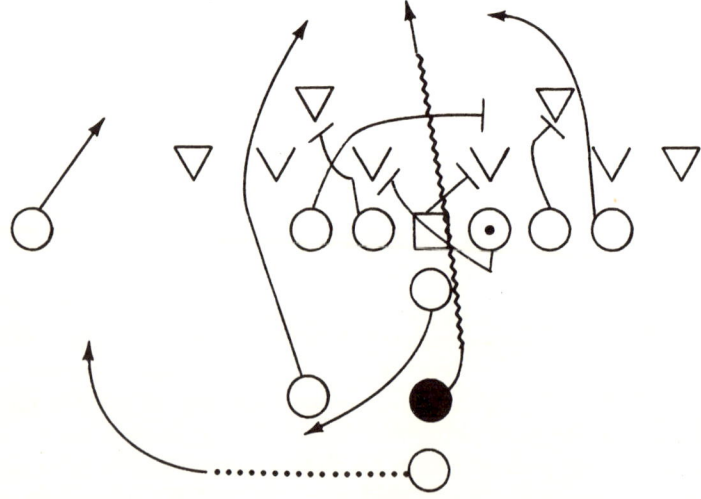

Fig. 3-45. Right—31 Trap vs. a 60.

USC RUNNING ATTACK

Toss Weakside—39 Toss

See Fig. 3–46.

Assignments

Y—Chop 6.
ST—Close.
SG—Pull and seal over hip of your Center.
C—Block onside. Or, zero.
WG—Pull and block the 1st man outside your tackle.
WT—Block inside gap. Or, block 2.
X—Crackback. Or, block 4. Or, inside safety vs. 4-deep.
Z—Post for X. Or, block 4.
QB—Reverse pivot and toss ball to F. Lead shallow.
F—Ball carrier.
T—Motion weak and block the HB.
R—Block the end man on the line.

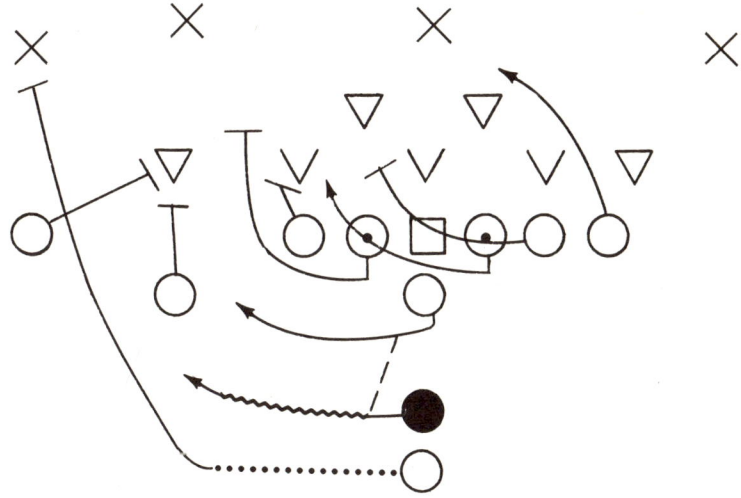

Fig. 3–46. Star—39 Toss vs. a 50 with a wide defensive end.

Coaching Points

ST—He must close quickly. He can clip in this area.
SG—He looks for any shooter over Center (even defense) or just past the Center (odd defense).
C—He steps quickly to the weakside to seal off the gap. He can clip in this area.
WG—He must get some depth and execute a low block at the knees of any defender who penetrates. We shall attempt to outrun this defender if the WG can stop his charge.

WT—He executes a cut-off block vs. a 50. He must prevent quick penetration of the inside gap if any defender threatens this area.
X—He will crackback if possible. He must prevent penetration in the area between himself and Z (or R if we are in right or left formation). He must check the defensive alignment.
Z—He sets up the crackback by X by getting on his man with a high, stand-up block.
QB—Same technique as on the sweep. A soft, two-handed toss and then he leads the play. He lets T get enough motion to be in position to block the HB out. This is a position approximately halfway to Z (5 or 6 yards from his original position).
T—He leads right at the HB and uses the junction-block technique.
R—He drives at the end man on the line and executes a cut-off block.
F—The play is designed to go wide. Initial speed is imperative.

We employ this play against teams who play loose vs. port and star in an attempt to stop our passing. We like it from left and right against teams that employ a four-deep with the inside safety covering the flat on flow.

Pitch Strongside—28 Pitch

See Fig. 3–47.

Assignments

Y—Block 3. Or, tackle call.
ST—Block 2. Or, tackle call.
SG—Pull and lead.
C—Onside. Or, 0.
WG—Pull and lead.
WT—Close.
X—Chop 6.
Z—To—4-deep, inside safety. 3-deep, halfback. Away, chop 6.
QB—Reverse pivot and toss ball to T. Lead play.
F—Block the end man on the line.
T—Ball carrier.
R—Swing away.

Coaching Points

Y—He will use a cut-off block. Trojan will be called vs. a 50 defense. Use far-shoulder technique.
ST—He calls Trojan vs. a 50 defense and over-blocks the defensive end.
SG—He attempts to sprint around the defensive end. If he cannot, he turns upfield.
C—Same technique as the toss.

USC RUNNING ATTACK

Fig. 3–47. Star—28 Pitch vs. a 50.

WG—He pulls deep, and if he succeeds in turning upfield outside the defensive end, he blocks out on the HB. Otherwise, his job is to cut-off pursuit.

WT—He closes quickly. Clipping is legal in this area.

QB—Same techniques as on the toss.

F—If, vs. a 50 defense, the defensive end is blocked by our ST, F should junction-block the defensive HB. Otherwise, he uses the junction-block technique on the end.

T—He should be ready to cut this play upfield for positive yardage. Again, initial speed is imperative.

We like this play against any defense that over-shifts to our slot in port and star, or towards X in left and right formations. It is also effective against defensive ends who are closing down when our Y-end blocks down on 24 Power. If the end flees to stop the pitch, 24 Power should be good for solid yardage.

Draw

See Fig. 3–48.

Assignments

Y—Block 3 if 2 on the line. Or, 1st LB inside.
ST—Block 2. Or, tackle call.
SG—Block 1. Or, tackle call.

C—Block on. Or, strongside.
WG—Block 1.
WT—Block 2.
X—Chop 6.
QB—Open weakside as if sprinting out to pass. Hand ball forward to R.
F—Block 3 to weakside.
Z—To—area. Away, chop 6.
R—Ball carrier.
T—Motion weak.

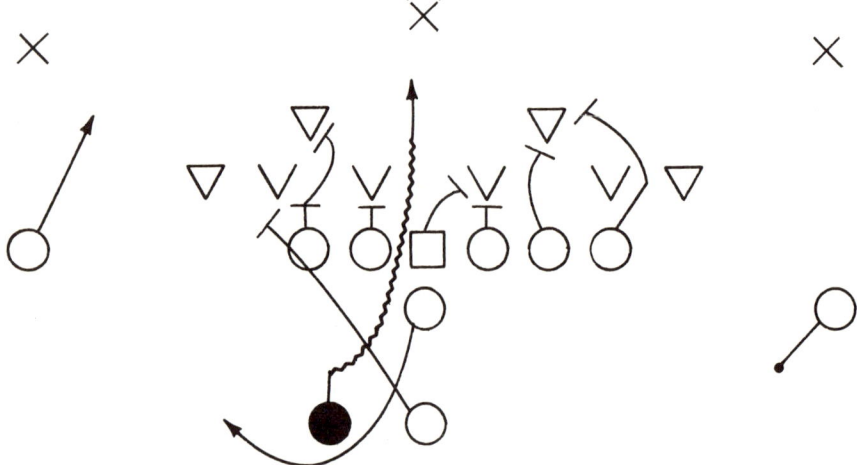

Fig. 3–48. Pro-Gee—Draw vs. a 60.

Coaching Points

Y—If 2 is on the line, Y uses the pin-block technique (Pass protection).
ST—He should call Pigeon vs. a 50 defense (Fig. 3–49). Otherwise, he should drive block on 2.

SG—He must expect help from the Center vs. an even front. He will post for his Center. If Pigeon is called, he must turn the defensive tackle out.

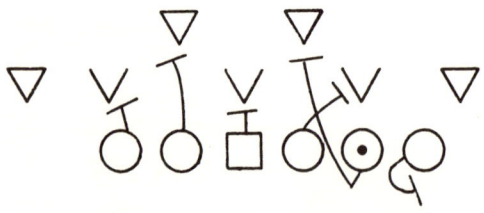

Fig. 3–49. Pigeon block vs. a 50.

C—If a defender is on, our Center must get on him and stay on him, allowing our ball carrier to cut off his block. We prefer our Center to take a man on him to our weakside, but we do not want the man on to penetrate.

R—He should key the block of his Center and break off the Center's block. He waits for the QB to reach him before he drives for the hole.

QB—The defense must read this initially as a rollout pass. He sprints out as if to pass, aiming at a spot behind his R-back. F must clear in front of the QB. After handing off to R, the QB continues to rollout.

We like this play against linemen and linebackers who are sliding quickly with flow. It is another play that keeps the linebackers "at home" for a while. It is also effective against linemen who rush hard when pass shows.

Weak-Tackle Trap

See Fig. 3–50.

Assignments

Y—2 on the line—1st LB inside. Or, out.
ST—2 on the line—block out. Or, 2.
SG—Block 1. Step Back.
C—Block 0. Or, off LB.
WG—Block 1.
WT—Trap 1st man past SG.
X—Chop 6.
QB—Reverse pivot as on 25 Power. Hand ball forward to R. Fake Green 25.
F—Block 2 weakside.
T—Fake 25 Power and block 1st man.
R—Ball carrier. Jab step outside and drive for the hole.

Coaching Points

ST—A Trojan call is a good false call on this play.
SG—He should expect the LB to slide inside. He must prevent penetration in his hole.
WG—He must prevent penetration in his hole.
WT—He should stay close to the line to give himself an inside-out angle on the defender to be trapped.
QB—This play must be executed to initially appear to be 25 Power. The ball must be hidden in the "third hand."

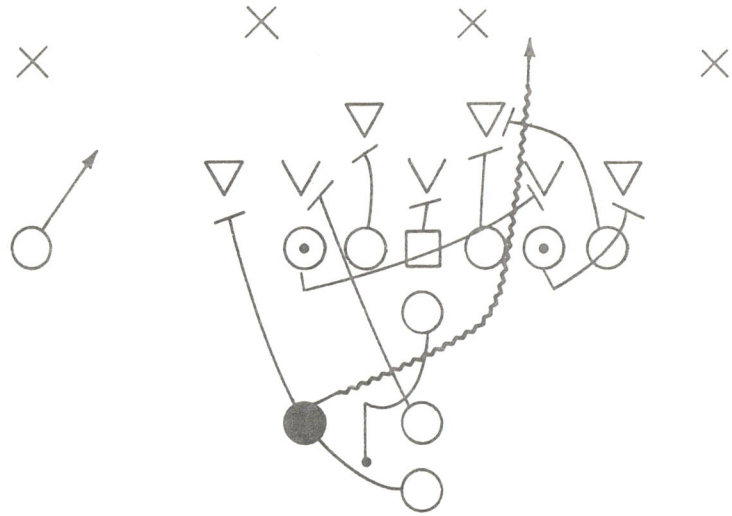

Fig. 3–50. Right—Weak tackle trap vs. a 50.

F—He leads tight to prevent any defender from chasing our pulling weak tackle.

T—A good fake is needed. In faking, we emphasize speed of movement and driving for the hole as if he were the ball carrier. Hand fakes, etc., are not as important as speed. Deception depends on speed.

R—He takes a short jab step and then drives for the outside leg of SG. He cuts inside the trap block of WT.

We like this play against a 50 defense best, and for the same basic reasons as the draw. It will also keep the defensive tackle honest. If he slides outside when ST pulls (Trojan call), he will now be trapped. This play can be effective in long-yardage situations.

4

USC Passing Attack

We believe that in order to win a team must pass, and that the only real danger in passing the ball is the threat of an interception. It is our belief that this threat can be reduced in three ways. First, by using a one-target passing attack. Secondly, by using an attack that is geared to maximum protection, and third, by giving freedom to our pass receiver in running his pattern.

I would like to cite our passing offense statistics for the past four seasons as an example. We have attempted 637 passes and have had 25 intercepted. However, 11 of the interceptions came on 4th down situations, and 2 others were on passes thrown by a halfback. The fourth down passes were mainly deep passes that served the same as a punt, or at least did not cause us to lose field position.

We have gained 4,853 yards passing the ball on 308 completions. This is an average gain of 15.6 yards per completion. For the 637 passes attempted, this averages to 7.6 yards for each pass attempt. Thus, each time we put the ball in the air the average gain was almost 8 yards, and each time we completed the pass the gain was close to 16 yards. We feel these averages more than offset the 25 interceptions, especially when our running average is also figured. Our QB has the option to run on most of our passes and has successfully done so on some occasions.

The table shows our figures for 1962, 1963, 1964, and 1965.

Year	Passes Attempted	Passes Completed	Passes Intercepted	TD Passes	Yards
1964	221	109	11	11	1,714
1963	219	108	11	11	1,495
1962	197	91	3	18	1,644
TOTALS	637	308	25	40	4,853

PASS PLAYS

We have four types of passes we throw, and their use depends to a great extent on the type of QB we have.

First, we must have play-action passes off our best running plays. We add the word, green, in front of 24 or 25 Power, and the plays become Green 24 and Green 25. We also use Green 35, Green 16, and Green 44 Counter.

Secondly, we have a sprint-out series, which is an option run and pass play for our QB. This is our 80 series with 84 and 88 passes going strongside, and 83 and 89 going weakside. The 83 and 84 employ motion by the T-back, and 88 and 89 are full-flow passes.

Third, we have rollouts off an inside fake. The 79 is one of our weakside passes, as is Waggle Weak. Boot Strong and Waggle Strong are two strongside passes of this type.

Fourth, we have the standard dropback pass, which we call our 90 series.

On all of these types of passes we emphasize the three factors mentioned previously, namely, that we intend to throw to one receiver, that we intend to give our passer maximum protection (by holding in our Y-end, plus backs, much of the time) and that our one intended receiver has freedom to get himself open.

PASS PATTERNS

We want our pass receivers to take an outside release route, especially if they are aligned in a wide position. We feel this is important for two reasons: First, it forces the defender to turn outside and away from the ball. Second, it greatly increases the area the linebacker must cover.

Hitch Pattern

We drive two or three steps to the outside of the defender, stop quickly, and face the QB in a football position. If possible, we fake inside and break outside. We must catch the ball before we start to run. (See Fig. 4–1.)

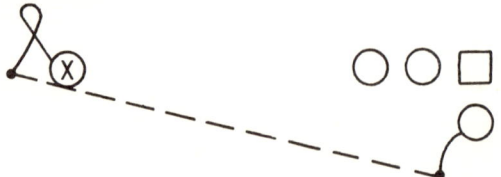

Fig. 4–1. Hitch pattern.

Delay Pattern

We delay on the LOS for a count of "one thousand one, one thousand go" before breaking to the outside of the defender three or four steps, and then cut to the inside, turning our shoulders to the QB (Fig. 4–2). We adjust depth of cut to the inside coverage.

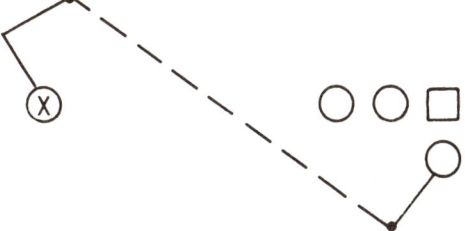

Fig. 4–2. Delay pattern.

Look Pattern

Y will drive up field making sure that he doesn't bend in toward LB coverage. He looks for the ball immediately. X and Z break directly to the inside, turn their shoulders to QB and adjust depth to coverage. (See Fig. 4–3.)

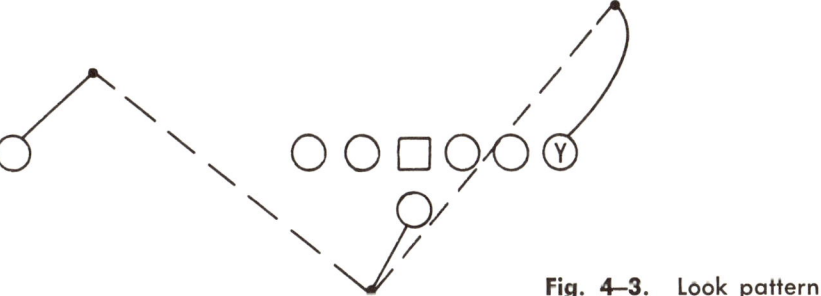

Fig. 4–3. Look pattern.

Quick Pattern

We drive to the outside of the defender and break out smoothly at a depth of four to six yards (Fig. 4–4). We look for the ball as soon as we break, and turn our shoulders to the QB as much as possible.

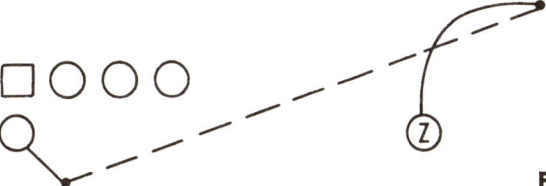

Fig. 4–4. Quick pattern.

Recon Pattern

We step up-field two steps and give the appearance that we are not involved in the play (Fig. 4-5). We face the QB and drift back behind the LOS. We expect the ball at any time.

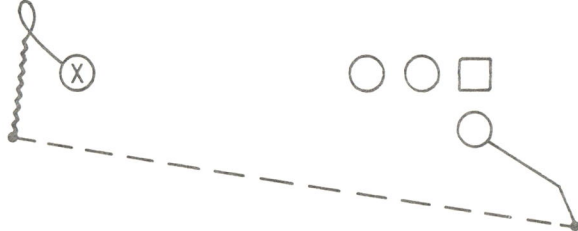

Fig. 4-5. Recon pattern.

Out Pattern

We drive up field, to the outside of the defender, to a depth of twelve yards then break out at a 90 degree angle, turning our shoulders toward the QB and looking for the ball immediately. Y breaks out and gains depth at the same time. He looks for the ball as soon as he can turn his shoulders to the QB. (See Fig. 4-6.)

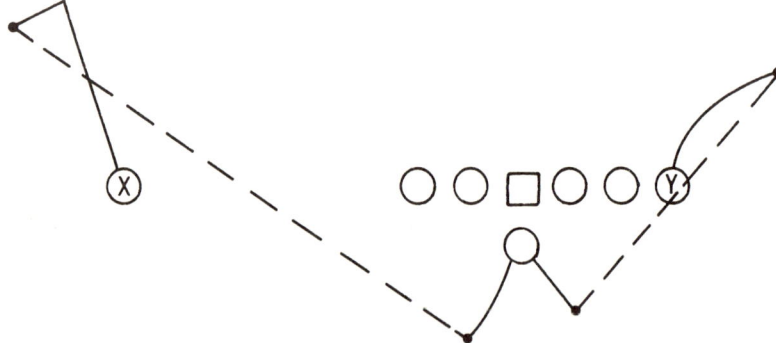

Fig. 4-6. Out pattern.

Cross Pattern

We break in and gain depth at the same time. We adjust depth of pattern to LB coverage. We try to catch up with the QB. Final depth of the pattern is between eight and twelve yards (Fig. 4-7).

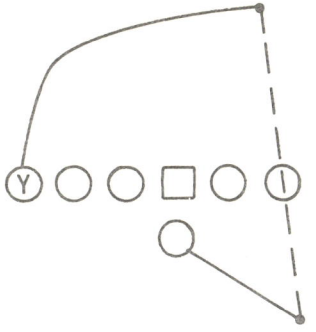

Fig. 4–7. Cross pattern.

Squirrel Pattern

We start to execute an out-and-up pattern, but turn inside two steps and come to a stop at a depth of fifteen yards. We face the QB in a football position ready to slide in or out (Fig. 4–8).

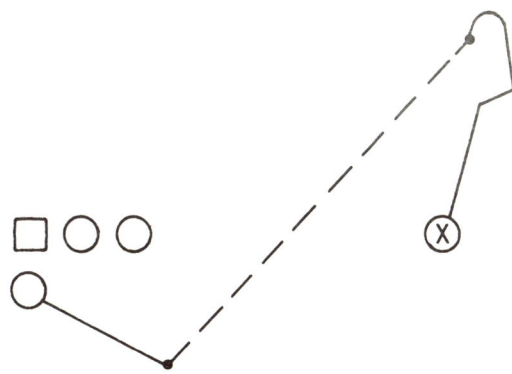

Fig. 4–8. Squirrel pattern.

Snake Pattern

We drive to the outside of the defender to a depth of twelve yards. We break in two steps and come to a stop in a football position facing the QB (Fig. 4–9).

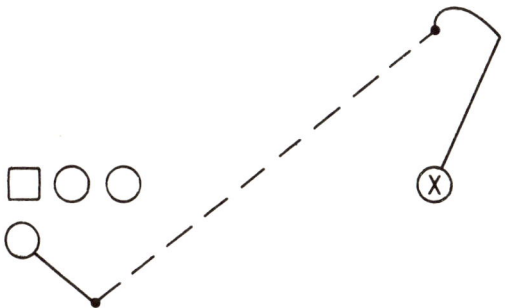

Fig. 4–9. Snake pattern.

Seam Pattern

We drive up-field, splitting the distance between the nearest 2 deep defenders (Fig. 4–10). The final angle of pattern will depend upon the defensive coverage. We look over our inside shoulder for the ball.

Crease Pattern

Y looks over his outside shoulder for the ball (Fig. 4–11). Similar to seam.

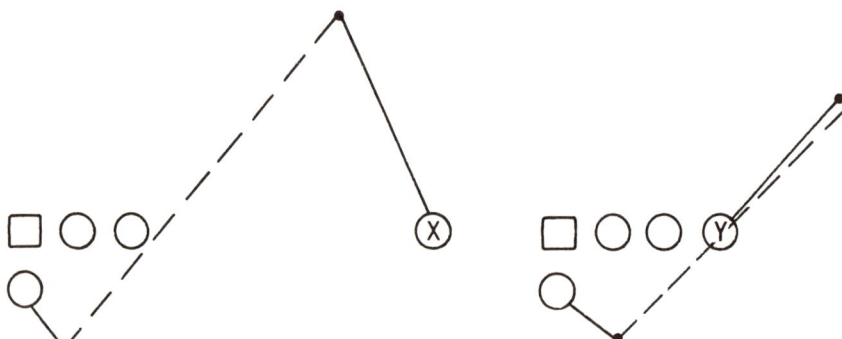

Fig. 4–10. Seam pattern. **Fig. 4–11.** Crease pattern.

Up Pattern

We drive directly up-field and outrun the defender (Fig. 4–12). We look for the ball over our inside shoulder as soon as we clear.

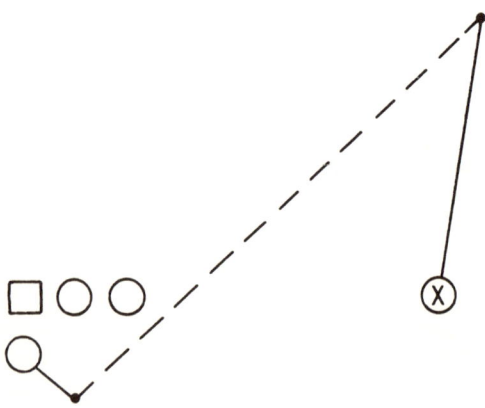

Fig. 4–12. Up pattern.

Corner Pattern

We drive twelve yards to the outside of a deep defender, fake toward the near post and break for the goalline corner, and look for the ball over our outside shoulder as soon as we break for corner (Fig. 4–13).

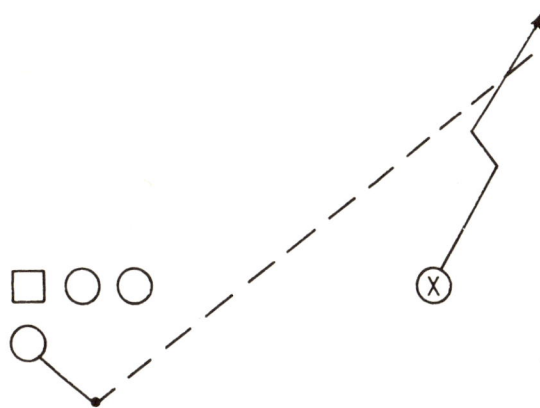

Fig. 4–13. Corner pattern.

Post Pattern

We drive outside the defender to a depth of twelve yards, then fake toward the corner and break toward the near goal post (Fig. 4–14). We adjust depth of final cut to the coverage making sure not to go too far toward safety man coverage.

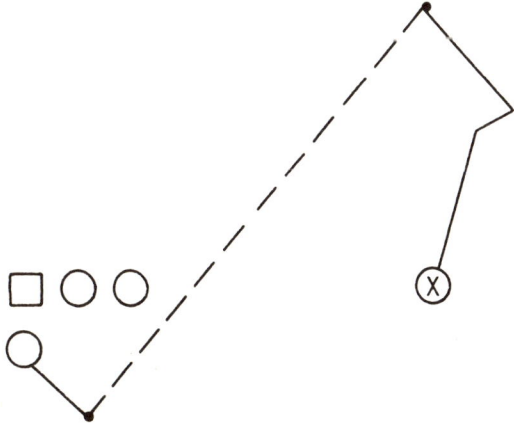

Fig. 4–14. Post pattern.

Flag Pattern

We drive directly at the near goalline flag, looking for the ball over our outside shoulder (Fig. 4–15). We look for ball as soon as we get clear.

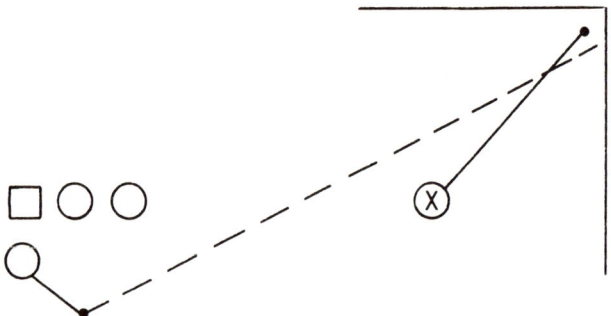

Fig. 4–15. Flag pattern.

Out and Up Pattern

We drive outside of the defender to a depth of eight yards, then fake the out pattern and then drive up-field past the defender (Fig. 4–16). We look for the ball over our inside shoulder as soon as we clear the defender. We do not bend back toward inside coverage.

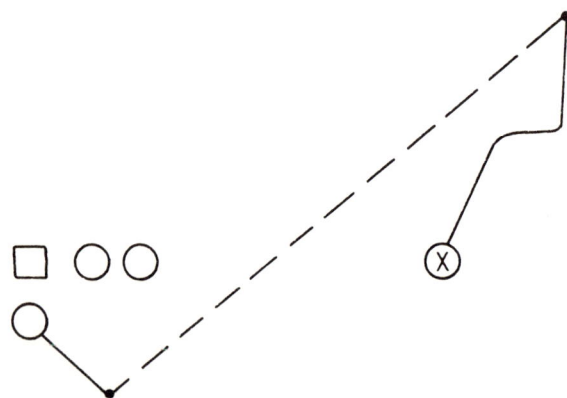

Fig. 4–16. Out-and-up pattern.

Banana Pattern

The R-back drives up-field, gaining width at the same time, to a position wider than LB coverage and deeper than end coverage, approximately 12 yards deep (Fig. 4–17). We look for ball over our outside shoulder as soon as we clear.

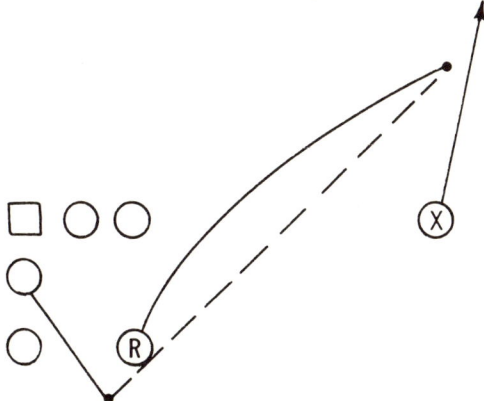

Fig. 4-17. Banana pattern.

Wheel Pattern

Z executes a quick pattern, breaking out four to six yards, and then breaks up-field, still gaining width (Fig. 4-18). He looks for the ball over his inside shoulder as soon as he clears. Width of initial cut will depend upon the defense being used.

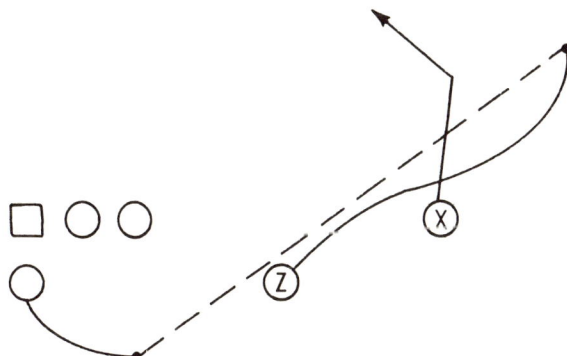

Fig. 4-18. Wheel pattern.

Swing Pattern

Z or R drives laterally (losing enough ground for good angle to catch ball) and looks for the ball over his inside shoulder as soon as possible (Fig. 4-19). He continues gaining width until he has flanked any inside coverage, then breaks upfield.

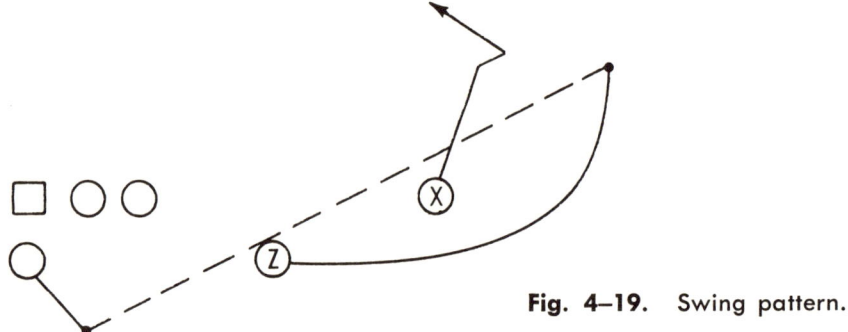

Fig. 4-19. Swing pattern.

Flare Pattern

R drives up-field, getting enough width to avoid contact with defensive linemen (Fig. 4-20). He looks for ball over his inside shoulder as soon as he clears LOS.

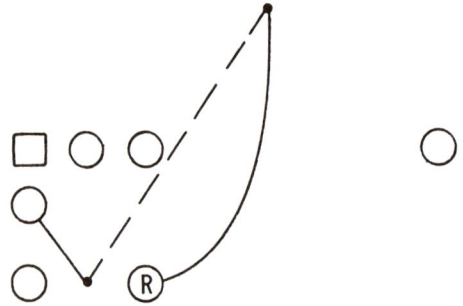

Fig. 4-20. Flare pattern.

Fan Pattern

R drives into the flat area four to six yards deep, running away from inside coverage and looking for ball over outside shoulder as soon as he clears the LOS (Fig. 4-21).

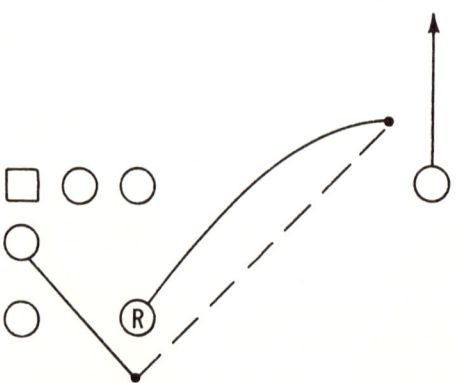

Fig. 4-21. Fan pattern.

USC PASSING ATTACK

Check Pattern

We step out and make contact with the defensive man, then slip by him and continue running toward the sideline, slightly behind the LOS (Fig. 4–22). We look for the ball over our inside shoulder.

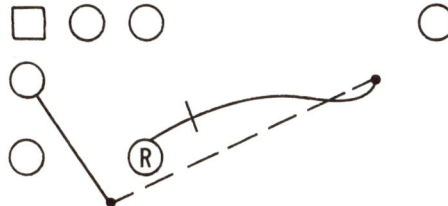

Fig. 4–22. Check pattern.

PLAY-ACTION PASSES

Green 24

See Fig. 4–23.

Assignments

Y—2 on the line, block in. Or, out. (24 Power rule.)
ST—If 2 is off the line, block out. Otherwise, block 2.
SG—Block 1.
C—Block on. Or, offside. Or, option.
WG—Block out. Or, option.
WT—Block on. Or, option.
X—Seam pattern.
Z—To—out pattern. Exception: Y out, 3-deep up, 4-deep post. Away, seam.
F—Block 3.
R—Swing.
T—Fake 24 and block onside LB.
QB—Fake 24 and execute run—pass option.

Coaching Points

Y—He blocks unless called into the pattern on Y-out. If Y-out is called, Y runs away from the LB (Fig. 4–24.) If the defensive end drops off, Y stays upfield and inside him.

ST—If Y-out is called, he executes a cut-off block. Otherwise, he expects a double-team vs. a 50 defense.

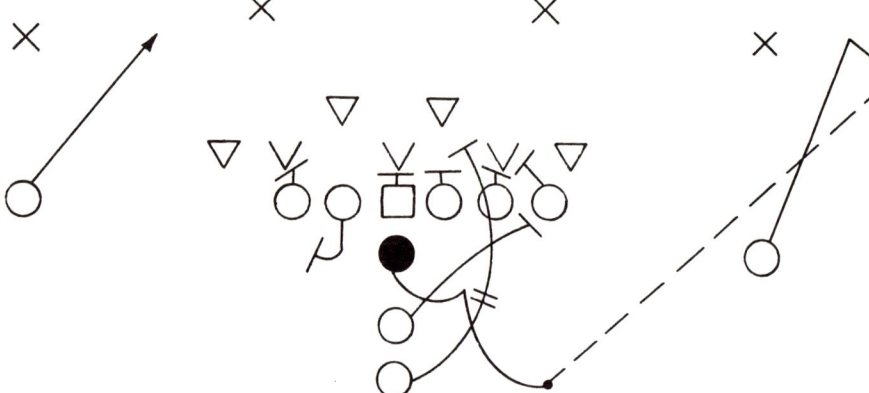

Fig. 4–23. Green 24. Intended receiver is Z.

Fig. 4–24. Y-Out pattern. Intended receiver is Y.

SG—He should take a hard step at the LB on a 50 defense, to try to draw him up. Vs. an even defense, he uses a hard drive-block to help on the play fake.

C—Against an even front, he is prepared to pick up the guard. But, he does not drive on the guard. We want solid backside protection. He steps strongside initially. (See Figs. 4–25 to 4–28.)

WG—He does not block the man on him, but rather the first man outside him. He steps strongside initially. (See Figs. 4–25 to 4–28.)

WT—He will block the man on him, letting our WG pick up the outside man. He fires on this man quickly. (See Figs. 4–25 to 4–28.)

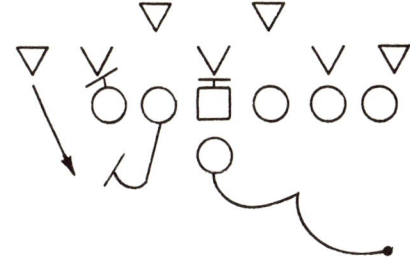

Fig. 4–25. Backside vs. 50; end shoots.

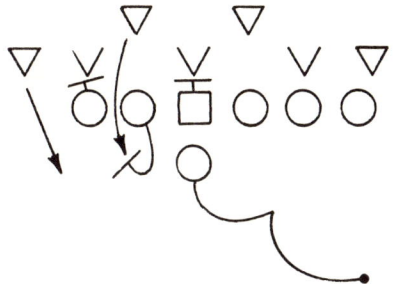

Fig. 4–26. Backside vs. 50; both end and LB shoot. We let the outside man go free.

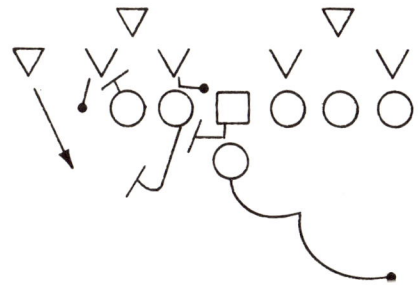

Fig. 4–27. Backside vs. 60; end shoots.

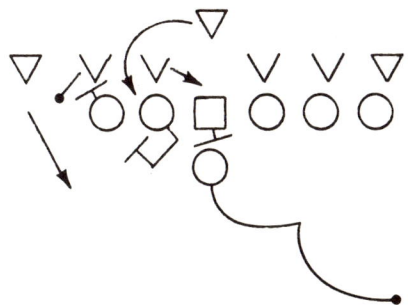

Fig. 4–28. Backside vs. 6-1; LB and end shoot. Outside man free.

Z—He runs an out pattern unless told to do otherwise. He must be alert to clear the area if Y-out is called. He then must recognize a 3-deep secondary (up pattern) as opposed to a 4-deep secondary (post pattern). (See Figs. 4–29 and 4–30.)

F—He executes a junction block on the end.

T—His fake can be a big help on this play. We have films showing him tackled on the fake, and we go to great lengths to point this

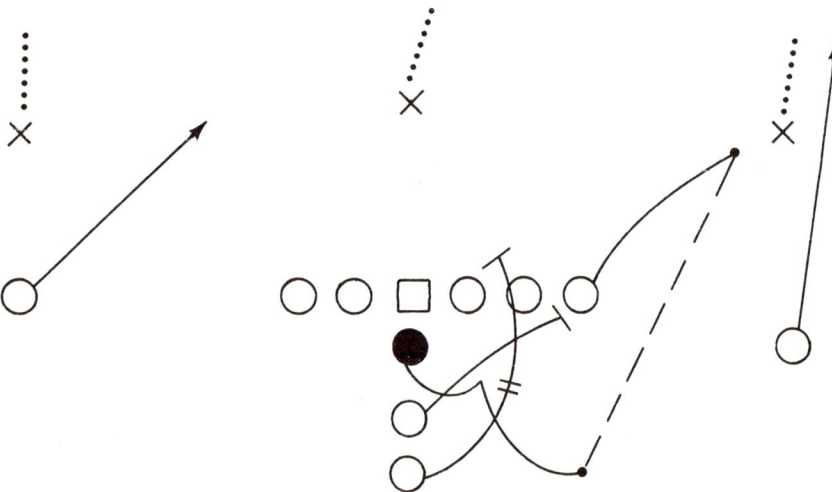

Fig. 4–29. Green 24—Y-Out vs. 3-Deep.

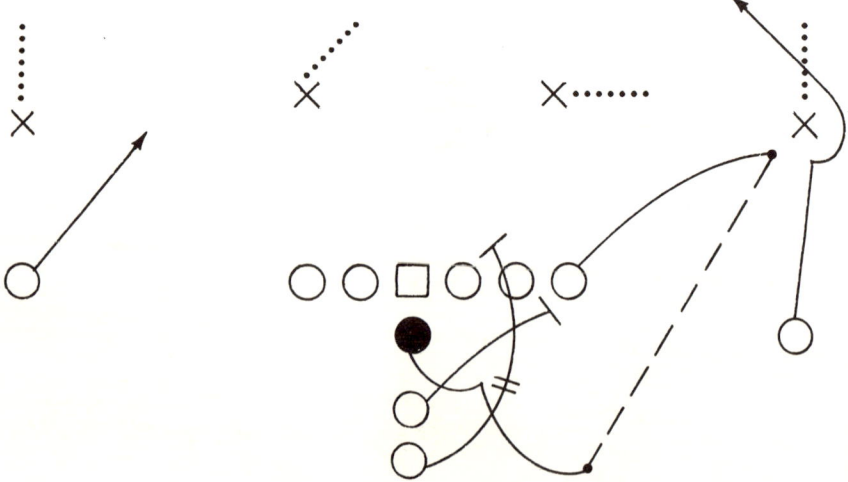

Fig. 4–30. Green 24—Y-Out vs. 4-Deep.

USC PASSING ATTACK

out to his teammates. He must also be alert for shooting linebackers.

QB—As stated previously, we feel the movement of the backs will be the key to the fake. The QB should third-hand the ball, let T pass, and then start rolling out. If the defensive end drops off, the QB can pick up an easy 5 or 6 yards. If he is throwing deep to Z on a post or an out-and-up, the QB sets up behind his strong tackle.

Against a team playing a 4-deep defense, we prefer to call a post pattern for Z. Against a 3-deep secondary, the out pattern should be effective. If we find an end who crashes in a 3-deep situation, we alter the blocking slightly and flip the ball to Y on the out. The Y out is also effective vs. a 4-deep that is rotating the outside defender to the flat and the inside safety to deep outside, provided Y does not run his pattern too far into the flat. However, Z is usually the intended receiver.

Green 25

See Fig. 4–31.

Assignments

Y—Block out.
ST—Block on. Or, out.
SG—Block out. Or, option.
C—Block on. Or, offside. Or, option.
WG—Block 1.
WT—Block 2.
X—3-deep, up. 4-deep, post. Note that Out may be called.
Z—Port and star, swing. Gee and haw, seam.
F—Block 3.
R—Swing.
T—Fake 25 Power and block the onside LB.
QB—Fake 25 Power and execute run-pass option.

Coaching Points

Y—He executes a pin block, stepping to the inside first to prevent penetration.
ST—He executes the same technique as our WT on Green 24.
SG—He executes the same technique as our WG on Green 24, but with our Y-end staying in to help our backside, our SG is most aware of shooting linebackers.
C—He executes the same techniques as on Green 24.

Fig. 4–31. Green 25—X-Out. Intended receiver is X.

WG & WT—They execute the same techniques as our SG and ST on Green 24.

X—His rule is written as such because we often run Green 25 from left or right formations (R swinging) or from Port or Star formations (Z swinging). If we call the play in Gee or Haw formations, the QB must call X into the pattern desired. X must be prepared to slide on the snake pattern (Fig. 4–32).

Z—If he runs a swing pattern (Port or Star formations) he stays wide until he has outrun the defensive end. He must not cut upfield too soon. He may also be called on to run an out pattern (Fig. 4–33).

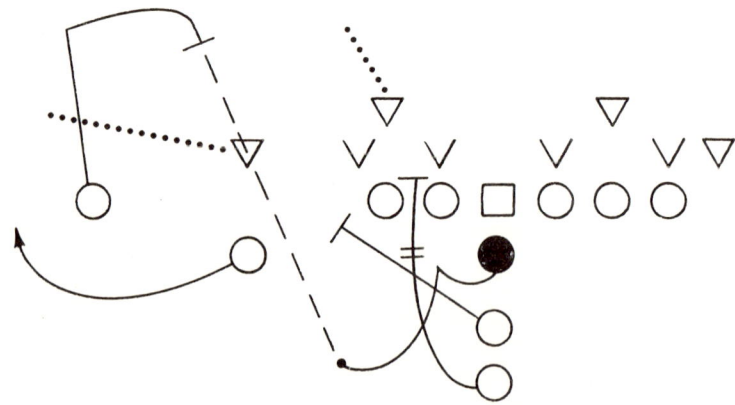

Fig. 4–32. Green 25—X Snake.

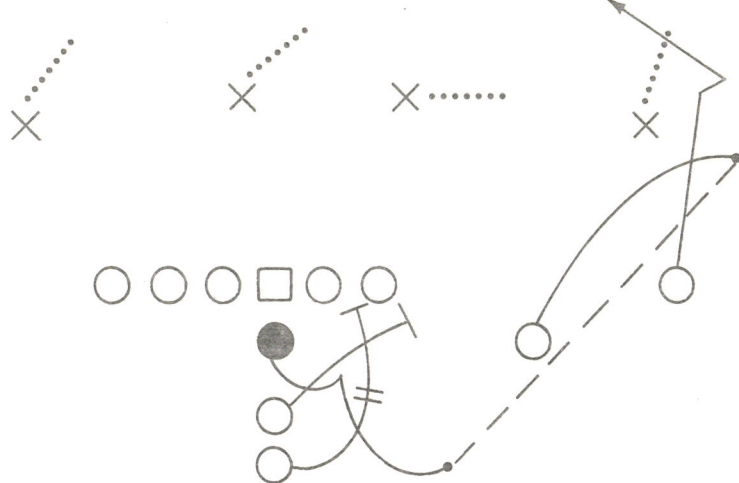

Fig. 4-33. Green 25—Z-Out.

R—His swing pattern involves the same techniques as mentioned for Z (Fig. 4–34). R may also be called on to run a fan pattern (Fig. 4–35). The first key is to release clearly. We would prefer that, on the fan, R release inside the defensive end so as to make F's block easier, but R must get clear by out-running the LB and this is his first job.

QB—Same techniques as on Green 24.

Against a 4-deep, 50 defense, we prefer this play from Gee or Haw or Left or Right formations. If the inside safety is covering

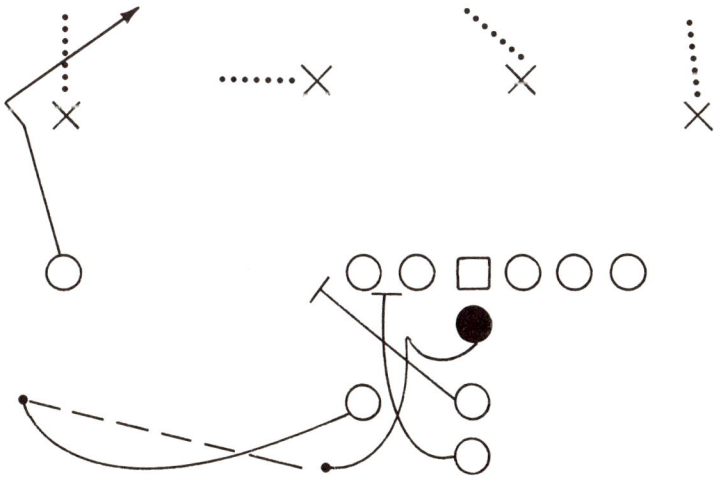

Fig. 4-34. Green 25 from right formation.

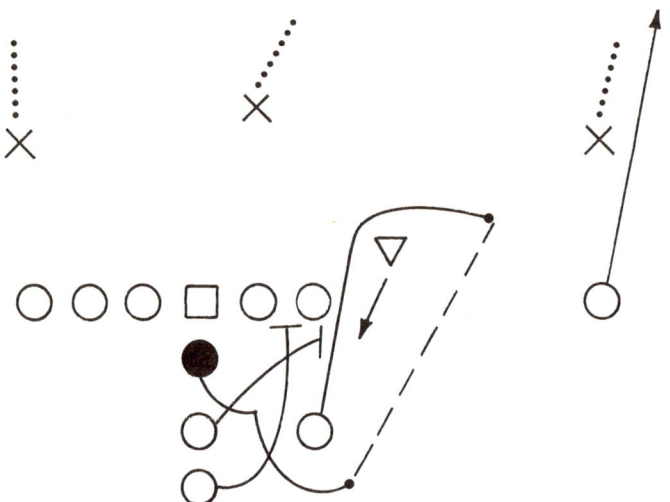

Fig. 4–35. Green 25–R fan.

the flat, we like to hit R on the swing, or X on the post in Left or Right, or X on the out in Gee and Haw formations. Against a 60 defense, the Z swing from Port and Star formations has been effective when combined with the X snake pattern. It places some pressure on the end and linebacker.

Green 24 and 25 are naturally more effective on first down, or some other running down, as the defensive end and linebacker are more liable to tighten up and play run first, thus being less effective vs. the pass.

Maximum protection is afforded our QB as we usually release only two receivers, and the fake of the run also holds potential pass rushers for an instant.

80 Series Passes

See Fig. 4–36.

Assignments

Y—Block 3. Or, tackle call.
ST—Block 2. Or, tackle call.
SG—Block 1. Or, tackle call.
C—Block on. Or, offside. Or, option.
WG—Block out. Or, option.
WT—Block on. Or, out.
X—Recon pattern.

USC PASSING ATTACK

Z—To—out pattern. Away, seam. Or, pick.
F—Block 4.
R—Flare pattern.
T—Motion strong.
QB—Sprint out strongside.

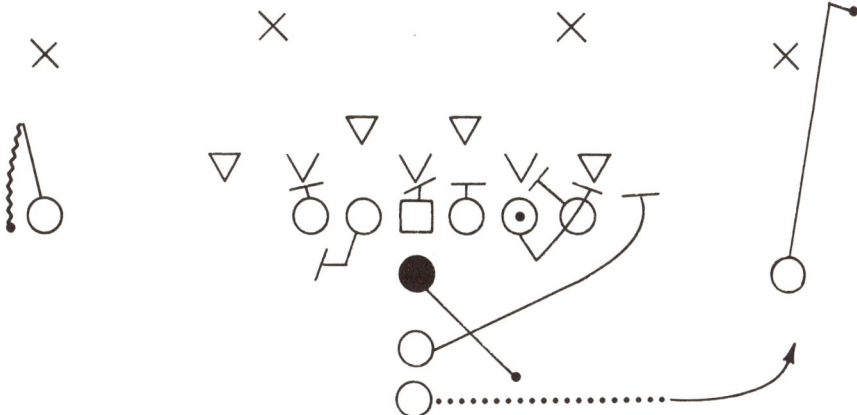

Fig. 4–36. 85 from Gee formation—Trojan call.

Coaching Points

Y—He must be alert for a tackle call. If it is a Trojan or George, he uses a far-shoulder technique. Vs. a 60 defense, he uses the reverse technique. He may also be called into the pattern.

ST—He must call to make his and the Y-end's blocks easier. We prefer Trojan vs. a 50, George vs. a 6–1, Eagle vs. a 60. He uses a far-shoulder block when blocking down. On the Trojan block he attempts to over block the end. He may receive help from F vs. a 4-deep secondary.

SG—On a Trojan call he steps at the LB and blocks him if he shoots. Otherwise, he turns inside to help his center. On a George call he over-blocks the end (Fig. 4–37). On Eagle he steps around his ST and looks for the LB to shoot (Fig. 4–38). If the LB does not shoot, the SG continues down the line leading the play.

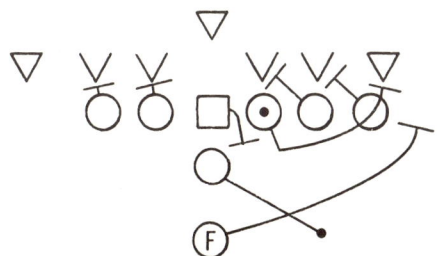

Fig. 4–37. 84 with George blocking.

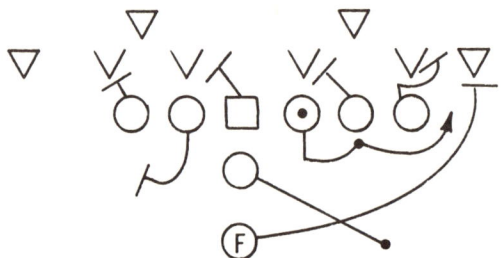

Fig. 4-38. 84 with Eagle blocking.

C–WG–WT—They have the same backside protection rules as on Green 24.

X—He should be alert on his recon pattern as we may throwback.

Z—He runs an out pattern unless called on to execute another pattern. Other patterns we like are: 2 snake, Z delay, Z post, Z out and up. The key is for Z to break off the line quickly. If 84 Pick is called, he blocks the man covering the motion, or the most dangerous man coming outside.

F—He drives directly at 4. If 4 drops off to cover our motion, F looks inside to help on 3 or a forcing LB, but does not stop running. Our QB may run if 4 drops off, and F must keep going and lead. And, F being downfield does not constitute a penalty for an illegal man downfield.

T—His motion must be full speed and he must stay wide. Once he gains his width he turns upfield full speed. He has broken open up-field, especially on 84-Z snake or post.

QB—He opens strongside after letting T get motion to a position behind our Y-end. Q gets about five yards deep so he can turn upfield and square his shoulders to throw. When sprinting out left, he throws sidearm.

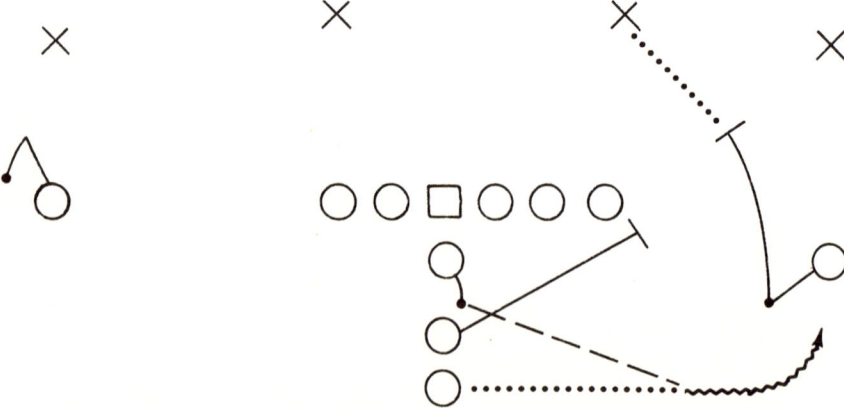

Fig. 4-39. 84 Pick vs. 4-Deep. Inside safety covers motion.

Our number one call off 84 is 84 Pick (Figs. 4–39 and 4–40). Our QB opens and throws to T in motion as quickly as possible, hitting him with as easy a pass as possible without taking too much off the ball. Z must read the pass coverage and be ready to block the most dangerous man.

We like the basic out pattern vs. 3-deep teams that force with their end. Our QB is instructed to immediately look at 4, and if 4 comes, to throw the ball to T right now (Fig. 4–41). We now have T, who we hope is a fine open-field runner, in the open vs. one defender where a missed tackle can mean a long gain.

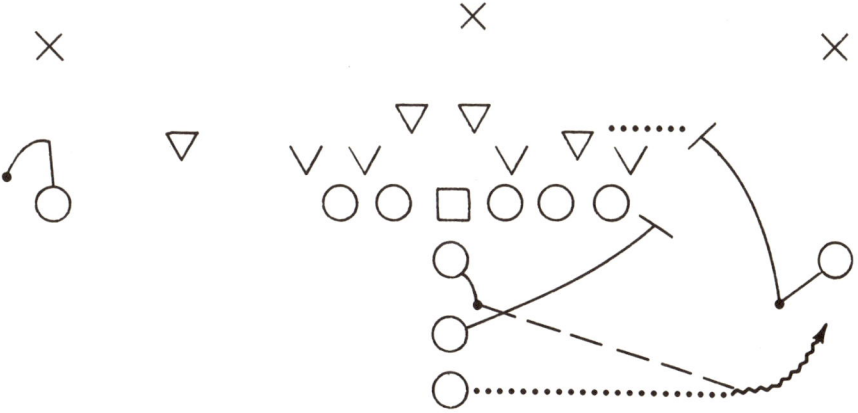

Fig. 4–40. 84 Pick. LB covers motion.

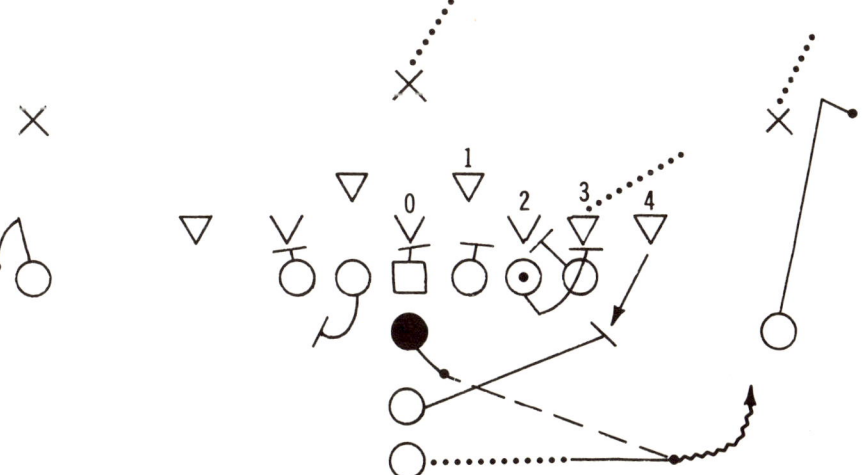

Fig. 4–41. 84 hitting motion man when 4 forces.

We like 84-Z delay vs. teams that play a 4-deep rotation or use man for man coverage (Figs. 4–42 and 4–43).

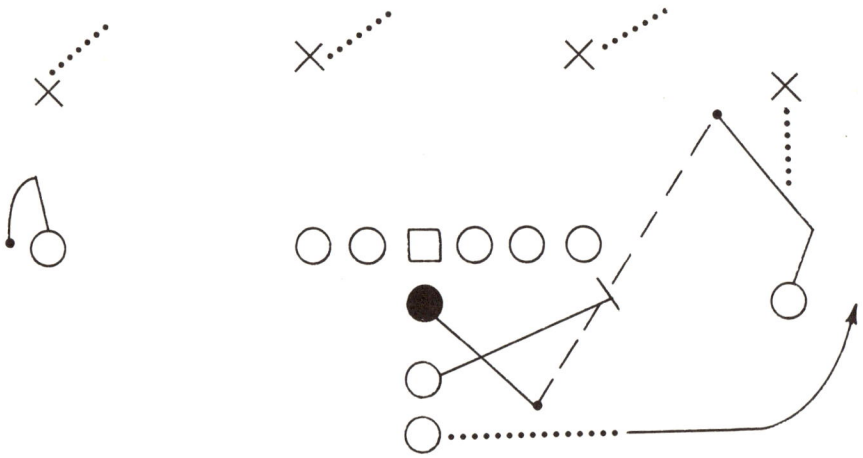

Fig. 4–42. 84–Z delay vs. 4-deep rotation.

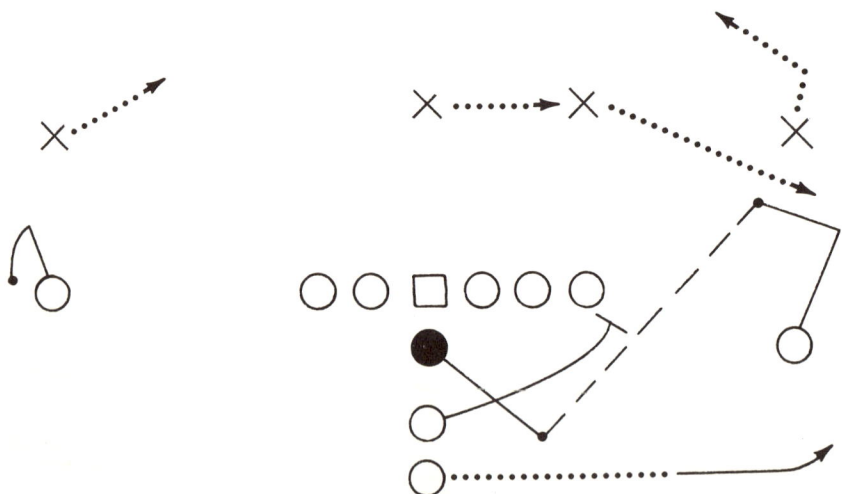

Fig. 4–43. 84–Z delay vs. man-for-man.

We like 84-Z snake versus teams that have their end drop off to cover the motion man (Fig. 4–44), and we like 84 Fly (Fig. 4–45) (Z out) vs. teams that rotate with motion.

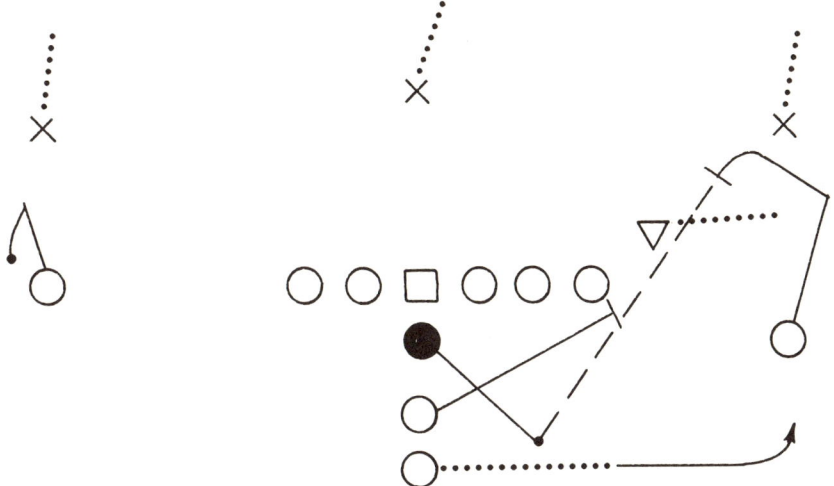

Fig. 4–44. 84–Z Snake vs. end drifting. QB should run here.

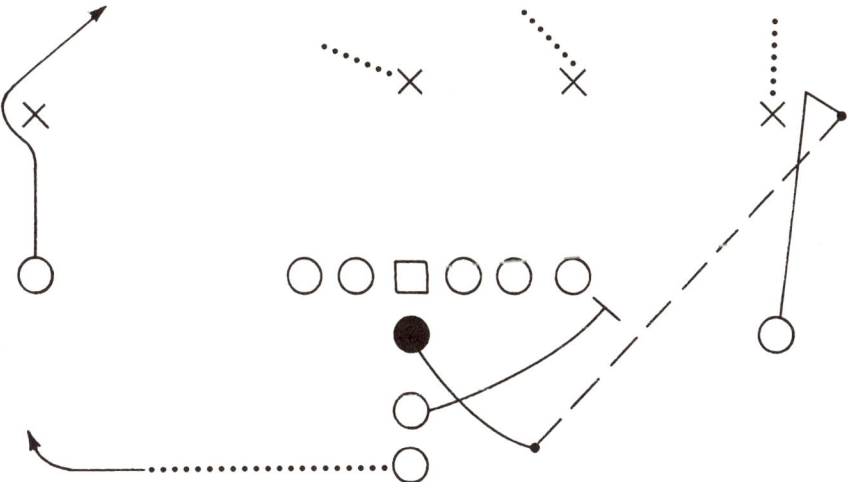

Fig. 4–45. 84 Fly vs. Motion rotation.

We like to run 84-Z out and up vs. a 3-deep defense that rotates in the secondary (Fig. 4–46). If the halfback covers Z, Z "squirrels" at 15 yards (Fig. 4–47).

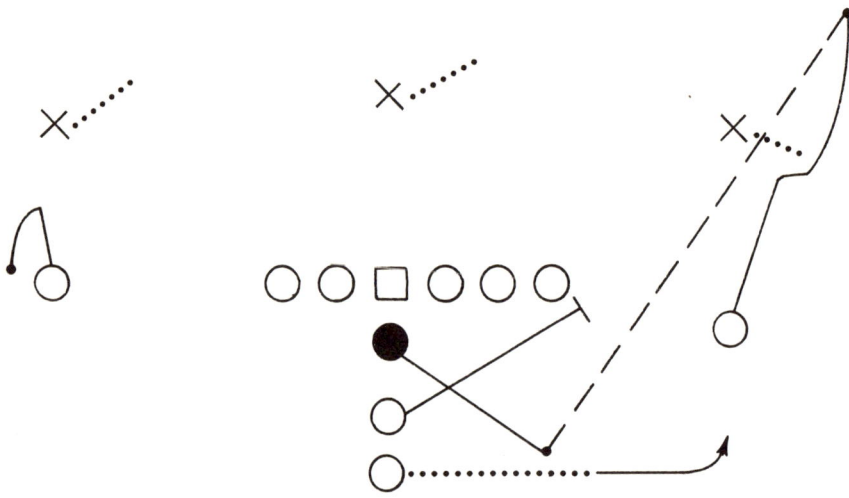

Fig. 4–46. 84–Z-Out-and-Up vs. 3-Deep rotation.

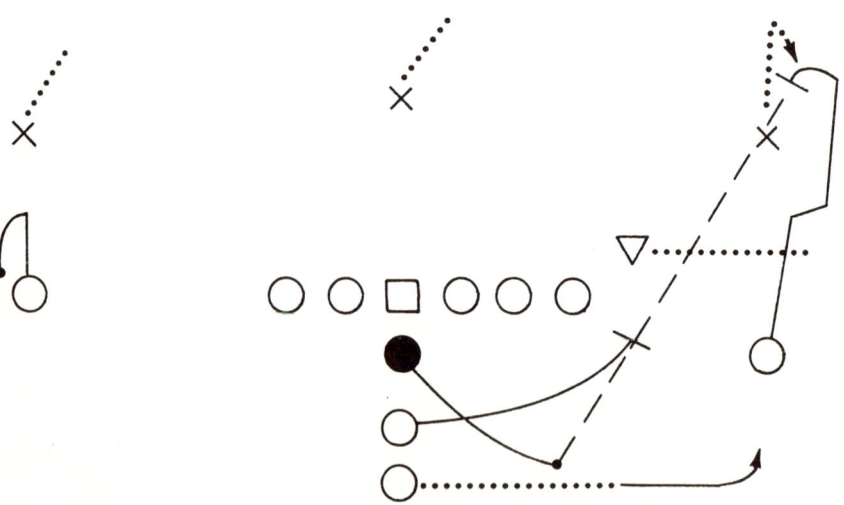

Fig. 4–47. 84–Z Squirrel. Halfback covers Z.

USC PASSING ATTACK

We like 84-Z post vs. a 4-deep secondary that covers motion with their inside safety (Fig. 4–48). We also like 84-Y crease vs. teams that are late in rotating the offside (Fig. 4–49). We usually combine this with X-post. F must block 3 if Y is in the pattern.

There are numerous options off this play, but the QB must keep in mind that we will take an easy 5-yard gain on any running situation. We hold Y in to block to provide maximum protection.

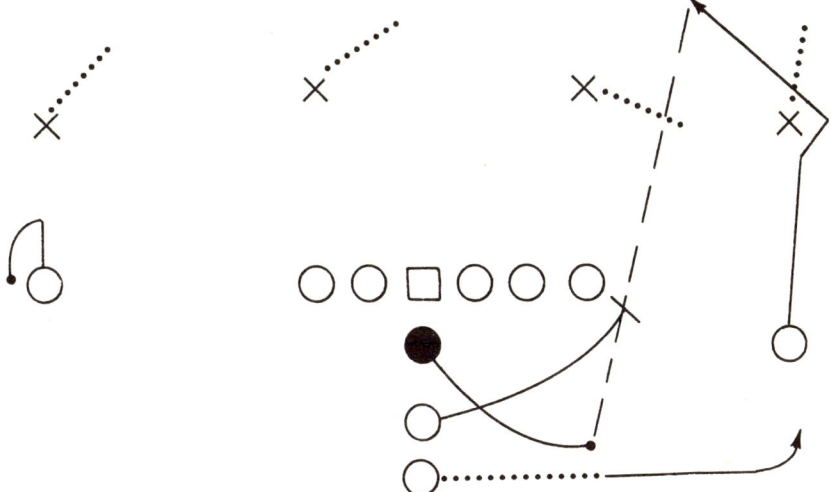

Fig. 4–48. 84–Z Post vs. 4-Deep rotation.

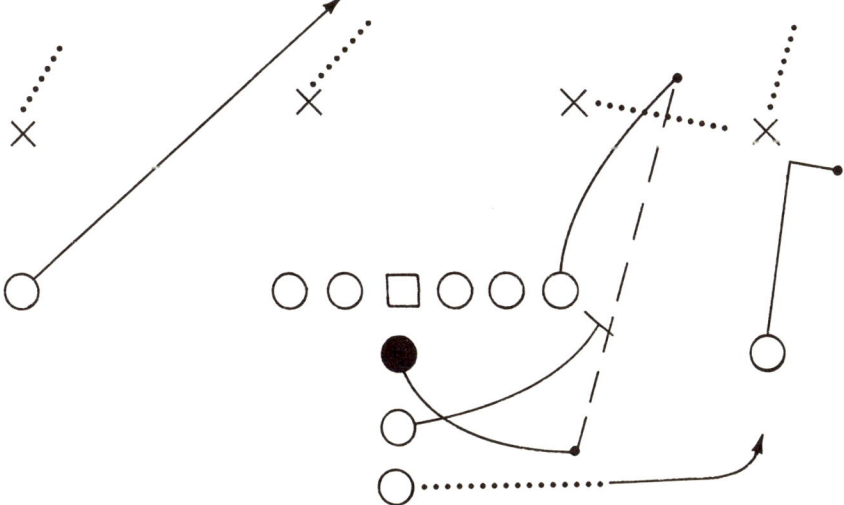

Fig. 4–49. 84–Y Crease (X post) vs. 4-Deep rotation.

83 Pass

See Fig. 4-50.

Assignments

Y—Block out.
ST—Block on. Or, out.
SG—Block out. Or, option.
C—Block on. Or, offside. Or, option.
WG—Block 1. Or, tackle call.
WT—Block 2. Or, tackle call.
X—Out pattern.
Z—To—look pattern. Away, recon.
F—Block 3.
R—Swing pattern.
T—Motion weakside.
QB—Sprint out weakside.

Coaching Points

Y—ST—SG—C—Same backside protection as on Green 25.
WG—If Eagle is called, he steps around the tackle and looks for the LB to shoot. If he does not shoot, he continues to lead.
WT—He calls Eagle vs. the 60 defense. Otherwise, he uses a cut-off block.
X—He must break off the line with great speed.
Z—If, in Port or Star formations, his look pattern should be wide enough so that the LB cannot cover him. He looks immediately for the ball.

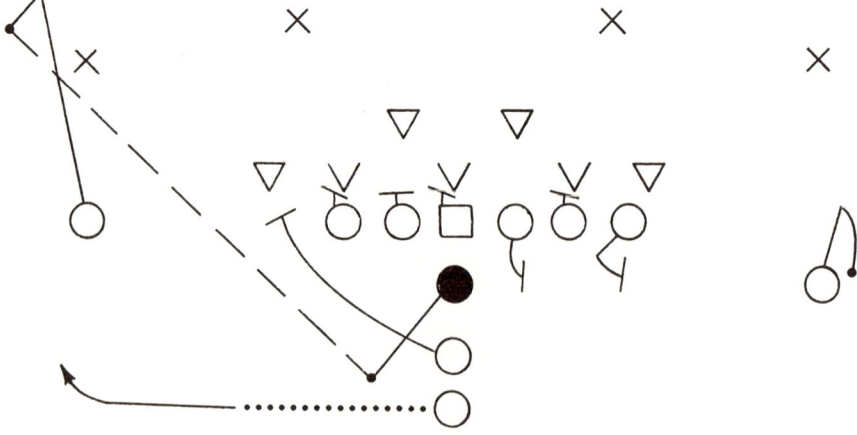

Fig. 4-50. 83 from Gee formation.

USC PASSING ATTACK

F—His technique is a low, body block to bring the end's hands down. We do not necessarily expect F to knock the end down, but we do want to give the QB a chance to throw and to do this we must bring the defender's hands down with a low block.

QB—He uses the same technique as on 84, but keys 3 instead of 4. If 3 runs off to cover the flat, Q is ready to run.

We prefer to run 83 against a team that over-shifts to our strongside, leaving only 3 men on the line to our weakside. We like to run 83 Fly (T motion strongside) to get a one-on-one situation for our X-end (Fig. 4–51). We also like 83 from Port and Star (Fig. 4–52) for a quick pass to Z on a look pattern.

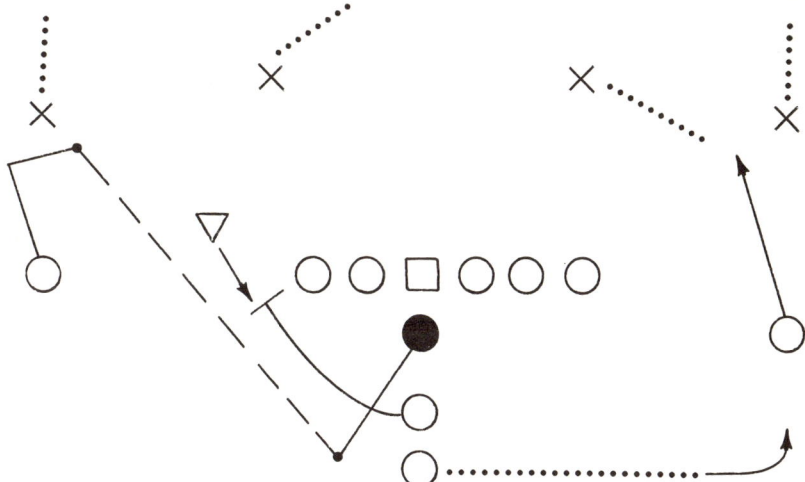

Fig. 4–51. 83 Fly–X delay.

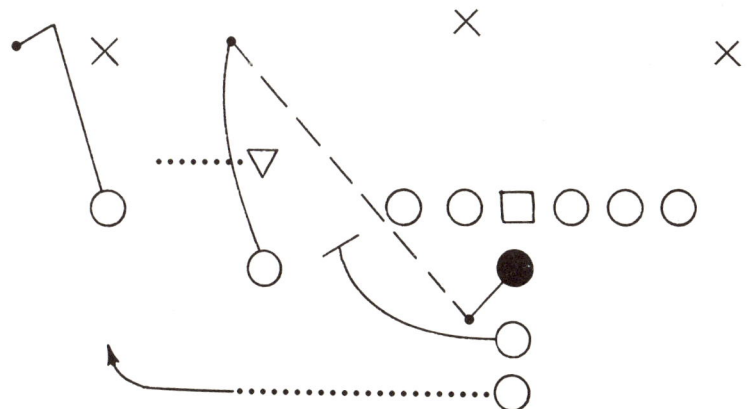

Fig. 4–52. 83 from Star formation.

88 Pass

See Fig. 4–53.

Assignments

Y—Out pattern.
ST—Block 2. Or, tackle call.
SG—Block 1. Or, tackle call.
C—Block on. Or, offside. Or, option.
WG—Block out. Or, option.
WT—Block on. Or, out.
X—Recon pattern.
Z—3-deep, up. 4-deep, post.
F—Block 3.
T—Block 4.
R—Swing.
QB—Sprint out strongside.

Coaching Points

Y—He should split enough to get free quickly. If possible, he should release inside the end in a 50 defense to make F's block easier. His pattern must be wide enough to run away from the linebacker, yet must bend upfield if the end drops off in the flat.

Line—Same protection as on 84. Exception: the ST cannot call Trojan or George as Y is in the pattern.

T—If 4 drops off, T looks inside and keeps running.

QB—If 4 drops off this can be a good gainer running the ball.

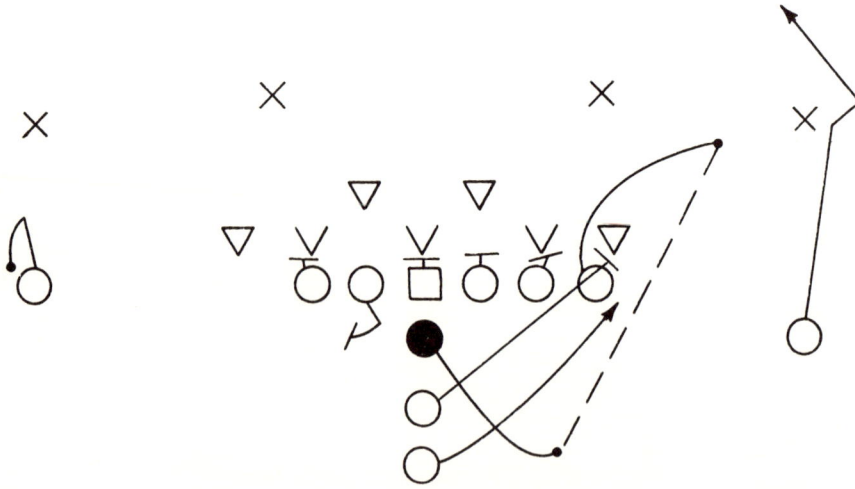

Fig. 4–53. 88 Y-Out.

We like this pass vs. teams that disregard Y as a receiver. 88-Y crease is effective against teams that shoot backers and use a zone pass defense. It is an effective run vs. teams that drop their end to the flat in a 60 defense.

89 Pass

See Fig. 4–54.

Assignments

Y—Block out.
ST—Block on. Or, out.
SG—Block out. Or, option.
C—Block on. Or, offside. Or, option.
WG—Block 1.
WT—Block 2.
X—Snake pattern.
Z—To—swing pattern. Away, seam pattern.
F—Block 3. Block 4 if R back.
R—Swing pattern in right and left. Or, block 3.
T—Block 4.
QB—Sprint out weakside.

Coaching Points

F—In left or right formations R will swing and T will block 4. F must know that if there is no T-back, and there is an R back, that R will block 3. Then, F must block 4. Our technique is always to "bring the hands down" with a low block.

R—He must know he swings in left and right, but blocks 3 in other formations.

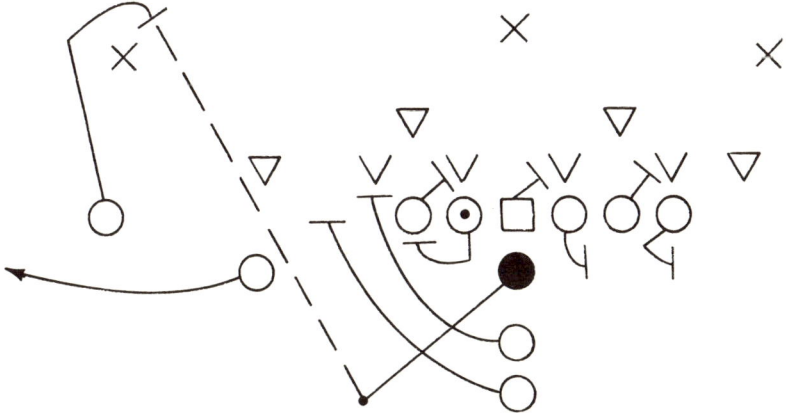

Fig. 4–54. 89–Z Snake.

QB—If we happen to catch a team with 4 off the line, this play should pick up good yardage by running the ball.

The play has been effective vs. 3-deep teams who drop their end off to cover Z on the swing in port and star formations. Two deep patterns that can be effective are 89-Z flag and 89-X post (Figs. 4–55 and 4–56) vs. teams that attempt to rotate on flow, or cover man-for-man. Once again, maximum protection is afforded our QB.

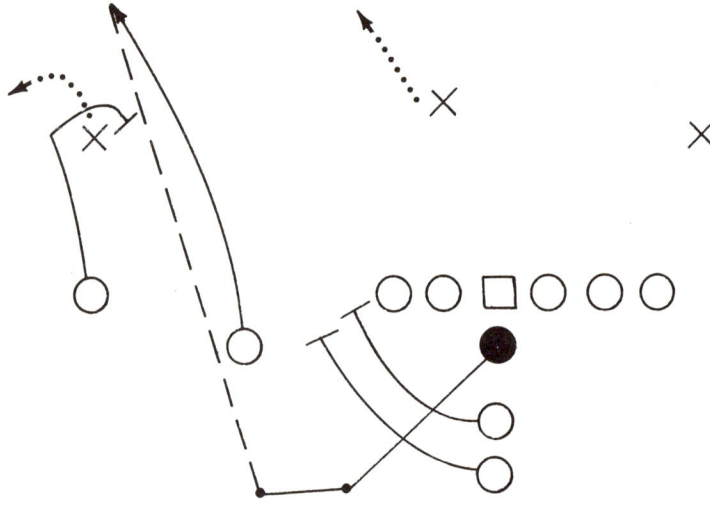

Fig. 4–55. 89—Z flag.

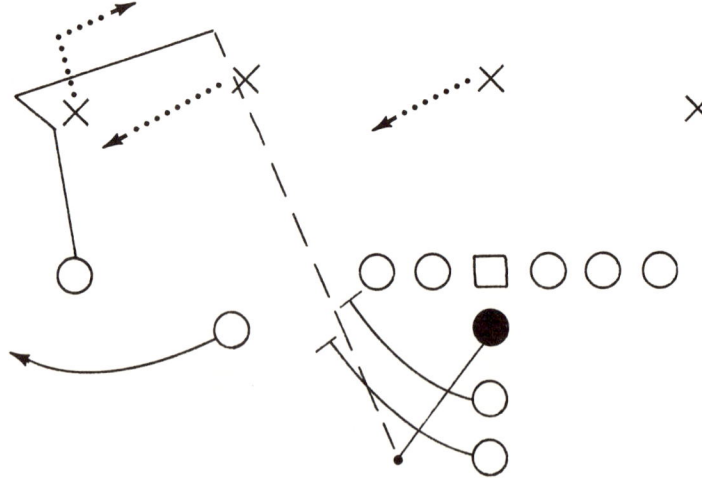

Fig. 4–56. 89—X post.

USC PASSING ATTACK

ROLL-OUT PASSES OFF INSIDE FAKES

Boot Strong

See Fig. 4-57.

Assignments

Y—Between. Or, on.
ST—Block 1st man inside on or off the line.
SG—Pull.
C—Block on gap. Or, on. Or, option.
WG—Pull.
WT—Block 2.
X—Cross pattern.
Z—Out pattern.
F—Fill block over weak guard.
R—Block 3 weakside.
T—Motion weakside.
QB—Open weakside and roll out strongside.

Coaching Points

Y—"Between" means any man between his ST and himself, on the line. He must know his tackle's rule (1st man inside). If he blocks down, he uses a far-shoulder technique. If the man is on, he uses the reverse technique.
ST—He uses a far-shoulder technique. Vs. a 50, he steps down, plugs the hole against shooting linebackers and then turns inside.

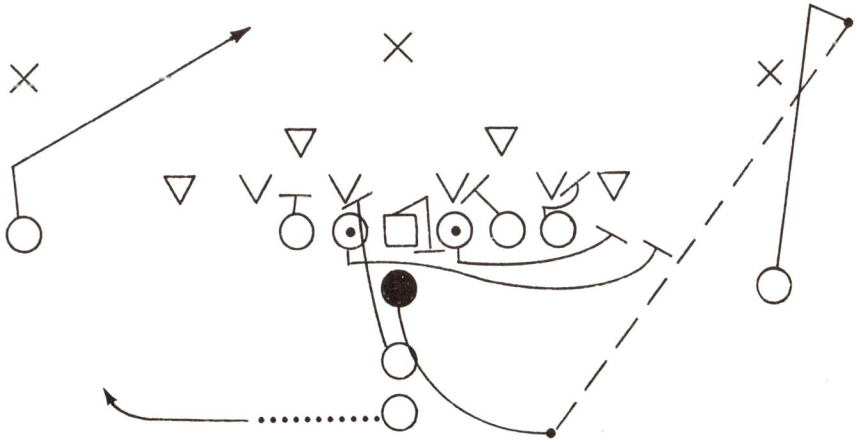

Fig. 4-57. Boot strong from Gee formation.

SG—As he pulls, he gets depth and also checks for any linebacker that may shoot (60 defense). He attacks the defensive end with one thought in mind, "bring his hands down" with a low block.

C—F will fill weakside, so our center thinks strongside. He must seal the gap to prevent any stunting linemen or shooting backers from getting our QB early.

WG—He pulls deep and attempts to get an outside position on the end who has been attacked low by our SG. Both guards continue downfield if the end drops off.

Z—He looks early as the QB will throw a little sooner than on 84, etc., because our guards are heading downfield.

QB—As he pivots to roll out he must get the ball up to throw as his guards may be going downfield. If 4 drops off, the run yardage should be substantial. He should not call a deep pattern on this play without telling his guards to hold up from going downfield. We do not want our guards to hesitate, because this cuts down their effectiveness.

This play causes a rotating secondary some problems and also is difficult on a defensive end who starts rotating back on motion away from him. Versus a man-for-man defense, the Z-delay pattern has proven successful. We especially like this play to allow our one receiver, Z, a one-on-one situation.

Waggle Strong

See Fig. 4-58.

Assignments

Y—Seam pattern.
ST—Block 2.
SG—Block 1.
C—Block on. Or, offside. Or, option.
WG—Pull and block the 1st man past our ST.
WT—Block 2.
X—Cross pattern.
Z—Up pattern.
F—Fill block over WG.
R—Swing.
T—Fake 25 and block 3.
QB—Half reverse pivot and rollout strongside.

Coaching Points

Y—He must split enough to get out quickly. We want him to clear the area.

USC PASSING ATTACK

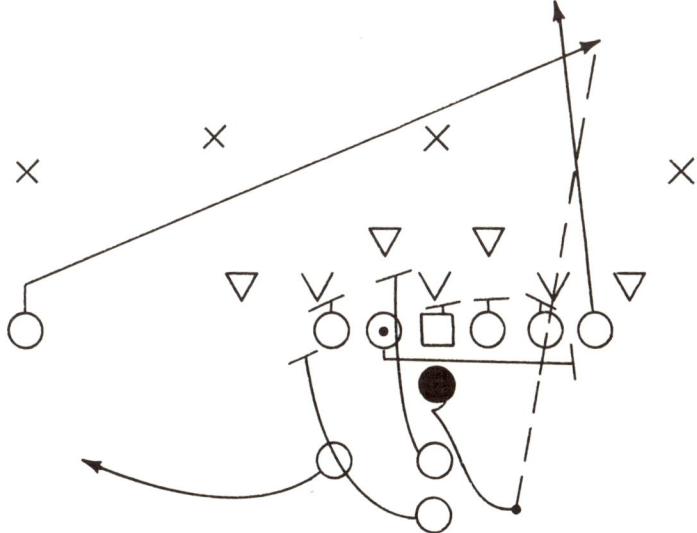

Fig. 4-58. Waggle strong from Right formation.

WG—He may have to block the end out. He must know that this play is a pass first and that his QB will set up to throw behind our ST; but if the end drops off, he goes and gets him.

X—He is the primary receiver. He wants to run deeper than the linebackers. His split should be near or pickle.

QB—He must not be in too big a hurry to hit X crossing. The linebackers should first bounce to our weakside. We would like to hit X at a spot relative to the area Y has cleared. If the defensive end drops back to this zone, we should be able to run.

This play serves as a counter-type pass versus teams that have fast pursuing linebackers. Other patterns that may break open are Y-out, Y flag, and X post. It adheres to our principles of maximum protection with one receiver as our target; and X is given freedom to get open.

79 Pass

See Fig. 4-59.

Assignments

Y—Block out.
ST—Block 2.
SG—Pull and lead.
C—Block on gap. Or, on. Or, option.

WG—Pull.
WT—Block the 1st man on the line.
X—Out pattern.
Z—To—swing. Away, seam.
F—Fill block over strong guard.
R—Block 1st man outside your tackle.
T—Motion weakside.
QB—Reverse pivot and rollout weakside.

Coaching Points

G's—Same techniques as on boot strong, except that the WG brings the man's hands down and the SG gets outside position.
WT—If he blocks down, he uses a far-shoulder technique. If blocking a man on or slightly outside shade, he uses a cut-off block.
C—He must protect the onside (weakside) gap.
R—He uses a low cut-off, scramble block and does not try to overpower the defender. His aim is to tie up the defender's feet.
QB—He looks immediately to the end man on the line, and if he runs off, the QB runs the ball.

If we find X covered by one man, this play gives us good protection to give X time to run a pattern to get free. We like the X out-and-up and X squirrel patterns from this. We also like this play vs. a team that overshifts to our strongside leaving one defender outside. If our WT can cut-off the defensive tackle, we can put three blockers on the defensive end. The play has proven to be an effective run in goalline situations, also.

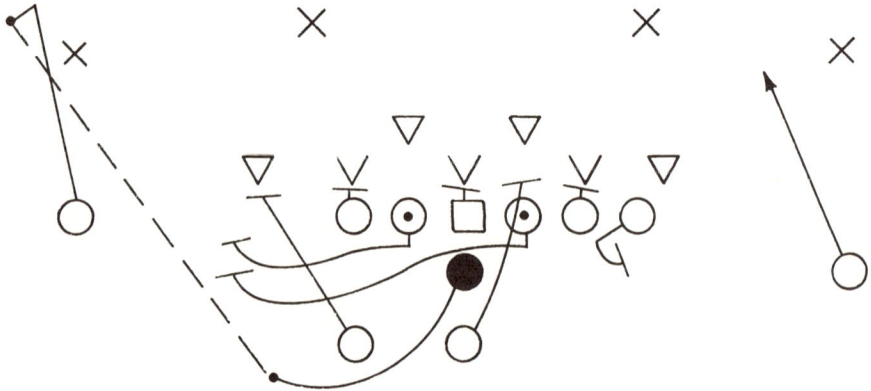

Fig. 4–59. 79 Pass from Pro-Gee formation.

USC PASSING ATTACK

Waggle Weak

See Fig. 4-60.

Assignments

Y—Cross pattern.
ST—Block 2.
SG—Pull.
C—Block on. Or, offside. Or, option.
WG—Block 1.
WT—Block 2.
X—3-deep, up. 4-deep, post.
Z—To—swing. Away, seam.
F—Fill block over strong guard.
R—Swing.
T—Fake 24 and block the 1st man outside our ST.
QB—Reverse pivot and roll out weakside.

Coaching Points

R—He must sprint quickly outside and get width. He looks immediately for the ball.
QB—He looks to the defensive end. If he forces, he throws to R immediately. If the end drops off, Q continues his rollout, looking for Y on the cross pattern.

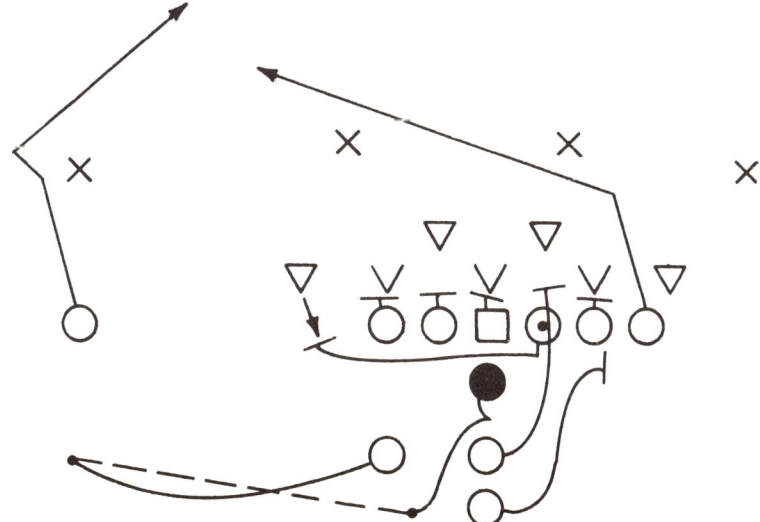

Fig. 4-60. Waggle weak from Right formation.

This play is effective against defensive ends who are forcing, and also against linebackers who are intent on stopping 24 Power. Occasionally against a team that keys R and rotates, X may get open deep.

90 Series Passes

The 90 series passes are our dropback passes. We do not employ dropback passes very often, as we prefer to threaten the defense with both the run and pass option by our QB. When we do throw dropback passes, we usually flood a zone, sending two and sometimes three receivers into the zone. Because of the scarcity of dropback passes in our offense, our blocking rules are quite simple. Our center blocks 0 that shows; our guard, No. 1 that shows; our tackles, No. 2 that shows; and our backs, No. 3 that shows. We drop our inside foot back and pin-block the defender that shows in our area. If we are releasing our R-back, our Y-end would block 3 that shows. (See Fig. 4–61.)

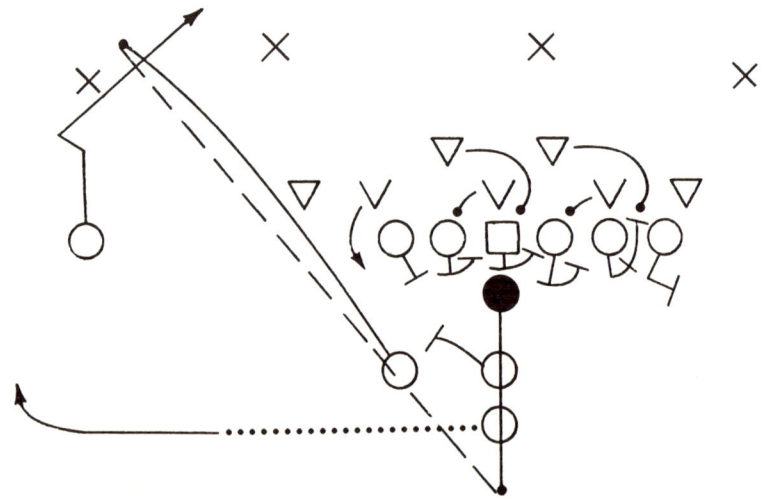

Fig. 4–61. Right formation—98-R banana.

5

Offense Drills

Much of our offensive work is done in team situations, especially after the season starts. We do have some basic drills we use to train our players for their offensive positions.

STANCE AND GET-OFF DRILL

We use the stance and get-off drill (Fig. 5-1) quite a lot in the spring and early fall. The coach signals the move he wishes the men to make and the QB calls the cadence. We practice five moves:

1. Straight ahead
2. Lead left and right
3. Open left and right (backs)
4. Pull left and right (line)
5. Pass protection

Important points to check for include weight concentration, body balance, explosive get-off and, of course, the original stance. The F-back always operates from a down stance, while our R- and Z-backs operate from both down and upright stance.

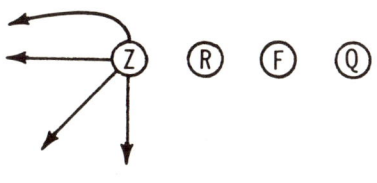

COACH

Fig. 5-1. Stance and get-off drill.

BAG DRILL

The bag drill (Fig. 5–2) helps develop power, balance, and ball awareness. The QB hands the ball off to a back who dives straight ahead at a man with a large dummy. This dummy is tilted left or right and the runner cuts the opposite direction and drives through two men holding air-flight dummies. These two men bang the runner quite hard. As the runner drives through, another man throws an air-flight dummy at the runner's feet forcing him to high-step to avoid tripping and falling.

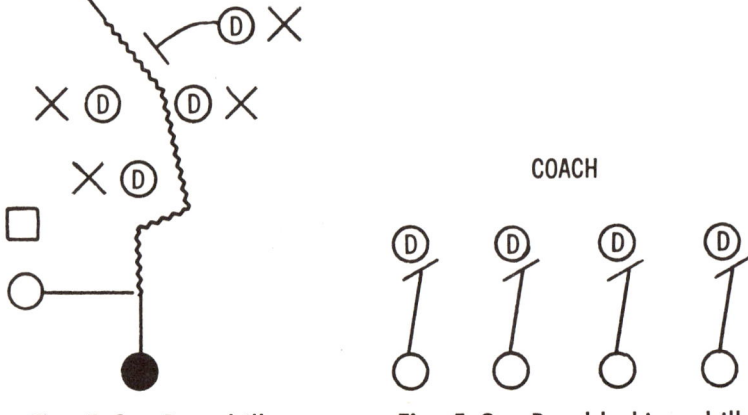

Fig. 5–2. Bag drill.   Fig. 5–3. Bag-blocking drill.

BAG-BLOCKING DRILL

Our bag-blocking drill (Fig. 5–3) enables us to teach the fundamentals of blocking without undue contact among our offensive backs. We practice our drive, body, and junction blocks on large dummies, stationing our backs at the proper angle to execute the various blocks. We emphasize stance and initial move here, also.

BLOCKING DRILL

After teaching the fundamental blocking techniques on dummies, we progress to "live" blocking on defensive ends and tackles (Fig. 5–4). We align offensive backs as our offensive Y-end and W-T, so that we can obtain the proper defensive alignment to execute our various blocks. We usually outfit the defenders in aprons.

OFFENSE DRILLS 107

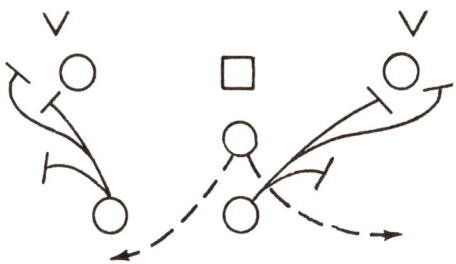

Fig. 5–4. Blocking drill.

OPTION AND KEEP DRILL

The option and keep drill (Fig. 5–5) is one of several pattern drills we use to develop the techniques of our various running plays. In this particular drill, the coach signals the defender to either play the QB or to play for the pitch, and our QB reacts accordingly. We also have drills to practice the sweep, the power, and the rollouts; and we sometimes add our offensive guards to these drills.

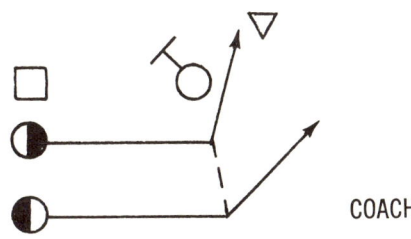

COACH

Fig. 5–5. Option-and-keep drill (patterns drill).

INDIVIDUAL PASS CUT DRILL

We operate two groups simultaneously, with the men switching groups after three receptions. One of the QB's is designated as the signal caller. We practice all of our individual pass cuts in this manner and the drill also provides a good deal of running for our receivers. (See Fig. 5–6.)

HALF-LINE DRILL—STRONGSIDE

We feel our half-line drills enable us to teach our offense with the utmost concentration on individual assignments. Our guards and backs must switch groups half-way through the drill so that they work on both strongside and weakside plays. We concentrate on our running attack in these drills. (See Fig. 5–7.)

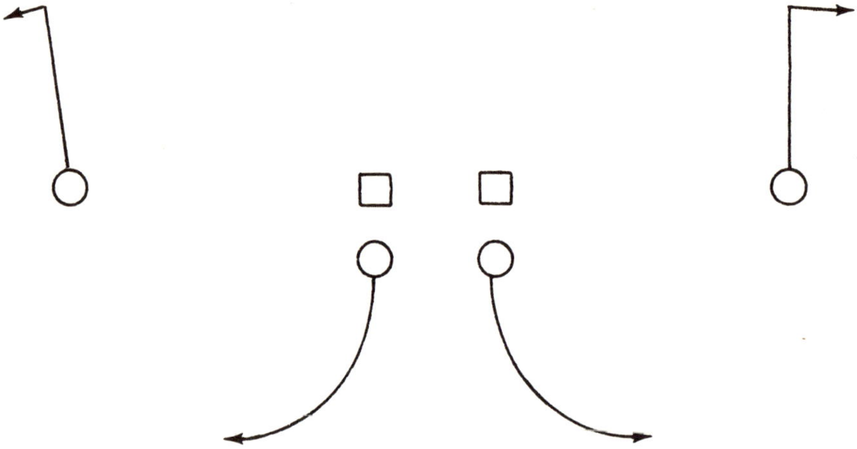

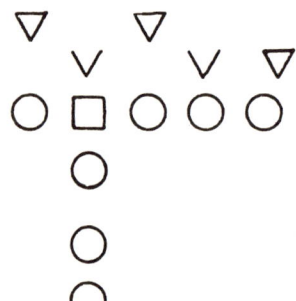

Fig. 5–6. Individual pass-cut drill.

Fig. 5–7. Half-line drill—strongside.

We have two drills for our QB's to develop their passing arms. In one drill, two QB's run parallel to each other as fast as they can. We want quickness of delivery in this drill. The distance between men increases as they warm up their passing arms. Our other drill is one that can be executed on and off the field. The passer lies on his back and merely flips the football up in the air and catches it. This requires much concentration and also requires the correct wrist snap technique to prevent dropping the ball.

Our line blocking drills are similar to our blocking drills for our backs in that we start with dummies and teach the techniques of our various blocks, and then progress to live drills against defenders in aprons. We attempt to have the defenders vary their charge, especially on our near- and far-shoulder blocks.

Our drill for double-team blocking has helped us learn to pick up stunts.

OFFENSE DRILLS

DOUBLE-TEAM DRILL

The coach behind the defenders signals which two offensive men he wishes to execute the double-team. The coach behind the blockers signals the middle defender to play straight or slant into or away from the double-team. The offensive blockers must get off hard and then block accordingly. If the defender plays tough, they double him inside. If the defender slants outside, they take him outside. If the defender slants inside, the post-man takes him in, and our lead-man picks up the linebacker. (See Fig. 5-8.)

As a rule, we try to keep our blocking drills short and moving quickly. We try to coordinate the blocking drills with the plays we are concentrating on that day. For example, when putting in the power play, our drills would include the double-team and the guard pulling through the hole, plus the fullback drive block on an end.

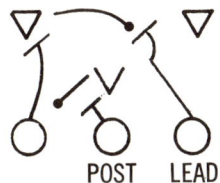

Fig. 5-8. Double-team drill.

Part II

DEFENSE

6

Defensive Fundamentals and Line Play

ALIGNMENTS

We believe defensive football is reaction football as compared to offensive football, which is mostly assignment football. Therefore, our objectives on defense are quite simple: Align ourselves and then slant or vary our positions so that (1) the offensive assignments change rapidly and do not remain as they appeared on the snap of the ball, and (2) our defenders are in a position to react to the ball.

We are not as interested in alignments as we are in reaction. Our key phrase is: "It is not where you line up, it is where you wind up." Therefore, we concentrate on recognition of offensive moves and then reaction to these moves. If we can teach our men to recognize offensive moves and then react to the play that develops, we can align them in various defenses but their basic moves will remain constant.

Our basic alignment is as shown in Fig. 6-1. On each play we will flop three perimeter men: rover, swing, and end. The two linebackers will also adjust their alignment, although not necessarily in accordance with the perimeter trio. Our tackles and middle guard are in a four-point stance, feet parallel. All others are in a two-point stance, outside foot back, except our halfbacks who have their outside foot up for better vision.

As the offensive team assumes its alignment, our weak backer makes a call of Left or Right to designate the strength of the offense (see Fig. 6-2). When the call is made, the side called becomes the strongside of our defense and the other side becomes the weakside.

If, for example, we call Left, our left side is our strongside and our right side is our weakside. If we call Right, the opposite is true. If the call is Left, our rover and swing man flop to the left and our end flops to the right. Our strong backer would probably go left, also.

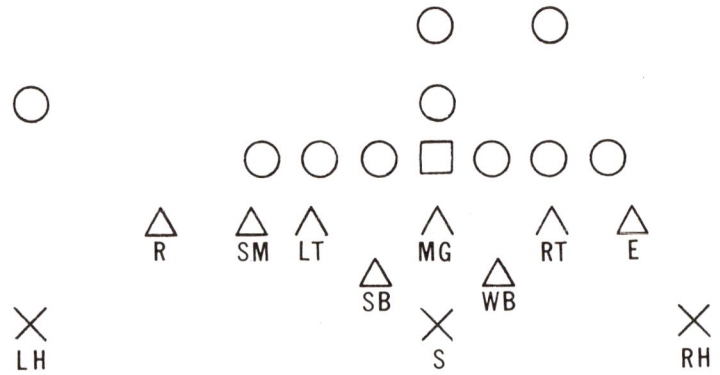

Fig. 6–1. 50 alignment.

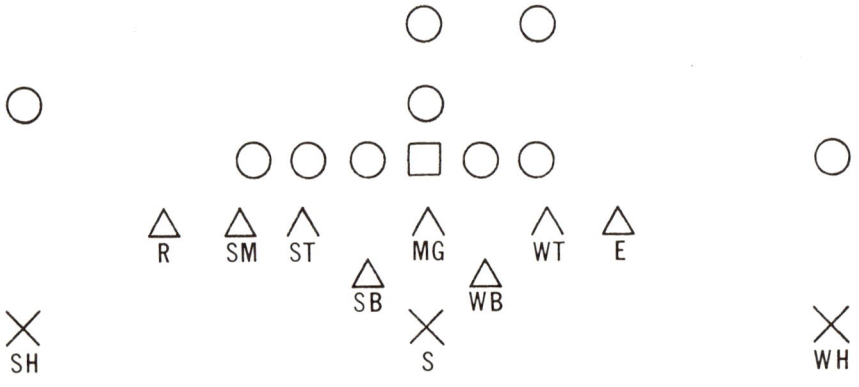

Fig. 6–2. Left call to offensive strength.

PERSONNEL

Rover. He must be agile enough to play good pass defense short, deep, and man-for-man, and also strong enough to fill tough on sweeps. He will flop from side to side with the strength of the offense.

Swing Man. He must be strong enough to stop power at him and agile enough for quick lateral pursuit on wide plays. He has

DEFENSIVE FUNDAMENTALS AND LINE PLAY

no pass responsibility. He assumes a two-point, upright stance. He flops with the rover and usually goes with the offensive tight end.

End. He is more agile than the swing man, as he will often be called on for pass defense. Yet, he must be strong enough to plug the off-tackle hole. He will flop to the side opposite rover and swing man.

Tackles. Our strongest defenders, able to break a double-team, yet quick enough to slant in or out effectively. We will place our quickest tackle to our right side as most teams seem to prefer to run to their right.

Middle Guard. Our quickest lineman, able to slant to and catch pulling guards. We would like him also to be able to play the center head on.

Strong Backer. Our strongest linebacker. He will flop with the strength of the offensive line. He must possess the necessary agility for pass defense and pursuit, but also be strong enough to play a guard tough on the line.

Weak Backer. Our best tackler and run defender who we hope can play some man-to-man pass defense on a halfback. We will attempt to free him on almost every play. Strength is a secondary requirement. He will flop to the offense's weak side so that he can pursue more plays.

Secondary. Agility, speed and reaction to a thrown ball are the prerequisites here. We will place our quickest, most intelligent man at safety, our quickest halfback to our right, and our best run defender to our left. They will not flop.

TACKLES

Our tackles have four basic charges they must learn to execute. On each of these charges they will read the move of an offensive lineman and react to these moves. These charges are:

1. Read charge
2. Crash charge
3. Slant charge
4. Gap charge

Read Charge

See Fig. 6–3.

Alignment: Outside shade of tackle (inside foot splits feet of the offensive tackle) on the LOS.

116   FOOTBALL COACHING

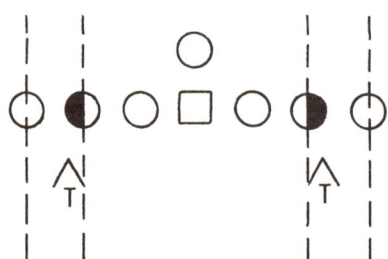

Fig. 6–3. Read charge—tackles' areas of responsibility.

Key: Ball to tackle.
Responsibility: Off-tackle hole. Cannot be hooked by the tackle.
Reaction: On snap, he takes a short jab step with his outside foot (for prevention of double-team) and he rips the tackle with his inside shoulder.
1. If tackle fires out, he rips hard and flattens (through the head) (Fig. 6–4).
2. If the tackle hook-blocks, he shivers and skates outside (Fig. 6–5).

   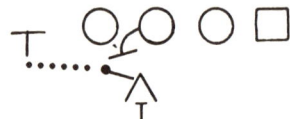

Fig. 6–4. Read charge—tackle blocks out.   **Fig. 6–5.** Read charge—tackle tries to cut-off.

3. If tackle blocks in, he closes flat and looks for trap.
   He does not penetrate; he keeps his feet parallel to the LOS. (See Fig. 6–6.)
   Note: We are susceptible to a block from the end, and we realize this. We will treat it similarly to the double-team.
4. If double-teamed by tackle and end, he rips the tackle (first job in any case) and drops his outside knee and rolls to ground to split the double-team (Fig. 6–7).
   Note: If we feel our tackle is an advanced defender, we may teach the spin-out technique. Otherwise, we only teach him to prevent the double-team from taking him in or back.

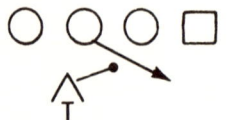   

Fig. 6–6. Read charge—tackle blocks down.   **Fig. 6–7.** Read charge—double-team block.

DEFENSIVE FUNDAMENTALS AND LINE PLAY

5. If the tackle pass blocks, our pass rush depends on whether the tackle is on the strongside or weakside.

   Strong Tackle. He jab-steps inside and keys the guard. If the guard releases, he looks for a draw. If the guard blocks out, he controls him with his hands. If the guard pulls for a screen, he goes with him. We expect our strong tackle to quickly get his hands on the offensive guard and control him. Our swing man will rush outside on our strongside. (See Figs. 6–8 to 6–10.)

   Weak Tackle. He rushes hard outside the tackle. Our weak tackle is the contain man, and we expect him to put on a tough outside rush. (See Fig. 6–11.)

We feel the read charge is the most difficult for our tackles to execute, and that it requires the most strength and natural ability. Therefore, we teach the techniques of this charge first. The use of this charge in game situations depends on our personnel, and, of course, the offensive situation.

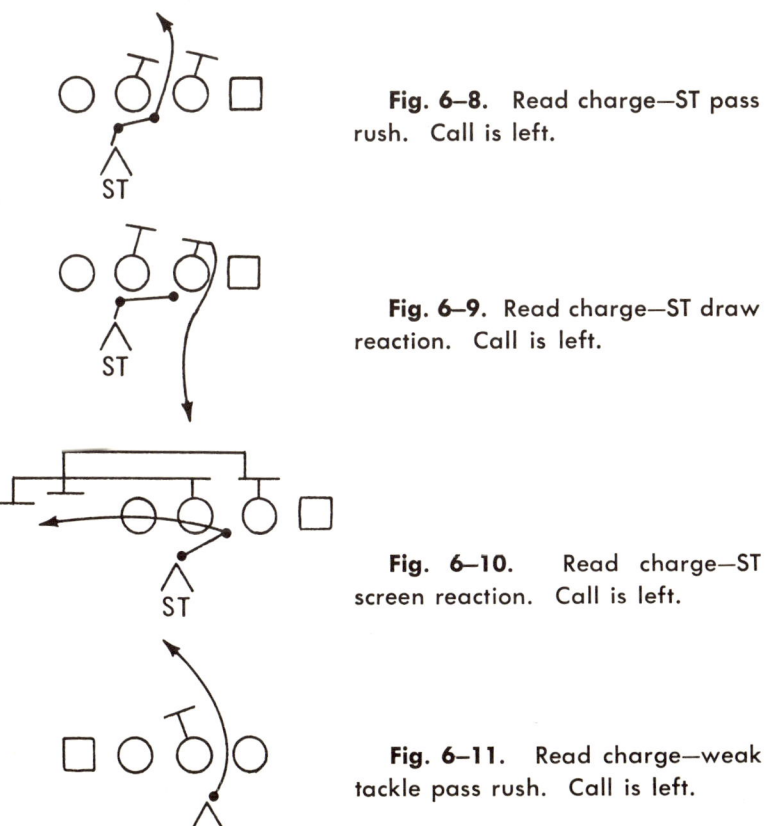

Fig. 6–8. Read charge—ST pass rush. Call is left.

Fig. 6–9. Read charge—ST draw reaction. Call is left.

Fig. 6–10. Read charge—ST screen reaction. Call is left.

Fig. 6–11. Read charge—weak tackle pass rush. Call is left.

Crash Charge

Alignment: Outside shade, on the LOS. (Same as Read.)
Key: Ball.
Responsibility: Penetration and off-tackle hole. He cannot be taken in by the tackle. (See Fig. 6–12.)
Reaction: On snap, he drives his inside shoulder to the outside hip of the offensive tackle. His reactions to blocks are exactly the same as in the read charge. The tackle should be able to react better to a fire-out or hook attempt by the tackle, and also to a double-team. The weak tackle should be able to put a better rush on the passer. The strong tackle will, however, have a more difficult maneuver to execute if his tackle pass-blocks. Both tackles are susceptible to traps.

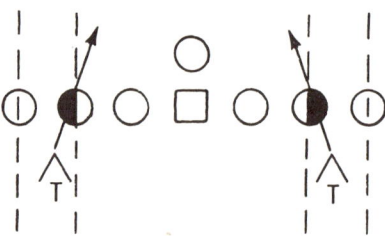

Fig. 6–12. Crash charge—tackles' areas of responsibility.

Slant Charge and Loop Charge

Our tackles will usually slant away from the defensive call. If we call Left, our tackles will slant right. If we call Right, they will slant left. Thus, they are slanting away from our rover and swing. We also have a call we can make to slant them toward our rover and swing if we so desire. When a tackle slants to a guard, we aim our inside foot to the back foot of the guard. Our outside slant is called a loop, because we step across the face of the end with our outside foot.

Strong Tackle—Slanting Inside

Alignment: Sneak in to head on the tackle. Try to disguise this.
Key: Ball to guard.
Responsibility: Inside hole. He cannot be blocked out by the tackle or guard.
Reaction: On snap, slant inside and key the guard (Figs. 6–13 and 6–14).
 1. If the guard blocks out, he flattens (Fig. 6–15).
 2. If the guard blocks in, he closes looking for a trap (Fig. 6–16).
 3. If the guard fires on our backer, our tackle tries to rip him and stay in the hole (Fig. 6–17).

DEFENSIVE FUNDAMENTALS AND LINE PLAY

Fig. 6–13. ST slant charge. Call is left.

Fig. 6–14. ST slant charge. Call is right.

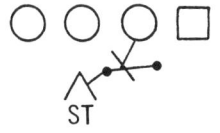

Fig. 6–15. Slant charge—guard blocks out.

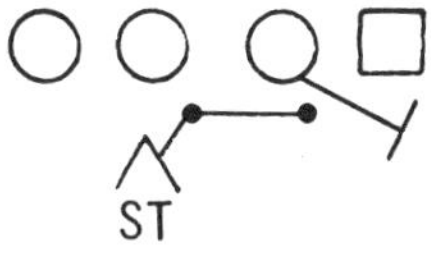

Fig. 6–16. Slant charge—G blocks down.

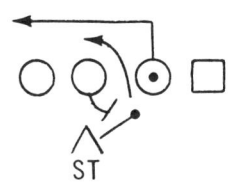

Fig. 6–17. Slant charge—G fires on our backer.

Fig. 6–18. Slant charge—G pulls outside.

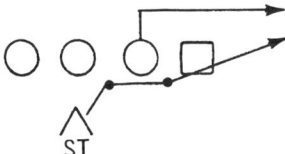

Fig. 6–19. Slant charge—G pulls behind the center.

4. If the guard pulls outside, we pull the tackle with our hands, go around the tackle, and follow the guard (Fig. 6–18).
5. If the guard pulls inside, he closes to the center and follows (Fig. 6–19).
   Note: When the guard pulls and we follow, we try to stay along the line, and do not penetrate and lose our pursuit angle.
6. If the guard pass blocks, we play him as we would on a read charge.

Weak Tackle—Looping Outside

Alignment: Outside shade of the tackle 18 to 24 inches off the ball.
Key: Ball to end. If no end, he keys near back.
Responsibility: Off-tackle hole and lateral pursuit. He cannot be taken in by the tackle or end. (See Figs. 6–20 and 6–21.)

Reaction: On snap, he loops to the end and hand-shivers him. If no end, he steps outside and keys the near back, ready to meet him with his inside shoulder.

1. If end blocks in, flatten (Fig. 6-22).
2. If end releases, he squares up, feet parallel, and finds the ball (Fig. 6-23).
3. If a back leads on him, he meets him with his inside shoulder. He cannot be taken in. (See Fig. 6-24.)
4. If pass shows, he rushes hard and contains the QB (Fig. 6-25).

One of the key factors in slanting or looping is getting off on the snap of the ball. This requires great concentration on the part of the weak tackle, as he must loop away from the ball. Above all, our slanting tackles must not be cut off by the offensive tackles.

Fig. 6-20. WT loop charge. Call is left.

Fig. 6-21. WT loop charge. Call is right.

Fig. 6-22. Loop charge—end blocks down.

Fig. 6-23. Loop charge—end releases.

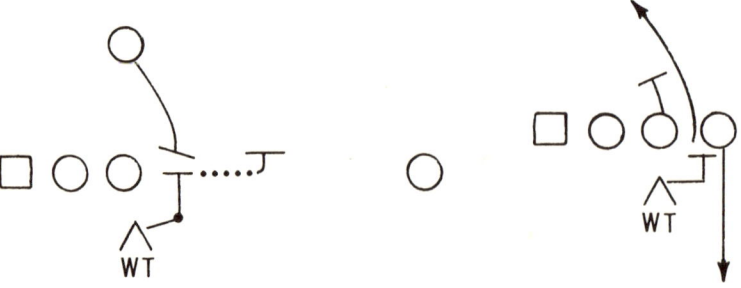

Fig. 6-24. Loop charge—end split, back leads.

Fig. 6-25. Loop charge—pass rush.

DEFENSIVE FUNDAMENTALS AND LINE PLAY

Gap Charge

On this charge, we align ourselves in the gap between two offensive linemen and drive hard for the backfield. We try to align ourselves in our normal position until the last possible second and then jump into the gap and go on the snap of the ball. We always jump to the first gap to our weakside away from rover and swing. Our technique is to get our tail up and nose down and place much weight forward for our initial charge, drive to a spot approximately even with the initial position of the back foot of the offensive linemen, come up to a solid football position. That way we prevent the ball-carrier from diving over us on short-yardage situations. Our middle guard executes this charge, also. (See Figs. 6–26 and 6–27.)

Fig. 6–26. Gap charge. Call is left.

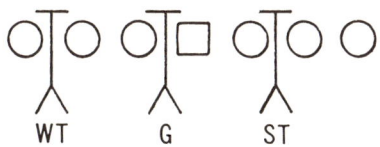

Fig. 6–27. Gap charge. Call is right.

MIDDLE GUARD

The middle guard must learn the same four charges as the tackles, but he is allowed to vary the read and crash charges somewhat.

Read Charge

Alignment: Head on Center. His distance off the ball depends on his ability to control the center's charge.
Key: Center's head.
Responsibility: Middle. He cannot be cut off by the center (Fig. 6–28).
Reaction: 1. On snap, he rips the chest of the center ready to flatten through the center's head. He does not go around the block of the center. (See Fig. 6–29.)
2. If the center pass-blocks, he checks for a draw, favoring the weak side—strong tackle is checking his inside. We do not expect a fast pass rush. (See Figs. 6–30 and 6–31.)

 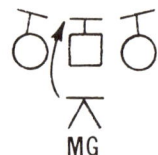

Fig. 6–28. Read charge—area of responsibility.

Fig. 6–29. Read charge—center drive-blocks.

Fig. 6–30. Read charge—pass block. Call is left.

Fig. 6–31. Read charge—pass block. Call is right.

Variation: In the Offset position (Fig. 6–32) the guard aligns himself in the weakside gap and then steps back to the center and rips him with his inside arm. He reads the head of the center as always. This alignment may cause the offensive guard to block on our guard further freeing our backer. If the guard does not block on our guard, our guard must be certain the center cannot hook him in.

If the center blocks hard on the guard, the guard flattens through his head (Fig. 6–33).

In addition, the middle guard may be called on to execute a gap-charge whereby he aligns himself in the gap and shoots.

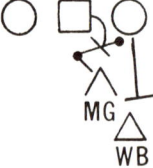 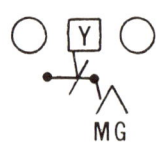

Fig. 6–32. Offset—center overblocking on our guard. Call is left.

Fig. 6–33. Offset—center drive-blocking on our guard. Call is left.

Crash Charge

This charge is an attempt by the guard to drive the center into the QB's lap. It is difficult to execute in that it requires the guard to overpower the center rather than to pick a side and shoot. The guard places more weight forward and drives his head for the chest of the center in an attempt to raise the center up and drive him back. Once the guard has whipped the center, he finds the ball and pursues.

DEFENSIVE FUNDAMENTALS AND LINE PLAY

Slant Charge

Like our tackles, the guard slants away from the call and away from rover and swing.

Alignment: Head on center.
Key: Ball to guard.
Responsibility: Inside hole to side of slant. He cannot be cut off by the center (Figs. 6–34 and 6–35).
Reaction: On snap, he slants to the guard and keys him.
1. If G blocks on him, he flattens (Fig. 6–36).
2. If G blocks out, he slides out and looks for a back or tackle block (Fig. 6–37).
3. If the G pulls behind center, we pull the center with our hands, go around center and follow (Fig. 6–38).
4. If G pulls outside, he slides out and follows (Fig. 6–39).
5. If G pass-blocks, he checks for a draw, then rushes (Fig. 6–40).

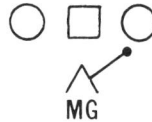

Fig. 6–34. Slant charge. Call is left.

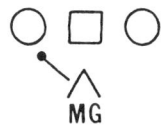

Fig. 6–35. Slant charge. Call is right.

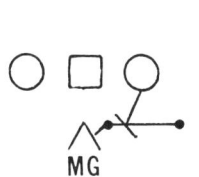

Fig. 6–36. Slant charge—flatten move.

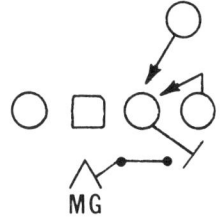

Fig. 6–37. Slant charge—guard blocks out.

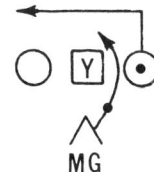

Fig. 6–38. Slant charge—G pulls behind center.

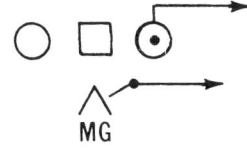

Fig. 6–39. Slant charge—G pulls outside.

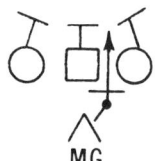

Fig. 6–40. Slant charge—pass-blocks.

Gap Charge

The middle guard executes this charge in the same manner as our tackles. In the gap-charge the guard jumps to the weakside gap and shoots on the snap. It is important that the guard come to a good football position if he gains penetration.

BASIC TECHNIQUES AND DRILLS

We feel there are four techniques a lineman must master, in addition to our charges:

1. Meeting a blocker and delivering a blow.
2. Shivering a blocker and going into pursuit.
3. Rushing the passer.
4. Tackling.

Meeting a Blocker

Our linemen meet blockers with a shoulder rip to the blocker's chest. We want the defender's shoulder to be lower than the blocker's shoulder. This becomes impracticable when the offensive blocker attacks beneath the knees. In this case, we will shiver with our hands.

We teach the rip initially by having our men deliver a blow to a sled. We emphasize the "football position" first; that is, the crouched position, feet spread and parallel, elbows bent, hands in front, ready to deliver a blow. The head is always up. We step hard with the foot corresponding to the shoulder with which we are ripping.

From the sled we go to form one-on-one drills (Fig. 6–41), from which we progress to full-scale contact. At all times, we emphasize the shoulder to the chest, and the destruction of the blocker's charge. From this we progress to the final stage, the addition of a ball carrier, which necessitates that the defender not only deliver a blow and destroy the charge, but that he get rid of the blocker and make a tackle.

One of our key drills for teaching this technique is our "machine-gun" drill, in which three blockers and a runner attack one defender (Fig. 6–42).

Blocker No. 1 is a lineman who fires out on the defender. The defender flattens through blocker No. 1's head. Blocker No. 1 sprints out quickly, just as blocker No. 2 attacks from a trapping position. When blocker No. 2 is destroyed, blocker No. 3 attacks

DEFENSIVE FUNDAMENTALS AND LINE PLAY 125

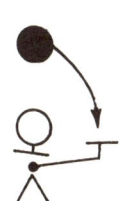

Fig. 6–41. One-on-One drill to teach rip.

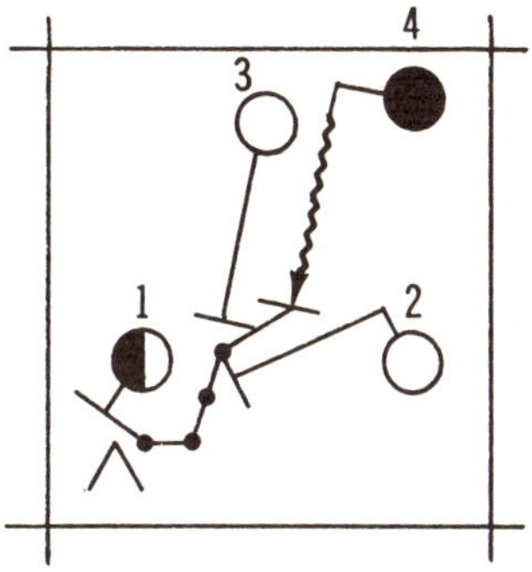

Fig. 6–42. Machine-gun drill for linemen.

from a backfield position. When blocker No. 3 is destroyed, the ball carrier (No. 4) approaches, and the defender tackles him. This drill is carried out in a 5-yard square marked by white lines. Should the defender be driven out of the square, he "loses" the match and returns for another go-round. The drill shown is for a right-shoulder blow. Each man should be required to go in the right and left shoulder drills, and perhaps should be in the left shoulder drill twice as we have found many players are much more proficient with their right arms and shoulders.

Shiver and Pursuit

We call this technique "skating" and find it is a technique most linemen need much drilling on to become proficient. Again, we start on the sled, emphasizing the football position and the hand shiver blow. We want to deliver the blow with the heel of our hands with a slight upward thrust at the chest.

From the sled we progress to one-on-one contact drills, with a blocker attempting a cut-off block on the defender (Fig. 6–43).

We then add a runner to give the defender an additional reaction (Fig. 6–44).

 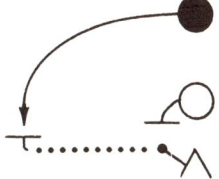

Fig. 6–43. One-on-One drill—cut-off block.

Fig. 6–44. One-on-One drill—cut-off block. Ball carrier added.

Finally we progress to our "skate" drill which involves three blockers and one ball carrier (Fig. 6–45).

Blocker No. 1 is an offensive lineman who attempts a cut-off block. The defender shivers blocker No. 1 and slides laterally. He must also work upfield to regain any ground he has lost. He tries to prevent his being driven deeper by each blocker. Blockers No. 2 and No. 3 attack with shin-high rolling blocks, and finally the defender tackles the ball carrier. A dummy is placed 15 yards from the defender, so that the width will not assume unrealistic proportions.

A point we emphasize in shivering is hand-feet coordination. We feel that the feet should jab to the rear as the hands jab forward. It is not an easy technique to master, but it can be the difference between being knocked down or making the tackle.

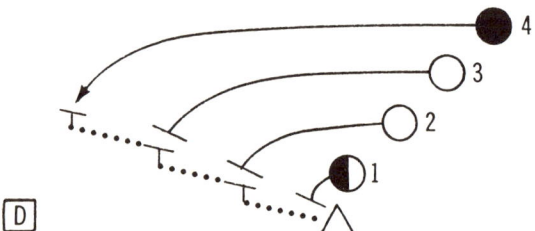

Fig. 6–45. Skate drill.

Rushing the Passer

One of the toughest techniques for a defensive lineman to master is rushing the passer. We teach two methods, yet feel that plain hustle and speed are the only real solutions to rushing the passer.

We start with one blocker and one rusher and teach the "hand-pull" method whereby the defender shivers the blocker hard to the inside or outside, then pulls him the opposite way and rushes by the blocker (Fig. 6–46).

We also teach the "shoulder-dip" method whereby the defender rushes as if he is going to shiver, and then drives his shoulder through the hip of the blocker, knocking him off balance and thus rushing by him (Fig. 6–47).

Fig. 6–46. One-on-One pass-rush drill.

Fig. 6–47. One-on-One drill—shoulder-dip pass rush.

DEFENSIVE FUNDAMENTALS AND LINE PLAY

One of the best drills we have found is to place three offensive blockers vs. one defender. We add a passer, and have him fade back and pass left or right, or, at times, run out of the cup left or right. We instruct the defender to get through somehow, and instruct the blockers to prevent the defender from doing so (Fig. 6–48).

We align the defender in different spots so as to teach both the inside rush and the contain rush. A point we emphasize is that it is important to watch the left hand of the passer, provided he is a right-handed passer. The passer cannot throw the ball until he releases his left hand. Until this release, it is unnecessary for the defender to raise his arms in an attempt to bat down the pass. It is also a wasted effort for a lineman rushing from the "offside" to raise his hands. If a passer is throwing to the other side, we want the defender to tackle him high. This is why we have the passer throw left or right in this drill.

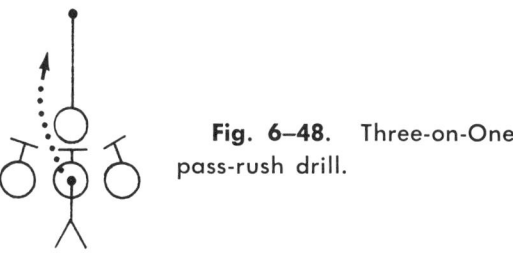

Fig. 6–48. Three-on-One pass-rush drill.

Tackling

We feel tackling is about 10 per cent ability and 90 per cent desire, and teach it as such. Our tackling sessions are short, but very aggressive and spirited. We teach the form and position slowly and with little hitting. Once we have mastered the form in the light drills, we feel that two or four tackles with alternating shoulders are enough in one drill. That is, if the tackling is solid and spirited.

Our initial drill is to pair our men and have one assume the tackling position with his forehead placed through the ball, feet spread, back arched, and wrists locked. A coach then moves behind the stationary ball carrier and gives him a hard shove to check the balance of the tackler.

Once the position is assimilated, we separate the pairs and have the runners approach the tacklers from about 5 yards away and jump up just as the tackler is about to strike. The tackler carries the runner a few steps and sets him down. The tackler's nose is imbedded in the ball and his tail is considerably lower than his shoulders. We call this our "lift" drill.

We then proceed to our "dump" drill in which the tempo picks up and we actually tackle the runner and dump him on his back. The tempo is at a trot at best, as we are still checking form. We then have the runners run diagonally left or right to teach the form of getting our heads across on tackles. We emphasize "squaring up" with the ball carrier, that is not letting him get an outside angle on us.

Finally we use our "square" drill, which is usually live and spirited (Fig. 6–49). Using our 5-yard squares, we have a contest between two sets of defenders; say, right and left tackles.

The runner must stay within the square and the tackler must prevent the runner from crossing the line by either tackling the runner in the square or knocking him across one of the lateral white lines. Each man starts in a corner of the square on the same side, and they should meet near the mid-point. The group allowing the fewest "touchdowns" wins the battle. The groups exchange sides of the square so that a tackler has shots at runners attacking both left and right.

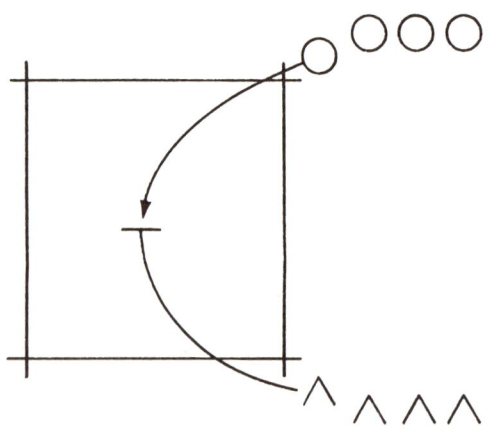

Fig. 6–49. Square drill for tackling.

McKay Drill

We have one final drill that combines the above drills with the exception of the pass rush (Fig. 6–50). I am not certain why the staff named the drill as they did, but we feel it is one of our most spirited drills. We require anyone not participating as the ball is snapped to yell for his position.

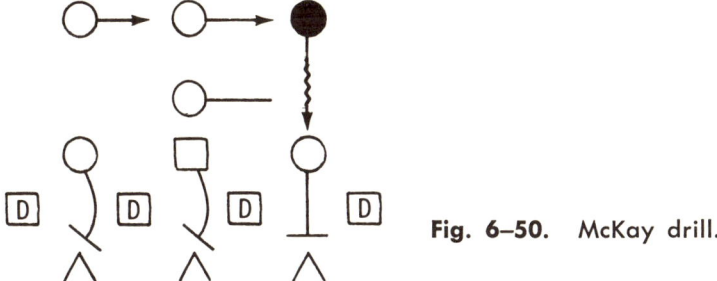

Fig. 6-50. McKay drill.

The offense consists of a QB and three backs, a center and two flanking blockers. The running lanes are about 3 yards wide, with dummies separating the lanes. Three defenders face the blockers. These can be backers, ends, or backs as well as linemen, of course. The coach signals the hole to be hit, the QB hands the ball to the designated back and the battle is on.

The drill gives us a good look at our ability to deliver a blow, to skate, and to tackle, plus a good look at our blocking and running ability. Short of full scrimmage, it is the most spirited drill we have, and we usually run two drills cross-field from each other and compete for spirit and the sound of pads hitting pads. The men come to the fore in this drill.

7

Defensive End Play

We have two types of end in our swing man and end, and some of their techniques are similar. In addition, our rover is a type of end at times, also, but I shall discuss his techniques under secondary play. When referring to ends in this chapter, I am referring to swing man and end.

Our ends have five assignments they can execute vs. a tight-end offense. They can:

1. Key the end
2. Key the QB
3. Shoot for the QB
4. Slant outside
5. Crash to the near back

Keying the End

Alignment: Outside shade of the end, on the line (Fig. 7–1).
Key: End's head.
Responsibility: Off tackle hole and lateral pursuit.
Reaction: His weight is on his outside foot. This foot is back with the toes pointed outside. His inside foot is "tied to the offensive end's head" and he is prepared to shiver the end with his inside arm.
  1. If the end blocks down, he steps down the line with his inside foot and turns his tail into the hole. His outside foot does not move. He looks for an inside-out block from a back or guard. He does not penetrate. He attempts to shiver the offensive end (Fig. 7–2).
  2. If, after the offensive end blocks down, a back or guard tries to over-block the defensive end, our end has his outside foot in a position where he can skate outside (Fig. 7–3).

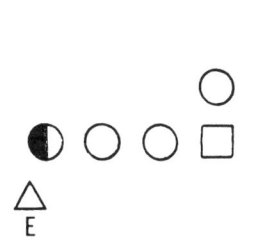
Fig. 7-1. Keying the end—alignment.

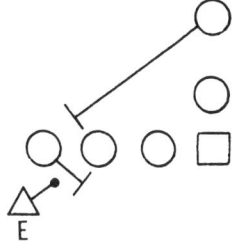
Fig. 7-2. Offensive end blocks down—defensive end closes down.

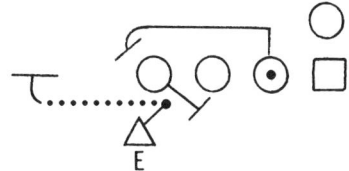
Fig. 7-3. End skates Outside vs. an Over-Block.

3. If the end attempts a cut-off block, our end shivers and skates outside, looks for the ball to determine whether the play is a run or a pass. If the play is a run, our end skates laterally along the line trying to maintain a position on the ball carrier to prevent a cutback (Fig. 7-4). If the play is a rollout pass, our end comes upfield and attempts to make the QB stop (Fig. 7-5).

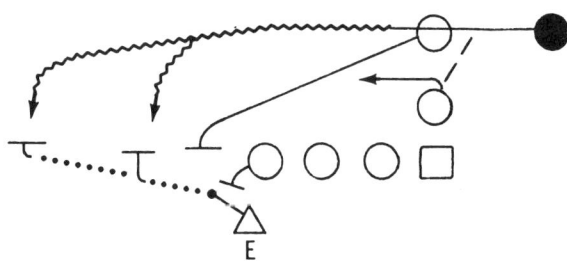
Fig. 7-4. Shiver and Skate vs. a Wide Run.

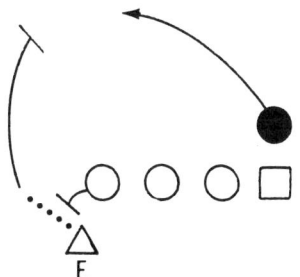
Fig. 7-5. Shiver and Force vs. a Roll-Out Pass.

4. If the end releases, and the play is away, our end trails the play slowly, staying as deep as the deepest back, to prevent reverses (Fig. 7–6).
5. If a drop back pass develops, our end rushes hard outside and contains the QB (Fig. 7–7). He uses the same rushing techniques as our weak tackle, that is, a contain rush outside all blockers. He must be careful not to open too wide a lane and allow the QB to step up and throw. We generally fake inside early as we rush.
6. If an option play develops, our end takes the QB. He should not declare himself too quickly, but should stay on the line and make the QB decide to keep or pitch. If the QB pitches early, our end skates for the ball carrier. If the QB keeps, our end tackles him. (See Figs. 7–8 and 7–9.)

Our swing man often executes this assignment, our end seldom keys the offensive end. This assignment is used most often when our tackle slants inside.

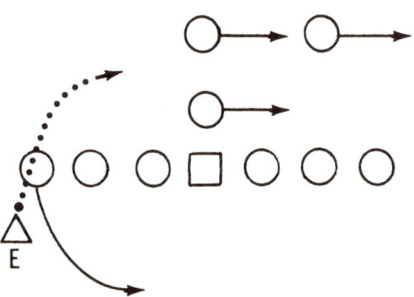

Fig. 7–6. End trailing play.

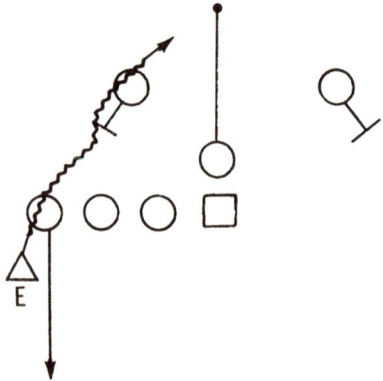

Fig. 7–7. End rushing a drop-back pass.

DEFENSIVE END PLAY   133

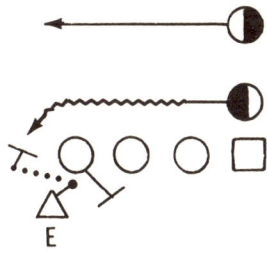

Fig. 7–8.   Option—QB keeps.

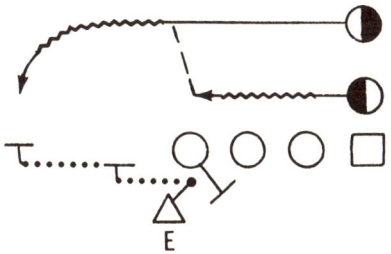

Fig. 7–9.   Option—QB pitches.

Keying the QB

Alignment: One foot outside the offensive end, on the line (Fig. 7–10).
Responsibility: Outside.
Reaction: His stance is the same as if he were keying the end, and he tries to shiver the end with his inside arm.
  1. If the ball is pitched deep, our end comes across hard to the outside shoulder of the lead blocker. He tries to close ground on the blocker. He turns the play in. (See Fig. 7–11.)

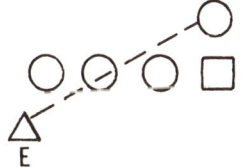

Fig. 7–10.   Keying the QB—alignment.

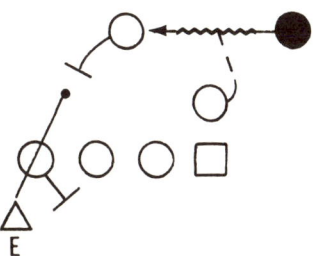

Fig. 7–11.   Pitch-out—end comes across to lead blocker.

2. If the ball is handed off, our end plays the same technique as if the offensive end had blocked down. He does not penetrate. He turns the play out. (See Fig. 7–12.)
3. If the QB rolls out, our end comes across to make the QB stop (Fig. 7–13). We use the same technique vs. all rollouts.
4. If the ball goes away, our end bounces back behind his tackle, looks to the far back for a counter, and if a counter does not develop, pursues the play (Fig. 7–14). If a pass develops, the end drops back 12 yards deep.

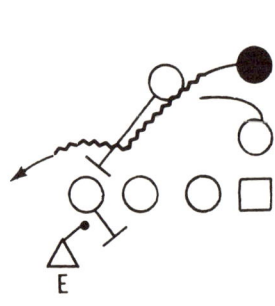

Fig. 7–12. Hand-Off—end closes tough.

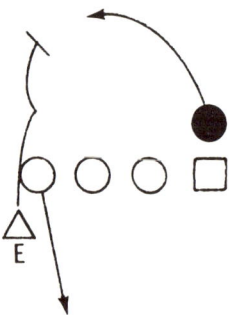

Fig. 7–13. QB Rollout—end comes across.

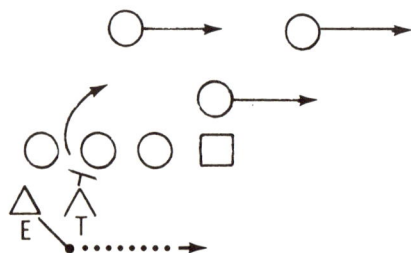

Fig. 7–14. End stacks on play away; then, pursues.

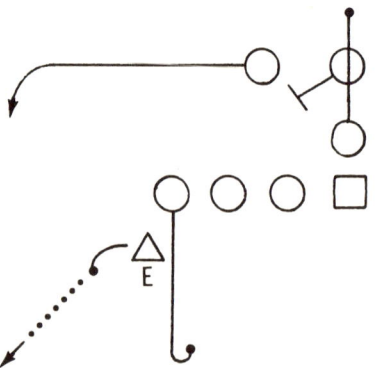

Fig. 7–15. Dropback pass; end must get wide.

5. If a drop-back pass develops, our end covers the flat zone, trying to get 8 yards deep. He turns to his outside, getting width with a few quick crossover steps, and then turns to face the QB and back pedals to the outside. His position depends on the pattern and the width of the field. (See Fig. 7–15.)
6. If an option play develops, our end is responsible for the pitch-man. He plays along the line trying to convince the QB that he will tackle him. But, our end must not be out-flanked. If the QB cuts upfield, our end tries to stay between the QB and the pitch-man until he is certain the QB will keep the ball. (See Figs. 7–16 and 7–17.)

Our end uses this assignment often, but our swing man seldom uses it.

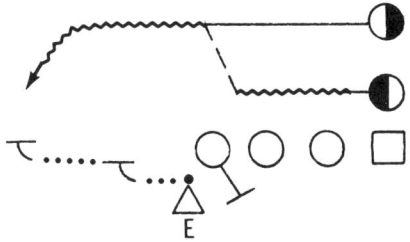

Fig. 7–16. Option—QB pitches.

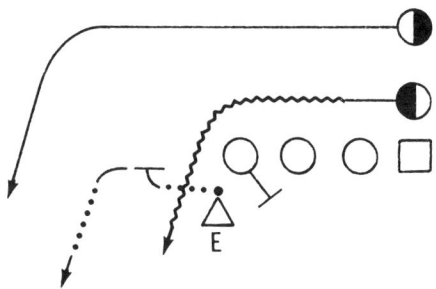

Fig. 7–17. Option—QB keeps.

Shooting for the QB

Alignment: One foot outside the offensive end, on the line.
Key: Ball to QB.
Responsibility: He shoots hard for the QB (Fig. 7–18). He has no outside responsibility.
Reaction: Our end should get his outside foot farther back to get a better start, and watching the ball out of the corner of his eye, shoot hard for the QB. We expect him to be able to stop inside plays. He should rush all passes on the inside of the blocker. He has a "free" rush. We prefer this assignment vs. a split offensive end. Rover executes this assignment on occasion, our swing man, seldom. (See Figs. 7–19 and 7–20.)

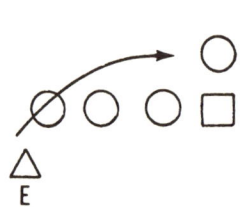

Fig. 7–18. Shooting for the QB.

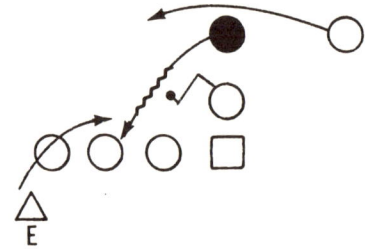

Fig. 7–19. Shooting end vs. an inside run.

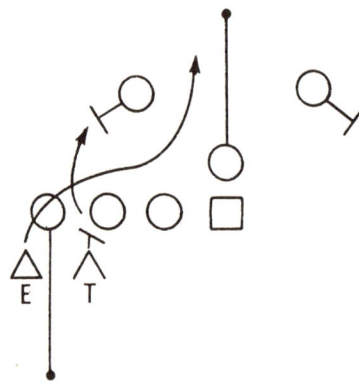

Fig. 7–20. Shooting end rushing a dropback pass.

Slanting Outside

Alignment: One foot outside the offensive end, on the line.
Key: Ball to QB.
Responsibility: Outside with penetration across the line (Fig. 7–21).
Reaction: Our end shoots outside and tries to get as deep as the deepest back as quickly as possible (Figs. 7–22 and 7–23). He has no inside responsibility and no pass responsibility. This assignment has proven effective against wide runs, options and rollouts and is used by both our swing man and our end. Our tackle or a linebacker usually fills the off-tackle hole.

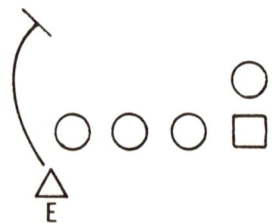

Fig. 7–21. End slanting outside.

DEFENSIVE END PLAY

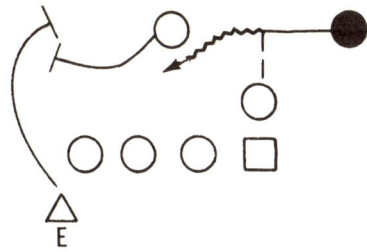

Fig. 7–24. End crashing.

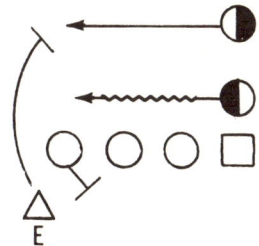

Fig. 7–22. End shooting outside vs. a sweep.

Crashing to the Near Back

Alignment: One foot outside the offensive end, on the line.
Key: Ball to near back to QB.
Responsibility: Turn all plays inside (Fig. 7–24).
Reaction: Our end staggers his stance for better get-off and crashes to the near back (Figs. 7–25 and 7–26). He has the same basic reactions as if he were keying the QB, but has no pass responsibility. He must contain wide plays, but we expect him to help on inside plays. He rushes all passes from the outside. Both our swing man and end execute this assignment on occasion.

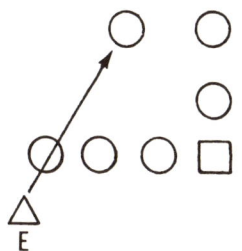

Fig. 7–23. End shooting outside vs. an option.

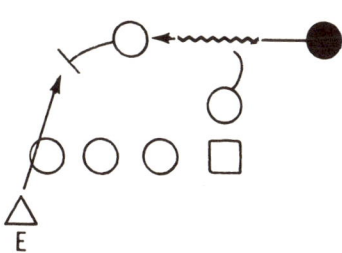

Fig. 7–25. End crashing vs. a sweep.

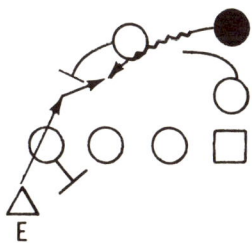

Fig. 7–26. End crashing vs. an off-tackle play.

Technique vs. a Split End

If the offensive end splits out wide our end can still play any of our techniques except keying the end. However, we have found that in many cases it is better to key the near back than the QB. Our end is responsible for outside containment if keying the near back.

1. If the near back leads wide, our end comes across the line deep, and turns his back to the split man so as not to be susceptible to a crackback block. Our end has the pitch-man on an option. (See Fig. 7–27.)
2. If the near back drives at our end, our end meets him as he would any inside-out blocker (Fig. 7–28).

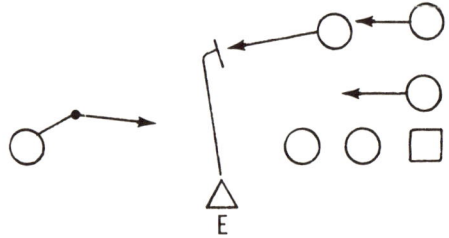

Fig. 7–27. Split end—near back leads wide, our end comes across.

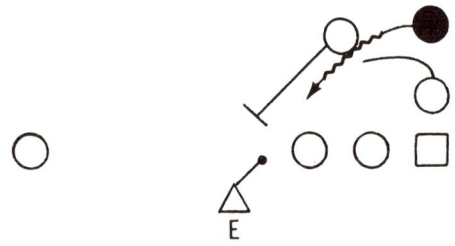

Fig. 7–28. Split end—near back drives, our end closes tough.

3. If a roll-out pass comes at him, our end either (1) plays along the line trying to stay between the passer and his intended receiver, or (2) forces hard. If playing along the line, our end must be no deeper than the QB, and if our tackle loses containment, our end must force the QB. His reaction depends on the pass coverage called. (See Figs. 7–29 and 7–30.)
4. If flow goes away, our end stacks behind his tackle and then (1) plug the inside counter hole, (2) pursues, or (3) drops back to his pass zone. His reaction depends on the play that develops.

DEFENSIVE END PLAY

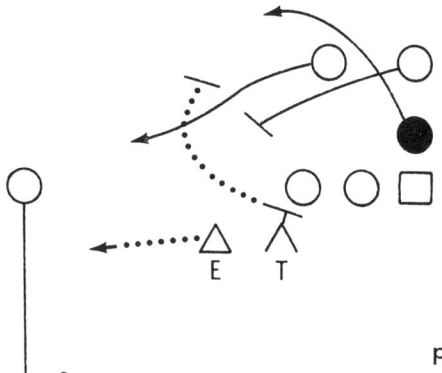

Fig. 7–29. Roll-Out Pass—end playing along the line vs. a split end.

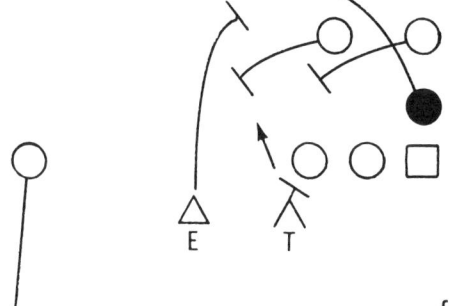

Fig. 7–30. Roll-Out Pass—end forcing vs. a split-end.

BASIC TECHNIQUES AND DRILLS

There are six basic techniques an end must master in addition to the previous ones discussed:

1. Meeting a blocker and delivering a blow
2. Shivering a blocker and going into pursuit
3. Rushing the passer
4. Tackling
5. Pass defense—zone
6. Pass defense—man-for-man

Meeting a Blocker

Our ends meet blockers from an outside-in position and there are three important points they must remember when meeting a blocker who is attempting to take them out. First, he must keep his feet faced upfield and his shoulders as close to parallel to the line as possible. Second, his outside foot should be back (toes pointing outside) the inside foot should be up and his tail should be turned inside. Third, he should not come across the line and open up a hole, but should close down the line and make the play go outside him.

Our best drill to teach this is another version of our machine-gun drill (Fig. 7–31). Blocker No. 1 drives on the end to take him out. The end meets him, sheds him, and blocker No. 2 attacks followed by blocker No. 3. Number 4 is the ball carrier who cuts inside the end. The end assumes his stance 2 feet inside the 5-yard square and 2 feet in front of the back line. If a blocker knocks our end beyond a line, or if the runner crosses the back line, our end "loses" the contest. We do not always go full speed, but at times work on the form, only.

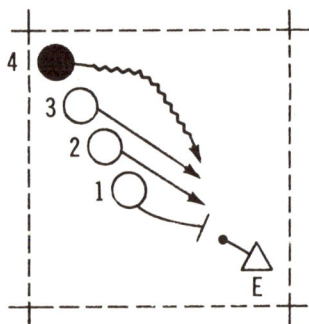

Fig. 7–31. Machine-gun drill for ends.

Shiver and Pursuit

Our "Skate" technique for our ends is similar to that for our linemen except that we try to emphasize the importance of closing ground to the lead blocker and then shivering him. We use the same skate drill for our ends as we use for our linemen.

Rushing the Passer

We teach our ends the same techniques we teach our linemen, but work more on rollout containment. We use the same drills.

Tackling

We use the same drills and techniques we use for our linemen.

DEFENSIVE END PLAY

Pass Defense—Zone

There are two factors involved in zone pass defense: First, getting to the proper zone and secondly, reacting to the ball. In going to zone we emphasize good body balance and recognition of field position, flow of the play and the pattern if a back is involved. In reacting to the ball we watch the QB, and go for his first move, hoping to cover five yards in any direction.

We start by having a coach face the end and execute a rollout, dropback, or bootleg pass.

If the QB rolls at our end (see (1) in Fig. 7–32) he plays along the line ready to bat down a thrown pass, and ready to come up and force if the QB turns upfield to run. Our end's depth should be no deeper than the QB's depth. If the QB drops back (2) our end crosses over to the outside, then backs away facing the QB. We back away so that we can react to a ball thrown inside or outside. If the QB rolls away (3) our end backs straight up.

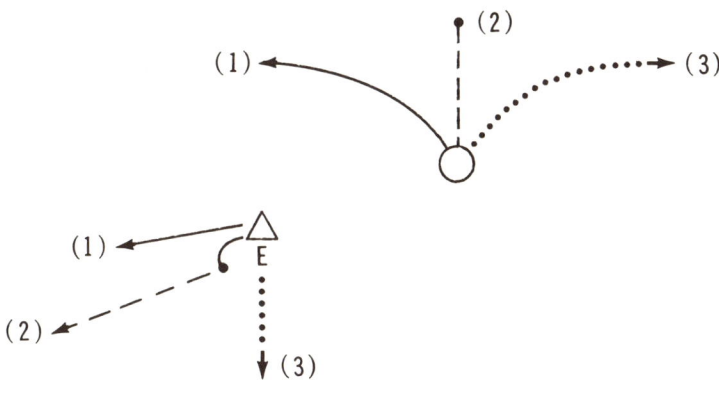

Fig. 7–32. To-Zone drill.

To teach reaction to the ball, we have three basic drills. The first we call the "spot drill."

The passer drops back to pass and the end back-pedals to zone (Fig. 7–33). The passer sets and throws to one of four spots, in front, left or right, or behind, left or right. The passer also rolls out toward and away from the end and throws to the spots.

In our shield drill, we add a man holding an air-flight dummy and he hits the defender just as he intercepts the ball (Fig. 7–34).

The man with the dummy hits the defender high with a good blow. This drill has helped our concentration on the ball.

Fig. 7–33. Spot drill. 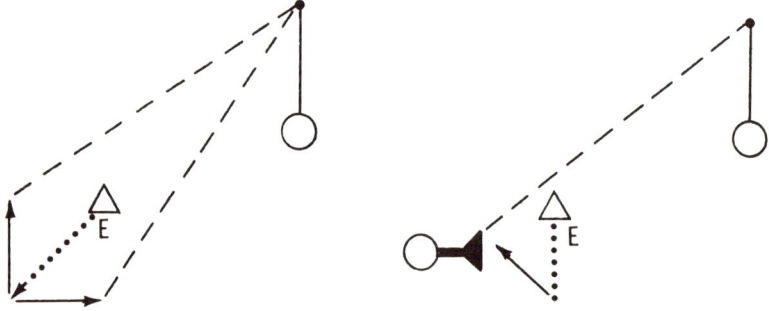 **Fig. 7–34.** Shield drill.

Our final drill is our Patterns Drill where we add two receivers who battle the defender for the ball (Fig. 7–35). We attempt to teach our end to adjust his zone position according to various patterns. This drill has good competitive merits when done live.

We then progress to unit (ends and backers) or team pass defense.

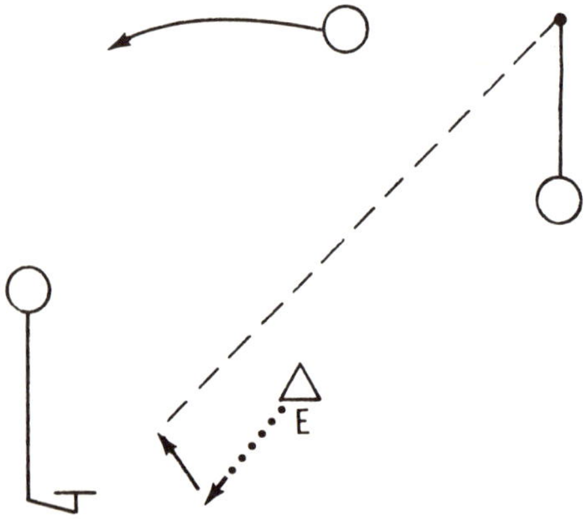

Fig. 7–35. Patterns drill.

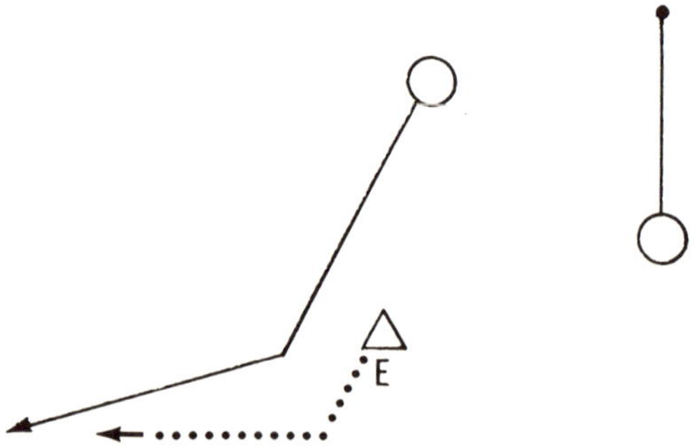

Fig. 7–36. Man drill—receiver breaks out.

DEFENSIVE END PLAY 143

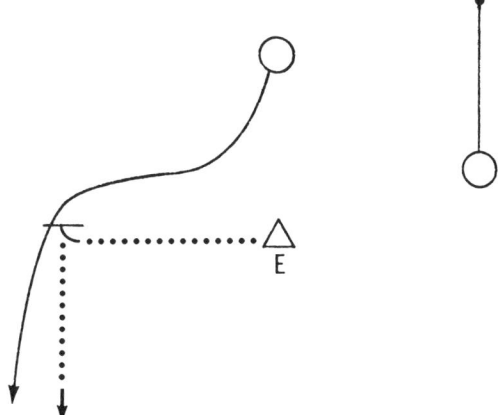

Fig. 7-37. Man drill—receiver breaks upfield.

Pass Defense—Man-for-Man

At times our end is called on to cover a back man-for-man. Our technique is to try to force the receiver to run outside us, then drive on him as soon as he makes a cut. If the receiver sprints upfield, our end tries to hit him and then turns and runs with him. We know of only one drill for this and that is to cover a back man-for-man in our Man Drill (Figs. 7-36 and 7-37).

8

Linebacker Play

As with most teams, our linebackers are key men on our defensive unit. Not only must they be quick, rugged, and sure tacklers, they must also be the leaders, and one of them acts as our defensive quarterback. The signal calling job is very important in our scheme of things, as many times we make adjustments after the offense lines up.

Our backers have five assignments they can execute, four when flow comes their way, and one when flow goes away.

1. Plug—Key flow
2. Scrape off—Key flow
3. Rip or follow a guard—Key the guard
4. Shoot the gap—Key flow
5. Bounce—Key flow

Plugging on Flow

Alignment: One and one-half to four yards off the line. Outside shoulder of the guard.
Key: Flow (QB or other back).
Responsibility: Dive hole (Fig. 8–1).
Reaction: The backer to the side of flow plugs the dive hole by stepping up and to the outside with his outside foot. He does not penetrate. He meets all blockers with his inside shoulder. His outside foot is back, toe to instep of his inside foot.
 1. If the ball comes through the dive hole, our backer meets blockers with his inside shoulder and turns the play in to our offside backer (Fig. 8–2). If a back is leading on him, the backer attacks him in the hole (Fig. 8–3).
 2. If the ball goes outside, our backer bounces along the line maintaining an inside-out angle on the ball-carrier and preventing the

LINEBACKER PLAY

Fig. 8–1. Plugging on flow.

Fig. 8–2. Plugging and turning the play inside.

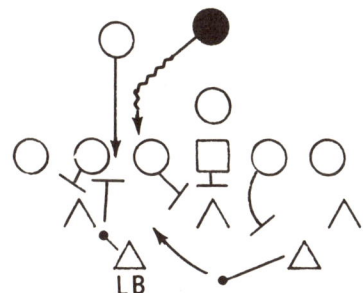

Fig. 8–3. Plugging and attacking a lead back.

    cut-back (Figs. 8–4 and 8–5). Our backer must adjust his speed to the ball-carrier's speed.
3. If an option play develops, our backer has the QB when he cuts upfield (Fig. 8–6). If the ball is pitched, he pursues (Fig. 8–7).
4. If a rollout pass develops, our backer covers the hook zone. His depth and width in his zone depends on the alignment and pattern of the offense. If there is a tight end to his side, our backer must slide laterally quickly to get across the face of an end running a crease or quick out pattern (Fig. 8–8). If the end blocks, or sprints outside, our backer fights back trying to get 12 yards deep (Fig. 8–9). If there is a split end to his side, our backer gets depth immediately when a rollout pass shows (Fig. 8–10). He is attempting to get in a position to react to any inside pattern by the end.
5. If a dropback pass develops, our backer fights for depth and initially glances at the back to his side. Our backer keeps a receiver in his zone to his outside (Fig. 8–11). An exception to this rule is when three receivers release. Our backer then covers a wider hook zone, and the off backer covers the inside hook zone (Fig. 8–12).

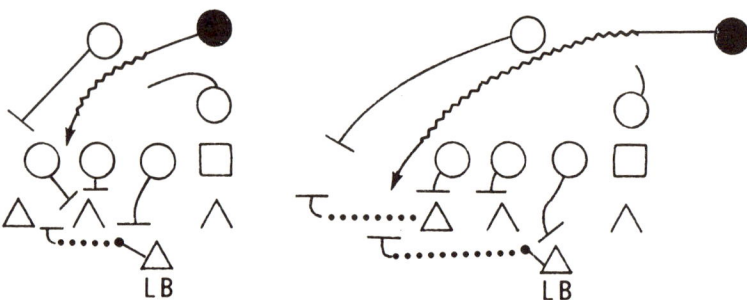

Fig. 8–4. Plug vs. off-tackle play.

Fig. 8–5. Plug vs. a wide run.

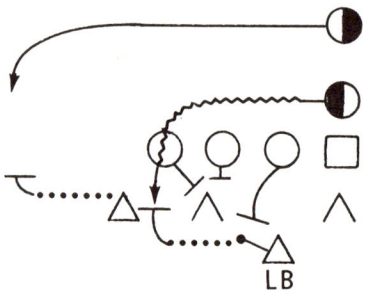
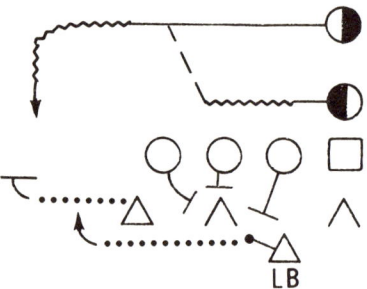

Fig. 8–6. Option—QB keeps.

Fig. 8–7. Option—QB pitches.

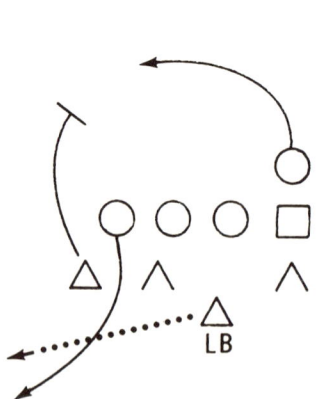
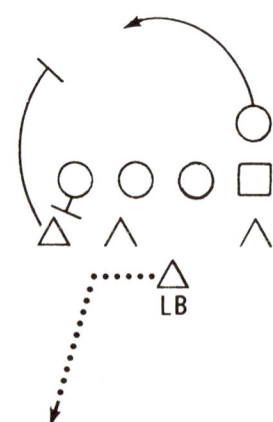

Fig. 8–8. Rollout pass—LB slides across the face of the end.

Fig. 8–9. Rollout pass, end blocks—LB fights for depth.

LINEBACKER PLAY

Fig. 8–10. Rollout pass—LB fights for depth vs. a split end.

Fig. 8–11. Dropback pass—LB keeps receiver outside him.

Fig. 8–12. Dropback pass—backers adjust to a 3-man pattern.

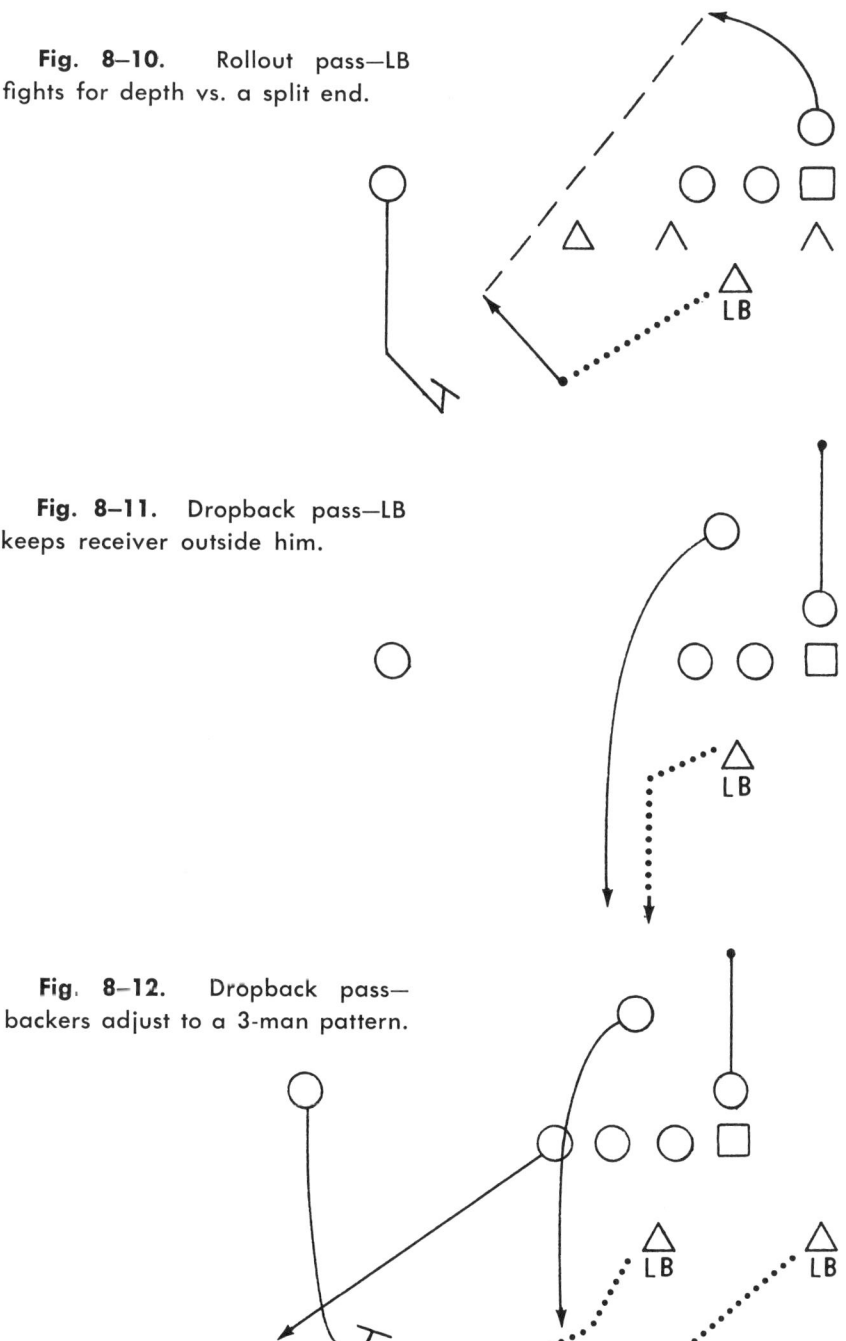

Scraping Off on Flow

Alignment: Outside shade of the guard with his feet slightly deeper than his tackle.
Key: Flow.
Responsibility: Off-tackle hole (Fig. 8–13).
Reaction: If flow comes his way, our backer shoots *tight* outside his tackle through the gap between the offensive end and tackle (Figs. 8–13 to 8–15). He should dip his inside shoulder as he scrapes-off and find the ball as soon as possible. If the ball is going outside, our backer goes into lateral pursuit (Fig. 8–15). He has no pass responsibility.

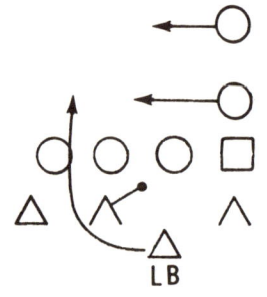

Fig. 8–13. Scrape-off on flow to.

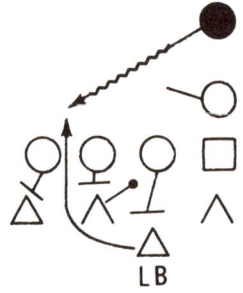

Fig. 8–14. Scrape-off vs. an inside play.

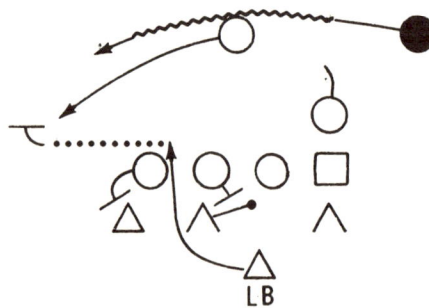

Fig. 8–15. Scrape-off vs. a wide play.

Ripping the Guard

Alignment: Outside shade of the guard, on or only slightly off line (Fig. 8–16); he must not show this too early.
Key: Guard.
Responsibility: Dive hole.
Reaction: On the snap, our backer delivers a hard rip into the guard with his inside shoulder. His technique is the same as our tackle on a read charge.
   1. If the guard drive-blocks, our backer rips the guard with his inside

LINEBACKER PLAY

shoulder. He cannot be taken in. If flow comes at him, our backer turns the play in to his fellow backer (Fig. 8-17). If the play breaks outside, our backer bounces along the line (Fig. 8-18).

2. If the guard blocks down, our backer steps down looking for a trap. He does not penetrate. He keeps his outside foot back and turns his tail into the hole (Fig. 8-19).
3. If the guard pulls, our backer follows him, attempting to "get in his hip pocket" (Figs. 8-20 and 2-21).
4. If the guard pass-blocks, our backer fights back to zone. If a flow pass shows, our backer attempts to cover his zone the same as if he were plugging.

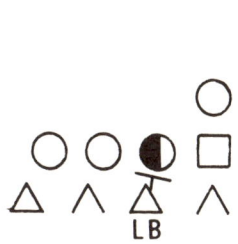

Fig. 8-16. Ripping the guard—alignment.

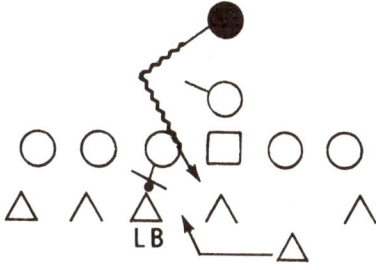

Fig. 8-17. Ripping the guard—flow inside.

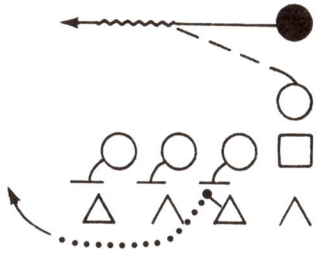

Fig. 8-18. Ripping the guard—flow wide.

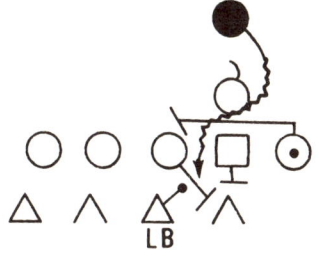

Fig. 8-19. Ripping the guard—guard blocks down. Backer closes.

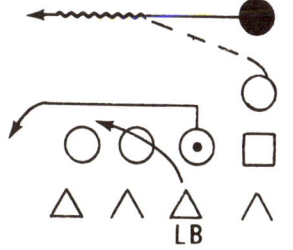

Fig. 8-20. Ripping the guard—guard pulls outside.

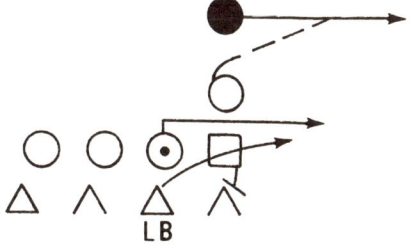

Fig. 8-21. Ripping the guard—guard pulls behind the center.

Shooting the Gap

Alignment: Either: (1) Normal, 1½ yards deep initially and then tightening, or (2) Stacked behind a lineman.
Key: Flow.
Responsibility: Gap to the side of flow (Fig. 8–22).
Reaction: When flow shows, our backers shoot the gap to that side. They penetrate, find the ball, and pursue. They have no pass responsibility and their reaction is similar to the scrape-off technique.

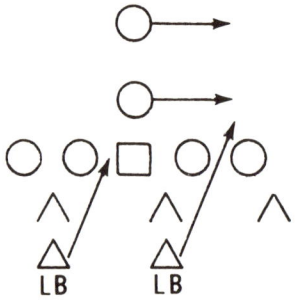

Fig. 8–22. Shooting the gap.

Bounce on Flow Away

Alignment: Depends on whether plugging, scraping, or ripping.
Key: Flow.
Responsibility: Middle and pursuit (Fig. 8–23).
Reaction: Our backer takes a step inside and back with his inside foot and then bounces until he definitely learns where the ball is going. He is careful not to cross his feet until actually in pursuit.
  1. If flow goes inside, our backer plugs and attacks the ball carrier (Fig. 8–24).
  2. If flow goes wide, our backer pursues, making certain of two factors: (1) that he stays deep enough so as not to be cut off, and (2) that he maintains an inside-out angle on the ball carrier so as not to allow cutback (Fig. 8–25).
  3. If a counter comes back, our backer should be deep enough to react back and plug his side, meeting all blockers with his inside shoulder and turning the play inside (Fig. 8–26).
  4. If a flow pass develops, our backer fights for depth in his zone. If he has a tight end to his side, he is conscious of either a hook (Fig. 8–27) or a cross pattern (Fig. 8–28). If a receiver crosses, he picks him up man-for-man until the receiver leaves his zone. He must yell Cross to his other backer.
  5. If a bootleg pass develops, our backer fights back to his hook zone and covers the play like a rollout. He should be especially conscious of crossing receivers on bootleg passes; thus we stress depth. (See Fig. 8–29.)

LINEBACKER PLAY

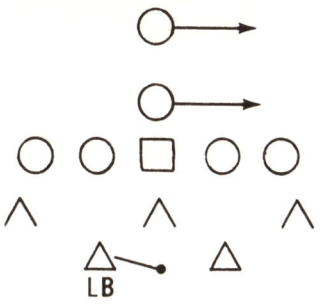

Fig. 8–23. Bouncing on flow away.

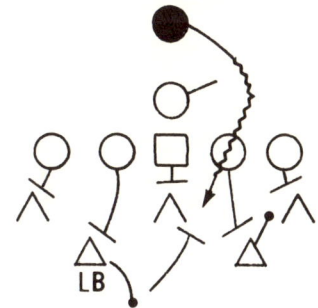

Fig. 8–24. Bounce and Plug vs. Inside Flow.

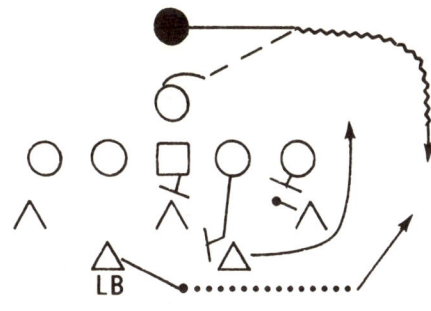

Fig. 8–25. Bounce and Pursuit vs. Outside Flow.

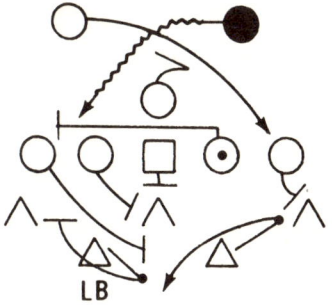

Fig. 8–26. Bounce and Plug vs. Counter.

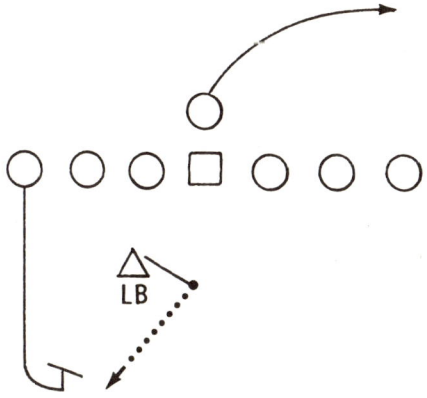

Fig. 8–27. Bounce vs. Flow Pass—end hooks.

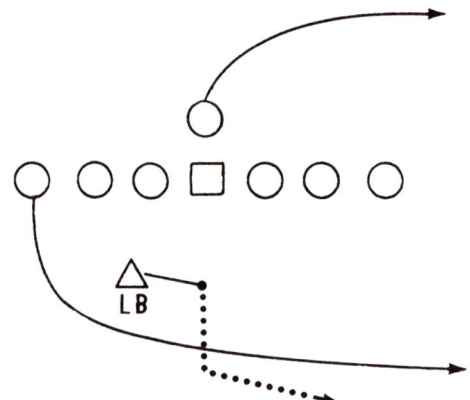

Fig. 8–28. Bounce vs. Flow Pass—end crosses.

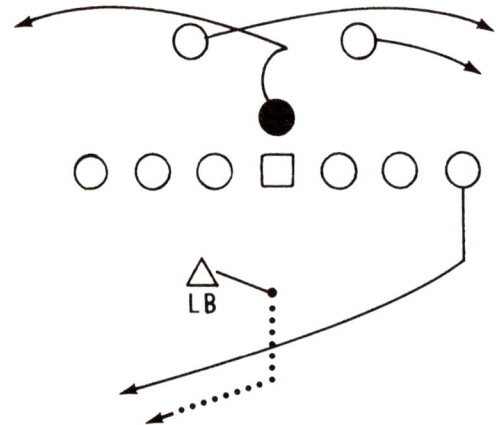

Fig. 8–29. Bounce vs. Boot Pass.

BASIC TECHNIQUES AND DRILLS

There are six basic techniques a backer must master. They are similar to those required of ends, and we work the two groups together much of the time.

1. Meeting a blocker and delivering a blow
2. Shivering a blocker and going into pursuit
3. Plugging or bouncing
4. Tackling
5. Pass defense—zone
6. Pass defense—man-for-man

LINEBACKER PLAY

Meeting a Blocker

Our backers meet blockers head on most of the time, or possibly at a slight side-angle. The two points they must remember is to meet blockers with their inside shoulder, and to keep their outside foot back. This is not always possible if we are scraping-off or shooting a gap, but then we feel our momentum should defeat the blocker.

Our key drill for teaching the technique of meeting blockers is our machine-gun drill (Fig. 8–30).

As in the machine-gun drills previously discussed, Nos. 1, 2, and 3 attack the defender and No. 4 is the ball-carrier. We operate inside our 5-yard square with the blockers attacking the backer at a distance of no more than 3½ yards. We station the blockers on one line, and align the backer 1½ yards in front of the other line. If a blocker or ball-carrier drives the backer over his line, they win and the backer is the loser. Before each attack, the coach commands which shoulder all participants are to use. We execute with the left shoulder more than the right because of the afore-mentioned right-hand proficiencies of most players. The drill is not executed at full speed until the fundamentals of foot, head, and body position are mastered. A backer seldom takes more than two sets a practice at full speed.

Shiver and Pursuit

We use the same "skate" drill for backers and ends.

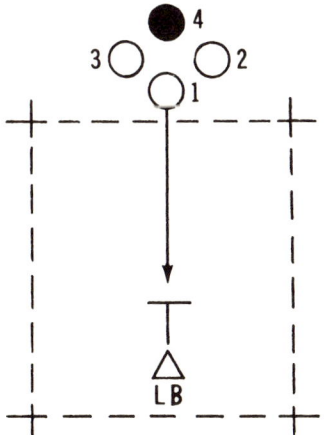

Fig. 8–30. Machine-gun drill for linebackers.

Plugging and Bouncing

We start by teaching the technique of the proper inside-out tackling angle on the ball-carrier with our Plug drill (Fig. 8-31). A QB hands off to the ball carrier who hits holes 1, 2, or 3 between dummies. The coach, aligned behind the backers, hand-signals the direction and the hole. The coach checks for the proper footwork and tackling angle. Form tackling is used, emphasizing forehead through the ball and a high tackle. By calling Left or Right the coach can have the scrape-off and gap moves executed also. Counters, rollouts, and bootlegs can also be executed in this drill.

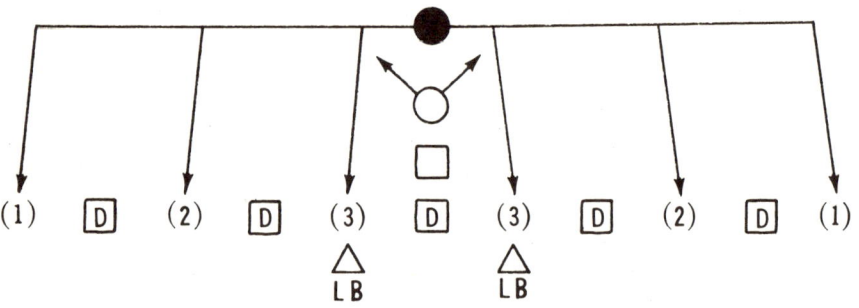

Fig. 8-31. Plug Drill.

Our Plug and Rip drill involves a little more recognition and also the meeting of blockers (Fig. 8-32). The offense consists of a QB and two other backs, a center, and both guards. Ends can be added for pass reaction, also. A variety of plays can be run, but we stress inside plays to teach the plug, scrape, and bounce. Often we have our swing man join this drill, and then add an offensive end for him to key.

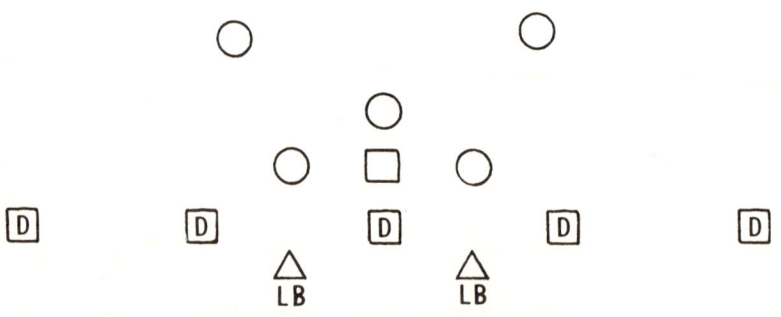

Fig. 8-32. Plug and Rip Drill.

LINEBACKER PLAY

Tackling Drills

Our backers use the same tackling drills as our line and ends.

Pass Defense—Zone

Our backers must master the same techniques as our ends, namely, going to zone, and then reacting to the ball. In going to zone properly, we emphasize flow and formation alignment, especially the presence, or lack of presence, of a tight end.

We use the same drills for our backers as for our ends, namely, the To-Zone (Fig. 7–32), Spot (Fig. 7–33), and Shield (Fig. 7–34) drills. The Patterns Drill for backers is different, however (Figure 8–33).

In the patterns drill we stress recognition of patterns. We concentrate on the points mentioned in covering flow and drop-back passes. Often we add the ends and rover and drill on short passes we expect to face.

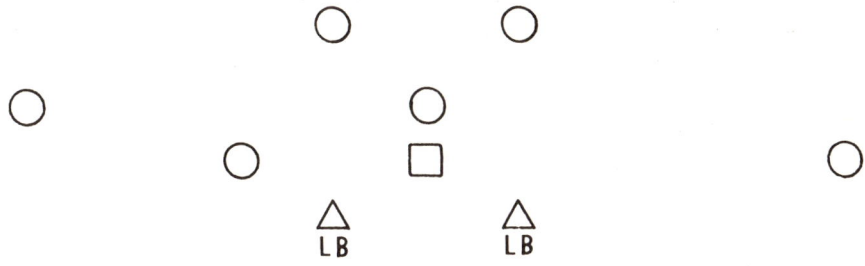

Fig. 8–33. Patterns Drill for linebackers.

Pass Defense—Man-for-Man

At times our backer is called on to cover a back man-for-man. Our technique is to try to force the receiver to run outside, and then drive on him as soon as he makes a cut. If the receiver sprints upfield, our backer tries to hit him and then runs with him. We use our Man drill for this (Figs. 7–36 and 7–37), with the same techniques as used by our ends.

9

Defensive Secondary Play

We use both zone and man-for-man pass coverage in our secondary. We use five zone coverages and two man-for-man coverages, and with the variety of passers and passing attacks we face, we need all this and then some to cope with our opposition. I shall discuss our coverages first, and then the techniques we use.

ZONE COVERAGES

Our five zone coverages are:

1. Cover One
2. Cover Two
3. Cover Three
4. Cover Four
5. Cover Prevent

Our linebacker coverage remains constant in all five coverages. Our end and rover adjust only to a flow pass weakside.

Cover One

In Cover One, we will rotate one way on flow, and that is to our weakside, away from the call and rover. Our weak halfback will cover the flat if a flow pass comes his way, with our safety covering deep outside, rover covering deep middle, and our strong halfback covering deep outside. Our end forces the QB in Cover One. (See Fig. 9–1.)

Our weak halfback aligns himself no more than five yards deep and four yards outside the offensive end. Our safety is nine to eleven yards deep depending on field position and down and distance, and is head on the offensive guard to our weakside. The strong halfback is seven yards deep and three yards outside the

DEFENSIVE SECONDARY PLAY

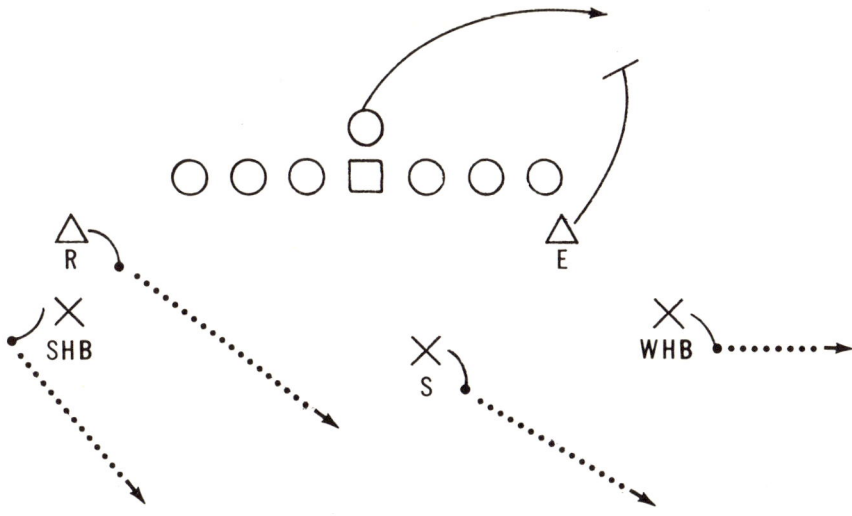

Fig. 9-1. Cover One—Flow Pass weakside.

offensive end and our rover is on the line, two to three yards outside the offensive end.

Our weak halfback levels in the flat at about seven yards deep, if flow comes his way. He keys the offensive end to the ball and is in a good position to give quick support on a running play. If a pass develops and no one shows in his zone, he drifts deep to help.

Our safety keys the ball to the receiver(s) to the side of flow. If any receivers come downfield our safety stays deep. If a run develops, he fills inside-out. If the end breaks deep inside, our safety must not rotate too far past him.

Our strong halfback covers deep outside, keeping the entire play inside him, but being careful not to open up too much area between himself and the ball when flow goes away.

Rover must cover deep middle on flow away. He must quickly rotate and key the end to his side. This end will not be able to release easily off the line if our swing man is doing his job properly, thus rover's job is somewhat easier than it appears.

If the offense presents a formation with a split end and a flanker back, we usually will call off Cover One and play Cover Three or Cover Four. These will be discussed shortly.

If the flow goes to our strongside, toward rover, rover covers the flat, our strong half covers deep outside, our safety, deep middle, and our weak half, deep outside (Fig. 9-2). In essence this is our Cover Three, three deep zones covered by our halfbacks and safety.

Rover gets width and depth depending on field position and formation. He crosses over for several steps to gain width and

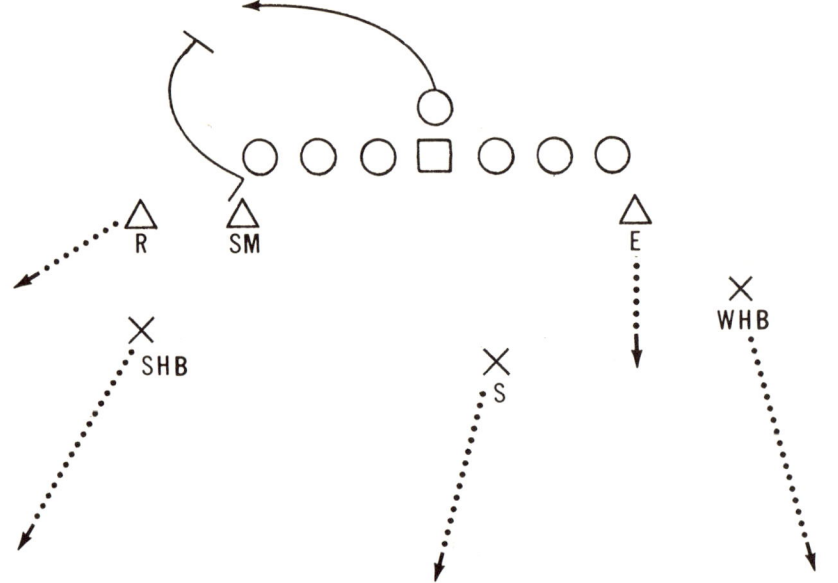

Fig. 9–2. Cover One—Flow Pass strongside.

then back pedals away from the QB. He faces the passer so as to be able to react either outside or inside to a thrown ball. If the swing man loses containment, rover is in a position to come up and support should the QB decide to run.

The strong half covers his deep outside zone, getting no closer than eight yards from the sideline. Our safety covers deep middle and does not cross the hash mark. Our weak half covers deep outside and keeps the entire play inside him.

Cover One is used against teams that like to run or rollout weakside to a tight end. We feel it places our weak half in a better position to support on runs.

Cover Two

In Cover Two we rotate two ways on flow. If flow goes weakside, we rotate exactly as in Cover One, except that rover drops straight back and our strong halfback covers deep half (Fig. 9–3).

If flow goes strongside we also rotate. Rover forces the play and our strong half covers the flat. Because we do not like to involve our end in too many pass coverages, we do not ask him to rotate to deep middle. Thus, our safety and weak half must cover deep halves of the field. They maintain a position relative to each other. Our end drops back to help on throwback passes. (See Fig. 9–4.)

DEFENSIVE SECONDARY PLAY

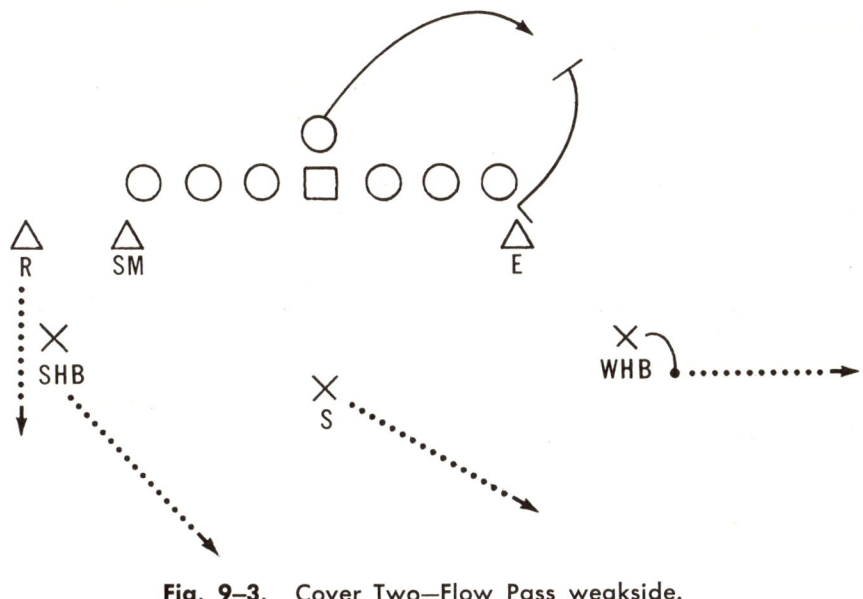

Fig. 9-3. Cover Two—Flow Pass weakside.

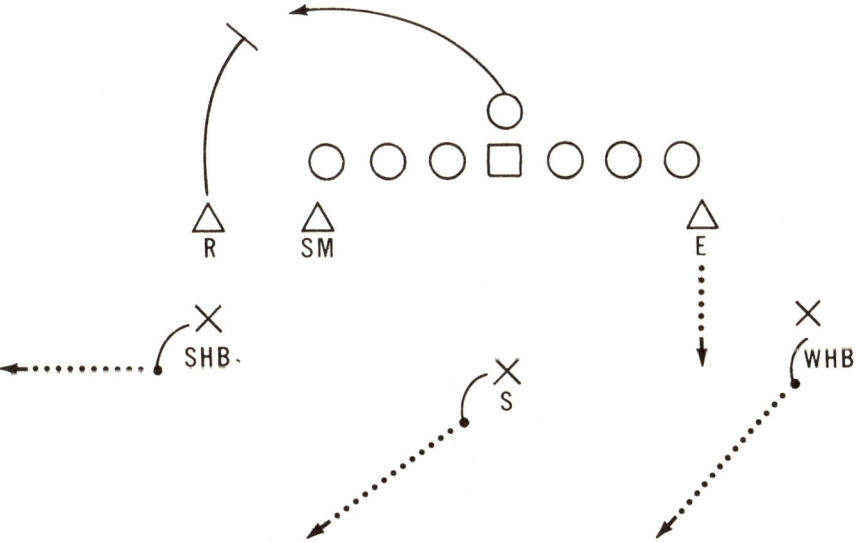

Fig. 9-4. Cover Two—Flow Pass strongside.

Our halfbacks line up seven yards deep and three yards outside the offensive end. Our safety lines up eleven yards deep on the center. The keys are the same as in Cover One. We prefer Cover Two over offensive sets that are tight, with no one split or flanked. We feel a halfback and safety can cover deep halves only against formations that are in a tight alignment.

Cover Three

This is the basic coverage we intially teach our secondary. In Cover Three our halfbacks cover deep outside and our safety covers deep middle against all passes. The alignment of our secondary varies according to field position, formation, and down and distance. Our basic alignment is seven yards deep and three yards outside the offensive end for our halfbacks, and eleven yards deep over center for our safety. However, we make adjustments to this at times. Our safety usually favors the weakside (Fig. 9–5) unless the wide side of the field is to our strongside, or two quick receivers are spread wide to our strongside (Fig. 9–6).

On running downs, our safety may be as close as seven yards, if the formation and situation dictate that there is a strong possibility

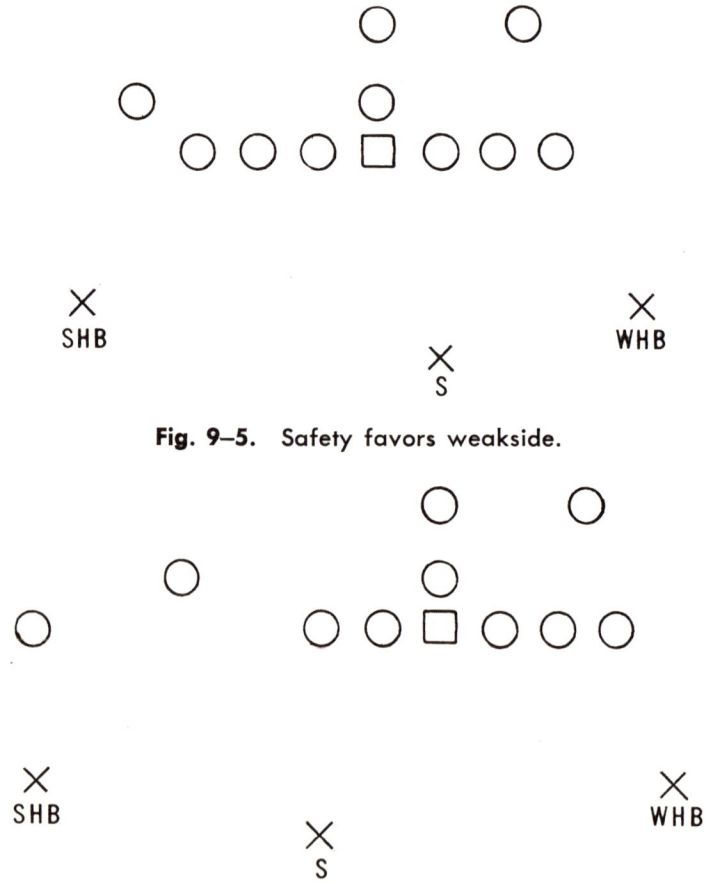

Fig. 9–5. Safety favors weakside.

Fig. 9–6. Safety favors strongside vs. two quick wide receivers.

DEFENSIVE SECONDARY PLAY 161

of a run. We feel he can still cover deep middle from this depth. However, we will not align him this close on Cover One or Two as we feel rotation is difficult from so deep.

Our weak halfback varies his depth according to the formation. If his end is tight, he moves up to a depth of five yards or closer on running downs (Fig. 9–7). If his end is spread, he stays seven yards deep and one yard outside him until he is eight yards from the sideline (Fig. 9–8). He gets no closer to the sideline than eight yards.

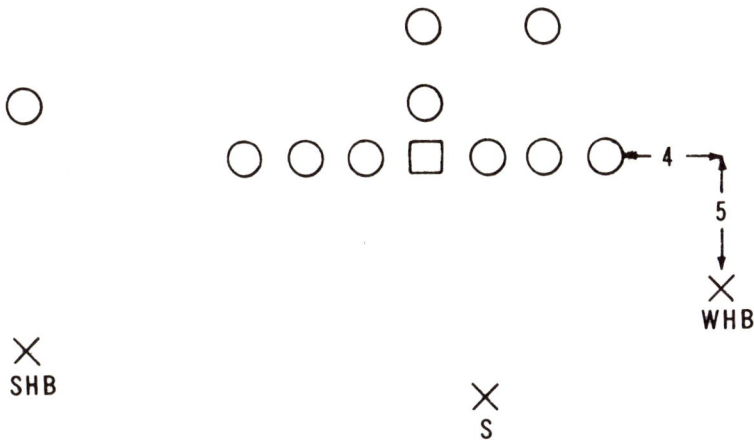

Fig. 9–7. Cover Three—weak half 5 & 4 vs. a tight end.

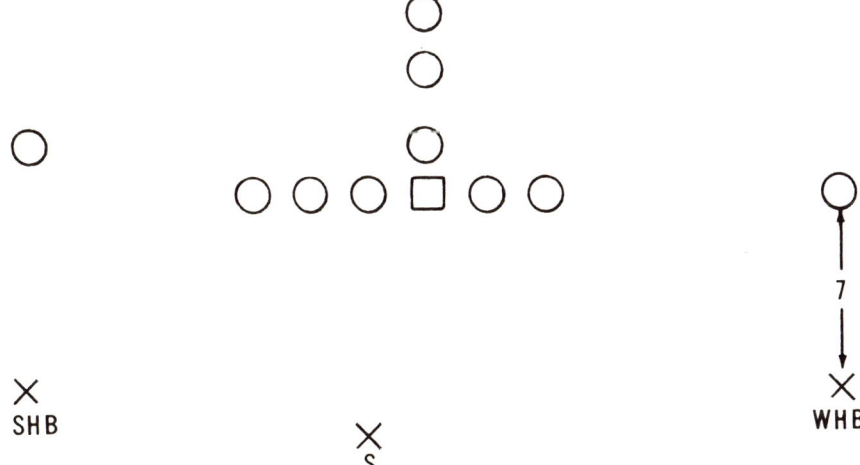

Fig. 9–8. Cover Three—weak half 7 deep outside a split-end. Safety favors the side of two receivers.

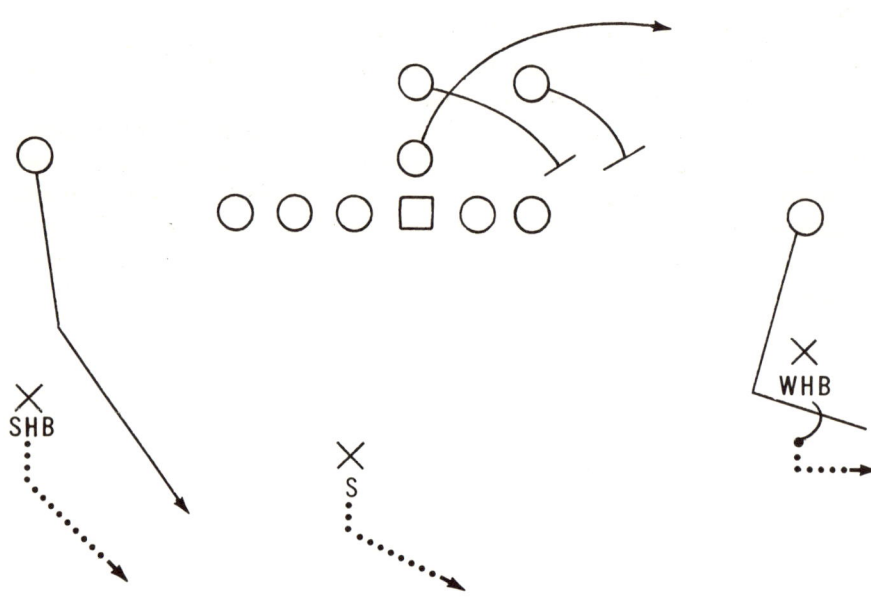

Fig. 9–9. Cover Three—Flow Pass. WHB can level with the receiver here, as only one man shows in his one.

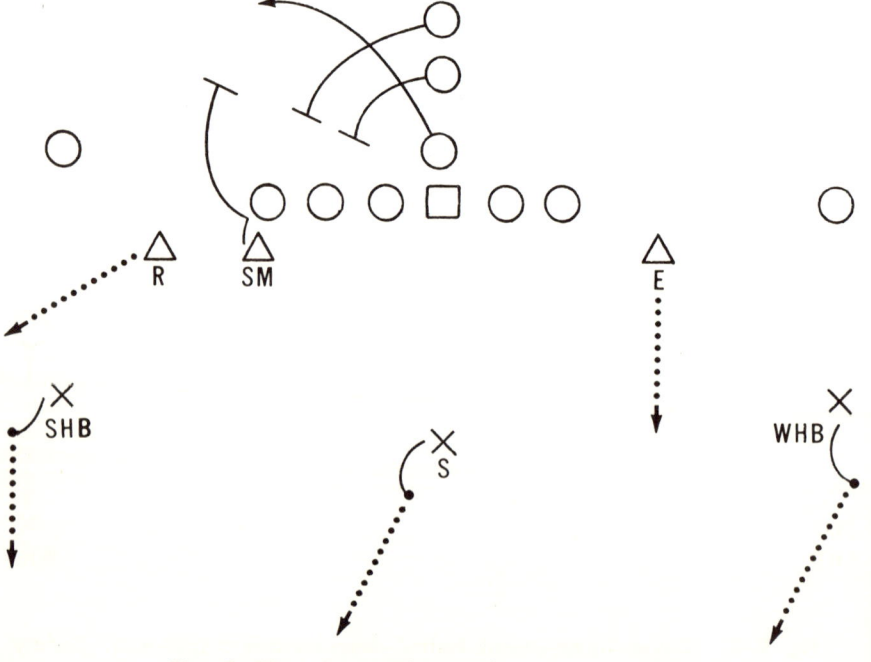

Fig. 9–10. Cover Three—Flow Pass strong.

DEFENSIVE SECONDARY PLAY

Our strong half is never closer than seven yards to the line in Cover Three. If a man flanks wide to his side he has the same rule as our weak half, one yard outside until eight yards from the sideline.

On flow passes, our three deep men move with the flow of the QB. The halfback to the side of flow stays deep outside, but can favor an outside cut by a man in his zone if only one receiver shows. The HB away from flow keeps a wide receiver outside (Fig. 9-9).

On flow pass to our strongside (Fig. 9-10), our rover covers the flat as in Cover One (see also Fig. 9-2). On flow pass weakside, our end forces the QB if the offensive end is tight, and plays along the line if his end is split (Fig. 9-11). Rover drops to the hook zone.

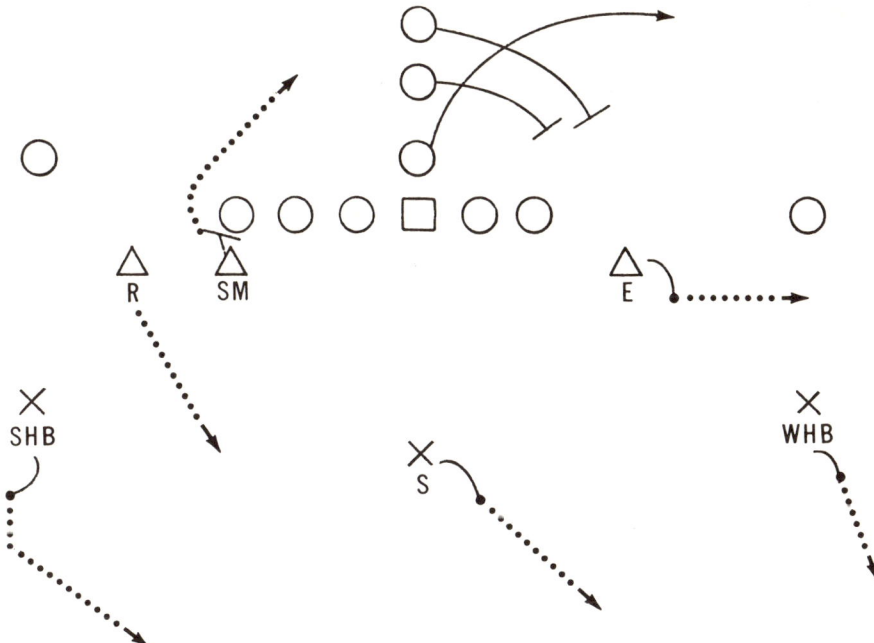

Fig. 9-11. Cover Three—Flow Pass weak with offensive end split.

Cover Four

This coverage is exactly the same as Cover One except for the alignment of our rover. In Cover Four, rover aligns himself four yards deep and one to two yards outside the offensive end. The coverage is used when we want to rotate weakside against teams

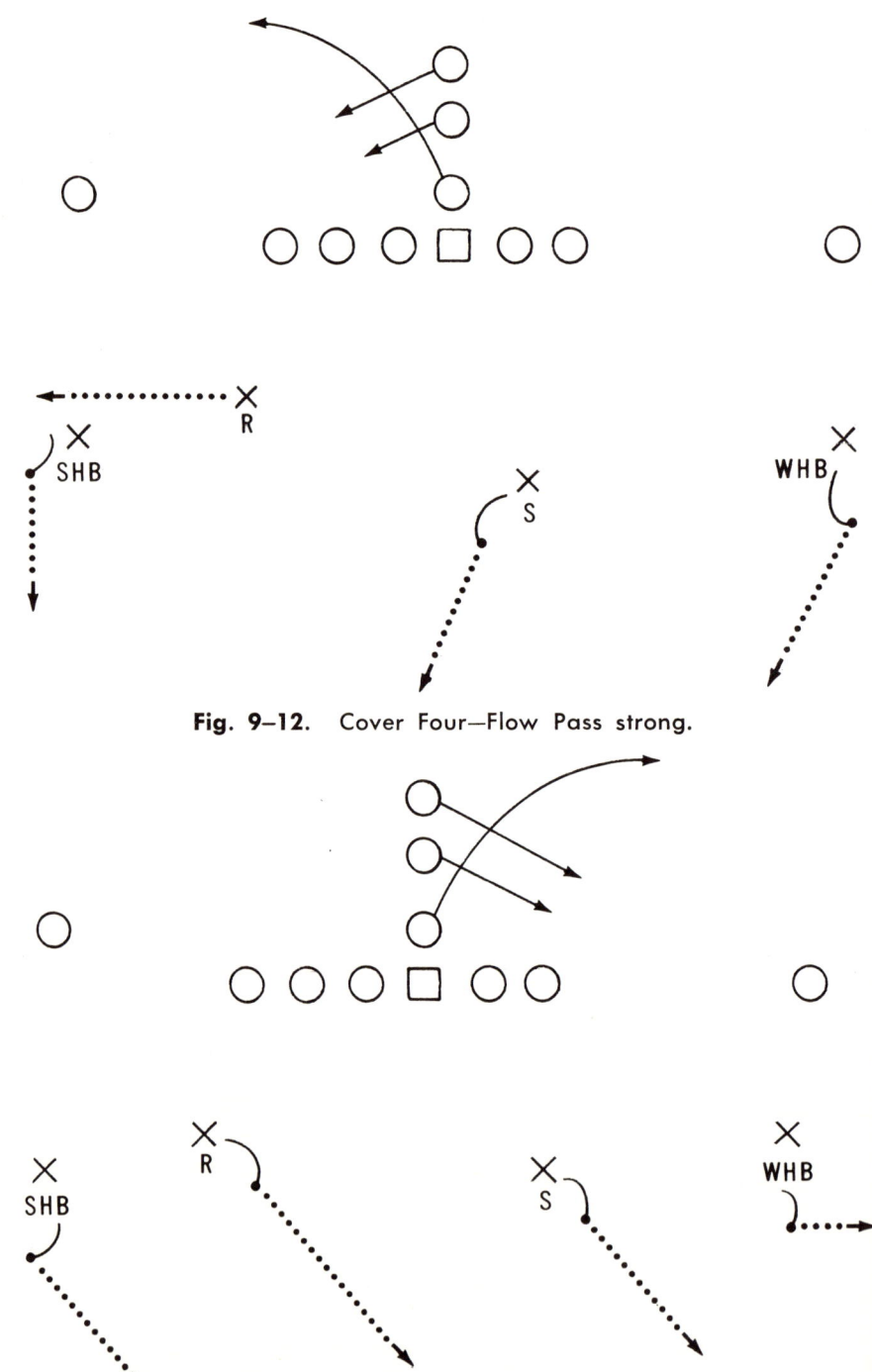

Fig. 9–12. Cover Four—Flow Pass strong.

Fig. 9–13. Cover Four—Flow Pass weak.

DEFENSIVE SECONDARY PLAY 165

that use a split end and flanker set. Zone coverage is the same as in Cover One on flow passes. (See Figs. 9–12 and 9–13.)

If the opponents use motion in their offense, our basic adjustment is to go to Cover Three if motion goes strongside (Fig. 9–14) and to Cover Four if motion goes weakside (Fig. 9–15).

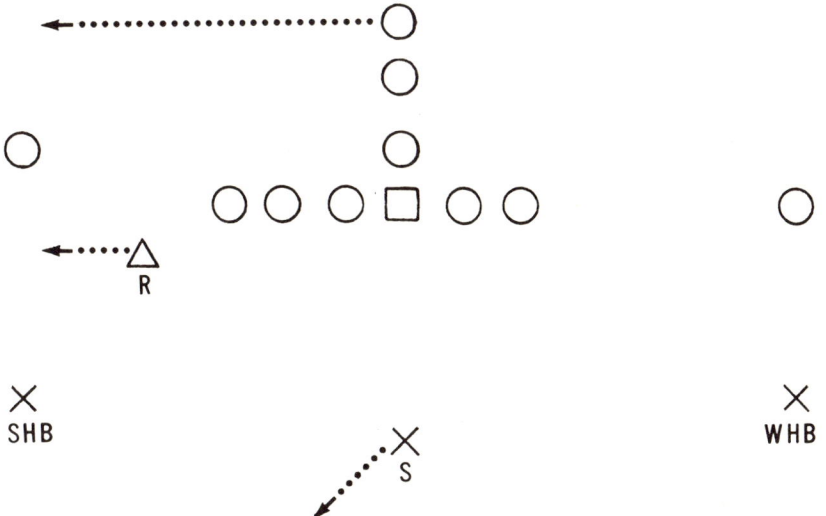

Fig. 9–14. Motion strongside. We adjust to Cover Three.

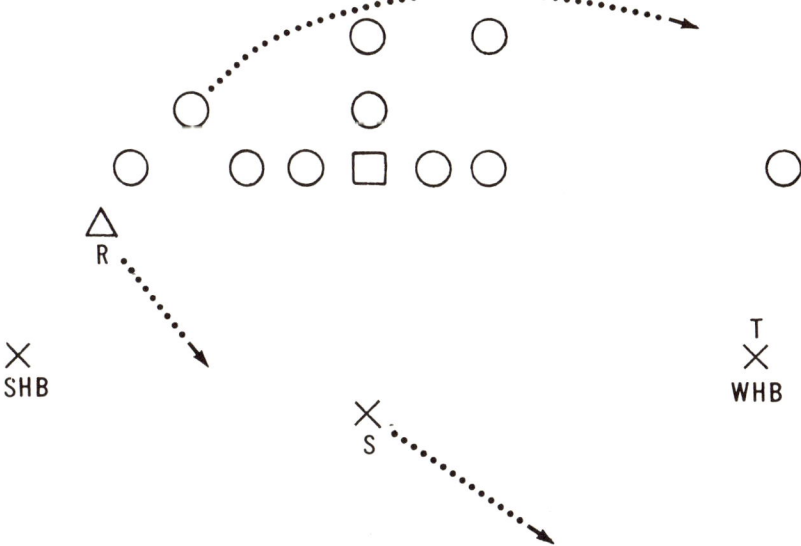

Fig. 9–15. Motion weakside. We adjust to Cover Four.

Cover Prevent

This coverage is used in obvious passing situations and when we are leading (or tied) at the end of the half or game and expect our opponents to throw the ball. (See Fig. 9–16.)

Our halfbacks line up at least ten yards deep, and our safety, at least fifteen yards deep. They cover their deep zones and keep all receivers in front of them. Our rover and end cover the split receivers man-for-man in the flat zone. If the receiver leaves the zone, rover and end play zone pass defense. Our strong backer racks the tight end and covers him man-for-man in his zone. If the tight end leaves the zone, our backer plays zone pass defense. Our weak backer covers the halfback if he runs a pattern to his side. If the halfback blocks, or leaves the backer's zone, our backer plays zone pass defense.

On occasion, we will remove a linebacker and replace him with a special safety. This safety lines up twenty-five yards deep in the middle of the field and blankets the entire field. Our remaining backer plays the middle zone short, and our original safety plays normal.

We feel our five zone coverages give us enough variety to cover the types of passes we face. The fact that our backers and end, who must also be key defenders against running plays, have basically the same assignment on all coverages makes it simpler to teach this variety of coverages. Any time we have called a rotating coverage in the huddle, our safety has the option to call it off, and go to Cover Three, if he feels he cannot cover deep outside because of field position or the offensive formation we are facing.

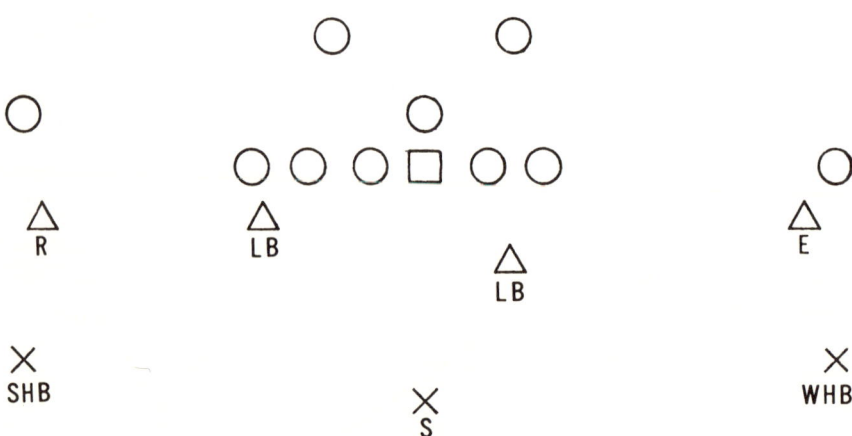

Fig. 9–16. Cover Prevent.

DEFENSIVE SECONDARY PLAY

MAN-FOR-MAN COVERAGES

Our two man-for-man coverages are cover red and cover blue.

Cover Red

Cover Red involves our three deep men, rover, and one linebacker (Fig. 9–17).

Our halfbacks cover the outside receivers. Our safety covers the offensive halfback and rover covers the tight end. Our strongbacker covers the fullback if he is used as a receiver. If the outside men are split out, our halfbacks stick with these men all over the field. Their basic rule is to take away the inside cut first; that is, make the QB throw the toughest pass.

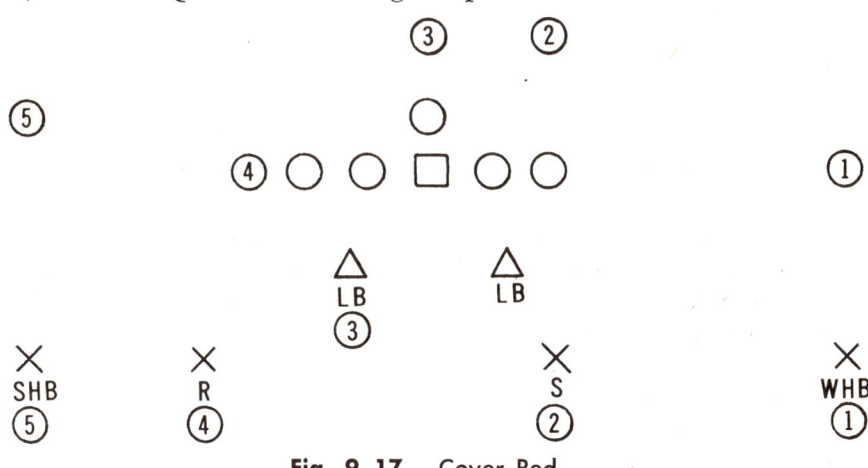

Fig. 9–17. Cover Red.

If an end is tight, or if two receivers are within five yards of each other, we use an inside-outside rule (Fig. 9–18). This rule tells the two defenders to play man-for-man only in their zone. Thus, the inside defender covers the receiver who breaks inside to his zone, and the outside defender covers the receiver who breaks outside to his zone. If both receivers go to one zone, each defender covers the man to whom he is originally assigned.

If motion shows in Cover Red, we go to our basic zone coverage rules and pick up the receivers man-for-man.

Cover Blue

Cover Blue is a man-for-man coverage where we free rover for pass rush and use our weak linebacker in the pass coverage. Rover and our end usually shoot and have a "free" rush. (See Fig. 9–19.)

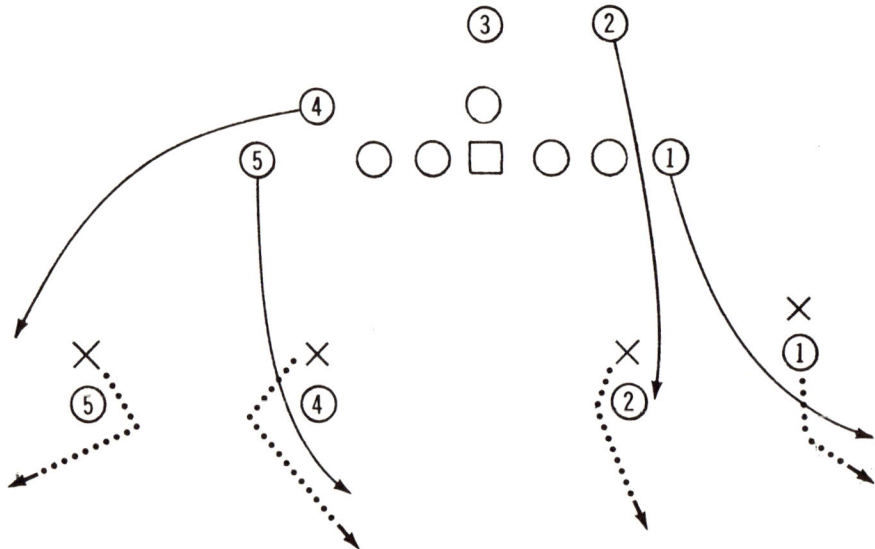

Fig. 9–18. Cover Red—inside-out on both sides.

Our halfbacks cover the outside men as in Cover Red. Our safety covers the inside receiver to the strongside, and our backers cover the remaining backs. On occasion, we will shoot our weak backer, and our end will cover the offensive halfback.

The only inside-out rule is between our strong half and our safety. Our weak half must cover his man all over the field.

If motion shows, we immediately go to our zone coverage. Rover must adjust to this, and this is not an easy task. We do not particularly prefer Cover Blue vs. teams that use motion to a great degree.

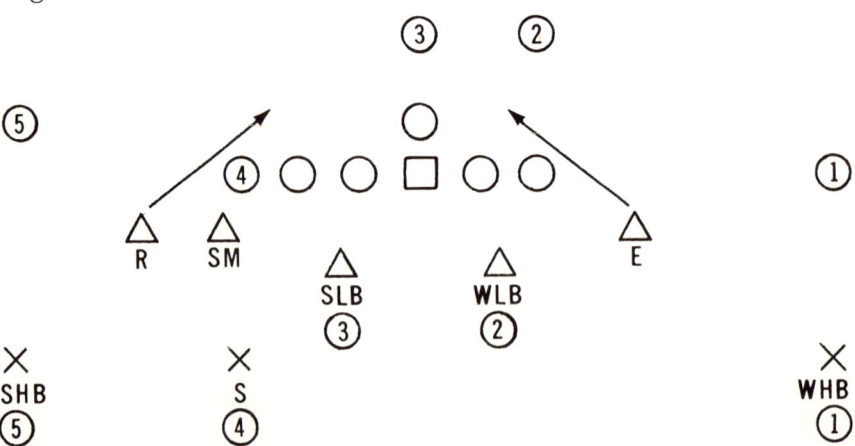

Fig. 9–19. Cover Blue.

DEFENSIVE SECONDARY PLAY

BASIC TECHNIQUES AND DRILLS

We feel there are five basic techniques our secondary men must master:

1. Initial move on key
2. Run defense filling and pursuit
3. Tackling
4. Pass defense—zone
5. Pass defense—man-for-man

Initial Move

Our halfbacks take a step out and back with their outside foot on the snap of the ball. Their outside foot is up as they align themselves. We feel that by having the outside foot up we align ourselves to better view the entire offensive formation. Most teams we face use at least one wide end or flanker, and it is a difficult task for a defensive halfback to view the entire formation if he is spread wide and has his outside foot back. He must then turn his neck and hips inside to see, and this slows his initial move. We want a quick initial move on the snap and feel our stance best gives us what we want.

Our safety's stance is one with feet parallel, as his initial move depends on flow. If the ball moves to his left, our safety takes a quick step out and back with his left foot. If the ball moves to his right, he steps with his right foot.

After their initial move, our secondary men glide until they recognize the play. If it is a pass (and we tell them every play is a pass at its inception), they cover their zone. If it is a run, they take their respective pursuit angles.

To teach initial move, we use our Shuffle Drill (Fig. 9–20).

The coach executes two moves to either side, (1) a run or (2) a rollout pass, and the secondary reacts accordingly. If it is a rollout pass, they glide to their zones. If it is a run, the halfback to the side of flow starts up to fill, the safety starts to take an inside-out angle to fill, and the halfback away from flow starts to glide deep to blanket the entire front.

We add rover to this drill when we wish to teach Covers One, Two, and Four. We start the secondary in Cover Three. Once the basic initial move is mastered, we add offensive ends and have our halfbacks key them.

Run Defense

To teach run defense we use our Fill Drill (Fig. 9–21).

We use an offensive end, a QB, and two backs on offense; and a

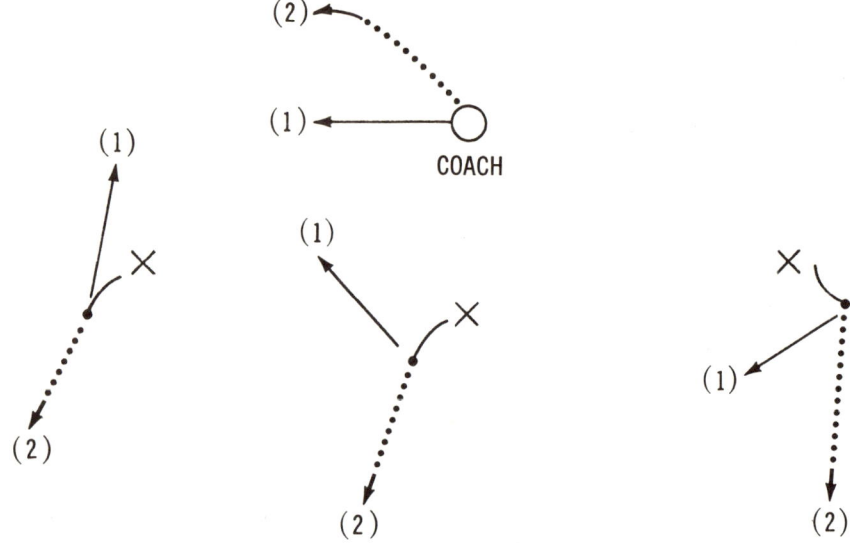

Fig. 9-20. Shuffle drill.

halfback and safety, on defense. We execute a wide run, either a sweep or option, and work on our halfback filling up and our safety filling inside-out. Our halfback comes up quickly, but must come under control in order to prevent a cutback. We want him to meet the blocker with his shoulders parallel to the line, feet facing upfield, and to use his hands in a shiver blow. Our weak halfback should fill faster than our strong halfback, because he is away from rover, and should take an angle to the inside. In most cases, our strong half should be reacting to a run that rover has turned inside and should take an angle straight upfield. Our safety fills inside-out, but his angle must be such that he can overhaul a back who happens to get outside.

If an option play develops, our halfback must maintain an outside-in angle and stay with the pitch man. He must never go for the quarterback. Our safety fills inside and is ready to meet the QB should the QB turn upfield.

Tackling

We use our aforementioned Tackling Drills for our secondary and also use the Fill Drill for tackling in the open field. We emphasize tackling high, as at times the secondary man may be our last defender in the path of a touchdown-bound runner and we do not want to miss!

DEFENSIVE SECONDARY PLAY

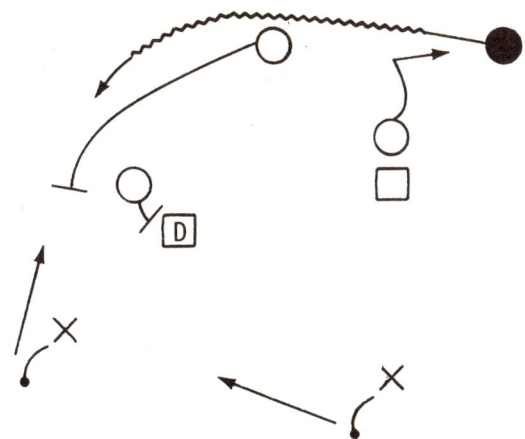

Fig. 9–21. Fill drill.

Pass Defense—Zone

As in teaching zone pass defense to ends and backers, we feel that our secondary must master two things: (1) going to zone properly, and (2) reacting to the ball. The aforementioned To-Zone Drill (see Fig. 7–32) teaches the initial moves of getting to zone in our various coverages. The difference in teaching zone pass defense to deep defenders is that they do not react to the passer's first move unless the ball is thrown, whereas defenders in the short zones must react to any move a passer makes that appears to signal that the ball will be thrown. A deep defender has a better chance to recognize a pattern as it develops so he has a better chance to anticipate where the ball will be thrown. Thus, our basic teaching point is to teach our deep defenders to react quickly to the ball while still being certain that they have their deep zone protected and that no pass can be completed behind them. Some players are capable of doing this while operating at less depth than other players.

We use the Spot Drill (see Fig. 7–33) and the Shield Drill (see Fig. 7–34) in our secondary. Another drill we like is the Hub Drill (Fig. 9–22).

Two receivers, fifteen yards apart (early in the season) sprint downfield vs. one defender. The coach, stationed deep behind the defender, signals the receivers to run one of three patterns: (1) up, (2) cross at ten yards, or (3) snake at twelve yards. One receiver always runs an up, and the other receiver will run one of the three patterns. The coach signals which receiver the passer is to hit and the defender tries for an interception. As the season progresses, we widen the distance between the two receivers to twenty yards, and finally to twenty-five yards. The defender stays deep enough to cover the deep receiver, and if the ball is thrown to a short receiver, reacts up as best he can. At times, we add linebackers to this drill.

In our Patterns Drill for the secondary, we usually add rover and our end and work on combination patterns involving deep and

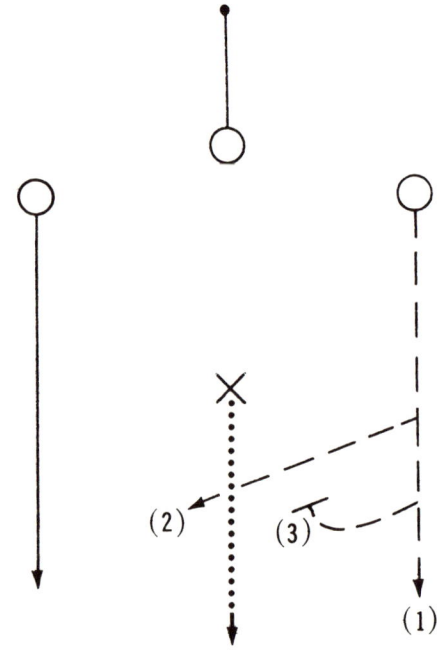

Fig. 9–22. Hub drill.

short men. We start with the premise that if an inside receiver breaks outside, then the outside receiver will break inside (Fig. 9–23). The opposite (Fig. 9–24) holds if the inside receiver breaks inside. We feel this can help our rover or end in covering the flat, and may give our halfback a better jump on the ball when it is thrown. Of course, many teams do not always operate on this general premise, and as the season progresses we must make adjustments against certain opponents.

Pass Defense—Man-for-Man

The variety of pass offenses we face force us to play man-for-man pass defense at times. We also feel we are much sounder playing

DEFENSIVE SECONDARY PLAY 173

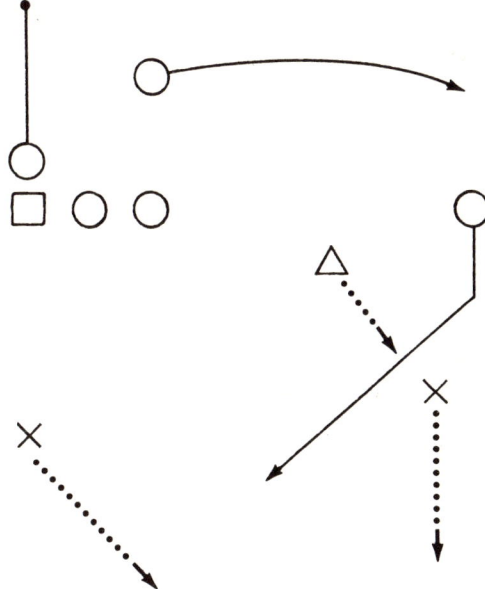

Fig. 9-23. Patterns drill—inside receiver breaks outside.

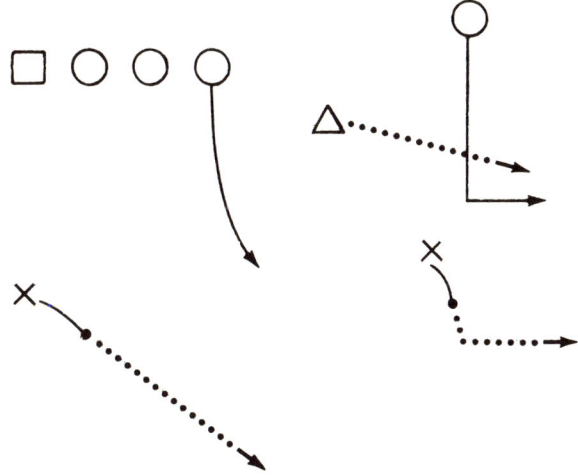

Fig. 9-24. Patterns drill—inside receiver breaks inside.

man-for-man inside our ten-yard line, unless the opponent is faced with a third or fourth and long yardage, when we do better with zone coverage. The best method we have found to teach man-for-man coverage is for our defenders to cover our best receivers as they practice their pass patterns. Much rivalry develops, especially when we move the offense inside the ten-yard line and go for a score. We emphasize taking away a split receiver's inside cut first, thus giving him only one way to go unless he runs into us. On the goalline, we want to drive on the receiver on the goalline and not let him drive us into the end zone where he has two directions in which to cut. In the middle of the field, we drive on the receiver when he cuts, staying in a position where we can hit him and turn and run with him if he breaks upfield (Fig. 9–25). On the goalline, we drive for his hands in front of him (Fig. 9–26).

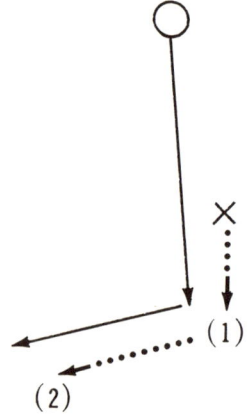

Fig. 9–25. Man-for-Man coverage. (1) Give the receiver one way to cut and then (2) drive for the ball in a position to get deep if he breaks upfield.

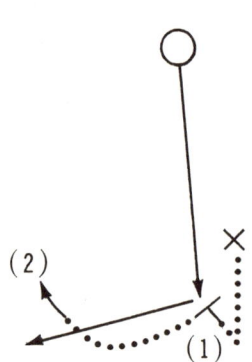

Fig. 9–26. Goalline Man-for-Man coverage. (1) Hit the man on the goalline and then (2) drive for his hands.

Part III

KICKING

10

The Kicking Game

PUNTS

Many close games are won or lost because of the kicking game. The major reason the kicking game breaks down is lack of hustle by the kicking team. Kicking the ball is the same as any offensive play—each man must carry out his specific assignment.

We use a spread punt and if the ball is back within three yards of our own goalline, we must get the ball out to at least three yards from the goalline, so that we can use our spread punt (Fig. 10–1).

We would always like to keep our opponent in his three-down zone so that he is forced to kick on fourth down. Ideally, we would like to force our opponent to kick from inside his thirty-yard line.

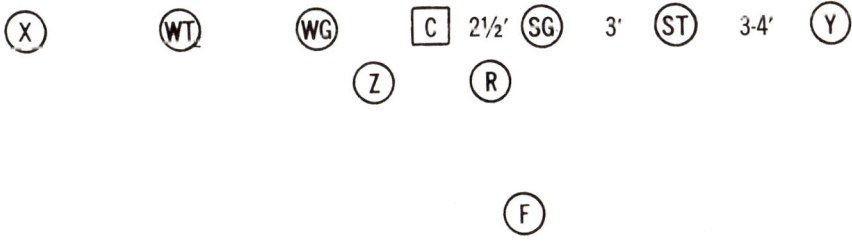

Fig. 10–1. Spread punt.

Our center must be able to snap the ball thirteen to fifteen yards deep in six-tenths of a second. The ball should be approximately waist high. In order to accomplish this, the center must work on snapping every day.

Our punter will line up thirteen to fifteen yards deep with his kicking foot on the ball. As the ball is snapped, he should take a short step with his kicking foot. He should receive the ball, and have it kicked in 1.3 seconds. If he is slow, chances are the punt will be blocked. We want height first and then distance. He should try and keep the ball in flight for four seconds. This will give us time for good coverage.

We take a one-yard split from tackle to tackle. Ends can split one to one and a half yards. They take a minimum split if the defense stacks up inside of them and their tackle. (See Fig. 10–1.)

Blocking Assignments

Center: 1. He snaps the ball waist high and gets his head up.
    2. He blocks area. If no one comes he covers.
    3. He is ready for a stack defensive set and/or shooting linebackers.

Guard: He takes a two-and-a-half-foot split from his center.
1. He blocks first man from nose on to his outside. He never blocks inside. If two men between him and his tackle, he calls Help-Tackle.
2. He keeps inside foot planted, drops outside foot back, and makes high forearm slam and then covers.
3. He does not fire out on-man or go outside after him, as he will create too big a gap between him and our up-back on his side.
4. He is ready for a stack defensive set and/or linebackers shooting over his area.

Tackle: He takes a one-yard split from his guard.
1. He blocks the first man outside, unless there are two men between him and his guard—then the guard will call Help-Tackle, and he will block inside.
2. If there are two men between him and his end, he calls Help-End.
3. He must be alert for a stack defensive set and/or shooting linebackers over his area.

End: He lines up one yard to one-and-a-half yards from his tackle.
1. If there are *two* men between him and his tackle or *three* men between him and his guard, the tackle will call Help-End, and he blocks inside.
2. If there is no one there, he *runs through* the man outside and covers.
3. He must be alert for a stack defensive set and/or shooting linebackers.
4. If he has an inside block, he cuts his split down to one yard.

THE KICKING GAME

Up-Back: He lines up in the gap between his guard and center, one yard back of ball.
1. He blocks area. He takes a well-braced stance and does not get blown back by linemen.
2. He must be ready for a stack defensive set and/or shooting linebackers through his area.
3. He does not leave until he has blocked his area for at least one second.
4. After he has blocked for one second, he covers behind his tackle. He is a safetyman on his side. He *stays head up on the ball and cannot get blocked.*

Personal Protector: He lines up six yards deep behind his right up-back.
1. He blocks the most dangerous man. He keeps his head on a swivel.
2. He never backs up.
3. He does not leave until ball is kicked.
4. He covers to his right.

Kicker: He lines up fourteen to fifteen yards from the ball.
1. He concentrates on ball.
2. He gets kick away and covers to his left.

Punt Coverage

Most punts are returned for long gainers or touchdowns because:
1. The kicking team loafs down under the punt.
2. Poor field coverage. We never follow same our own color jersey.
3. Low or poor punt.
4. Missed tackles.

See Fig. 10–2.

Lineman. As soon as he has sustained his block for at least one second, he sprints downfield, fanning out as he keeps about five yards between him and his teammate next to him. He comes under control about three yards from the receiver. He never crosses over, and he keeps his body pointed upfield. We *keep the ball carrier inside our coverage. We tackle high!*

Up-Back. He sustains his block for one second and then becomes a safety man behind his tackle. If the ball carrier breaks, it is his responsibility to make the tackle. He cannot get blocked. He keeps out of the heavy traffic.

Personal Protector and Kicker. After the ball is kicked, they become second ends to the outside on the sides on which they are aligned. They do not let the ball carrier outside of them.

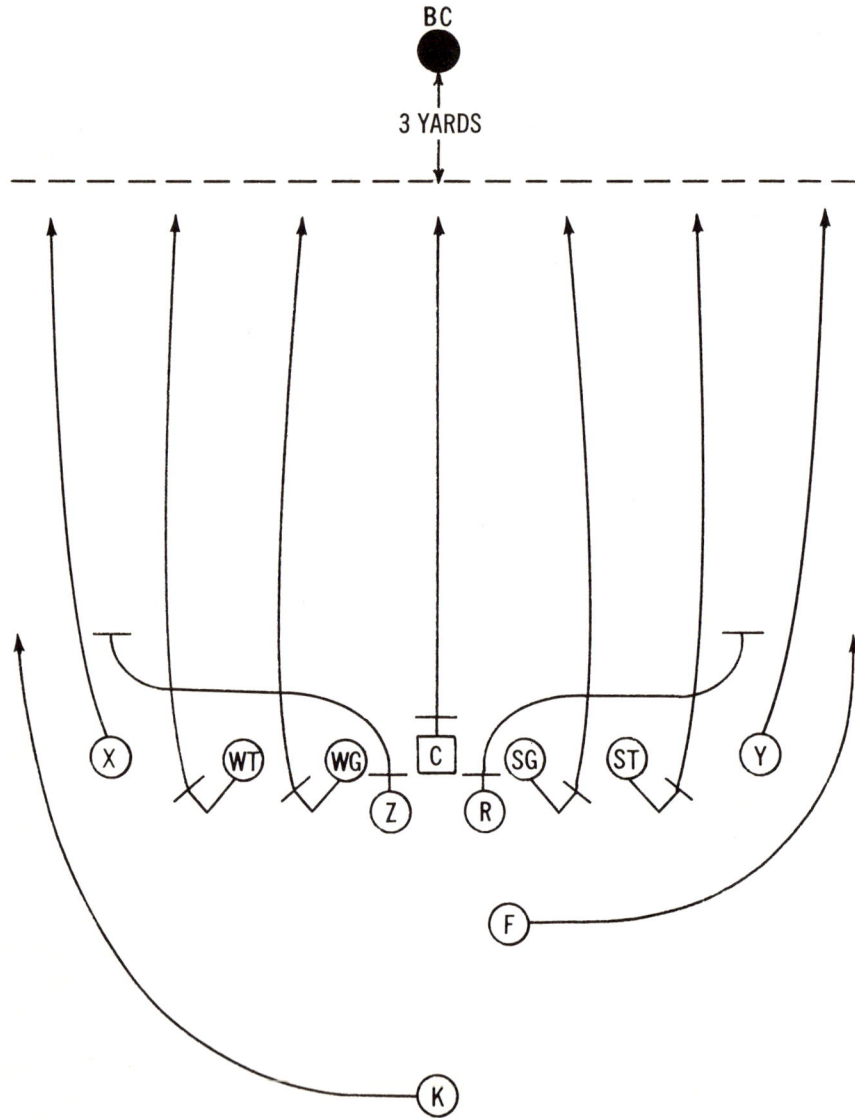

Fig. 10-2. Punt coverage.

PUNT RETURNS

We must try to get the ball into our four-down zone or be able to kick the ball and keep our opponents in their three-down zone. This can be done if every man does his assignment and hustles. If one man loafs, it breaks down our whole return pattern.

See Fig. 10-3.

THE KICKING GAME

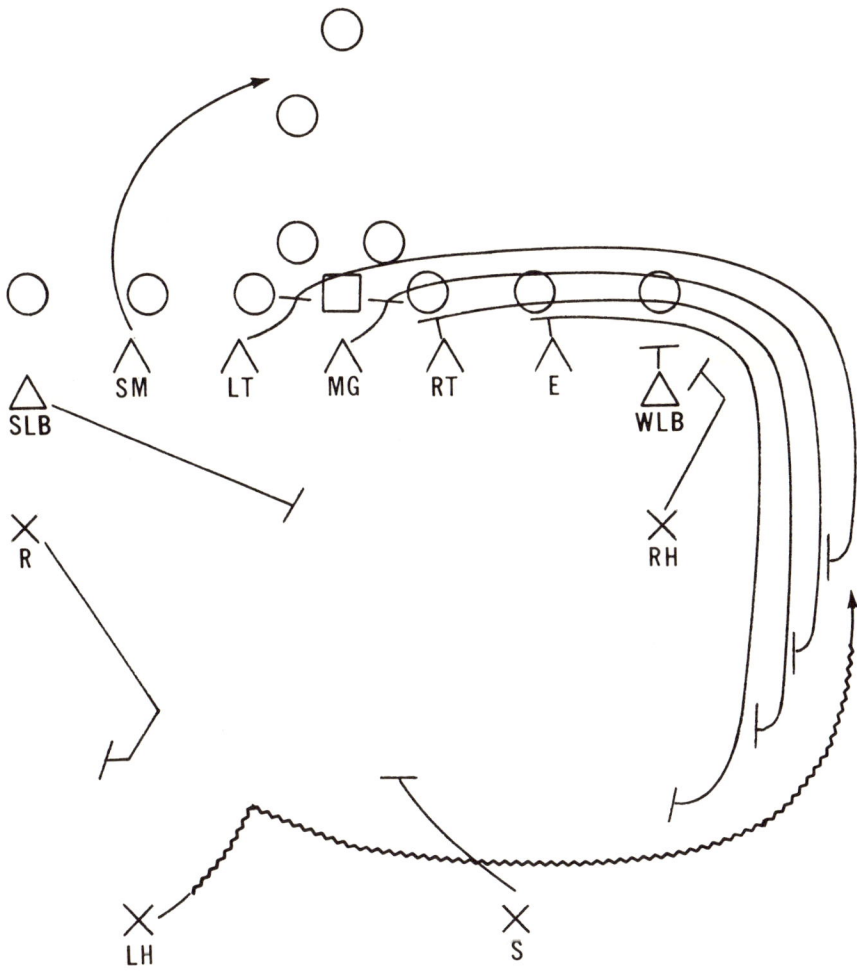

Fig. 10–3. Punt return—right.

Responsibilities

E: He lines up on the outside shoulder of the tackle. He strikes a blow on the tackle and then sprints around an imaginary post seven yards from where he lines up. He heads directly at our receiver and blocks the first opponent he encounters. He becomes the first man in our picket line.

RT: He lines up on the outside shoulder of the guard. He strikes a blow on the guard and then sprints around an imaginary post seven yards from where he lined up. He becomes the second man in our picket line. He sets up about five yards from our RE and blocks the first opponent encountered.

MG: He lines head up on the center. He makes a slant move through the up-back to his right. He then sprints around an imaginary post seven yards from where he lined up. He sets up five yards from RT and blocks the first opponent encountered.

LT: He lines head up on the guard. He makes a slant move through the head of the up-back to his side. He then sprints around an imaginary post seven yards from where he lined up. He sets up five yards from MG and blocks the first opponent encountered.

SM: He lines up on the outside shoulder of the tackle. He drives through the shoulder of the tackle. He watches for a fake run or pass and/or poor snap. He keeps outside leverage on the ball. After the ball is kicked, he becomes the last man in the picket. He blocks the first opponent encountered.

WLB: He lines up about two yards off the ball over the offensive end. As the end releases, he puts an aggressive block on him and attempts to knock him down. Our right half will also come up and hit him. After he blocks him, he gets up and blocks him again. He continues blocking him until the ball is dead.

RH: He lines up about six yards deep. He checks for a fake punt and run or pass. He then double teams on the offensive end with our WLB. He continues blocking the end until the ball is dead.

SLB: He lines head up on the offensive end about two yards deep. After the ball is snapped, he takes off to the inside and blocks the first man coming down the middle. It will probably be the center or one of the up-backs.

R: He lines up six yards deep, and two yards outside the offensive end. He checks for a fake punt and run or pass. As the offensive end releases, our LH drops back getting an inside-out blocking angle on him. He blocks him to the outside.

LH and **RS:** They line up forty yards off the line of scrimmage. They *field the ball in the air.* Whoever fields the ball calls for it, catches it and heads up field a few steps, then loses ground and gets into the picket alley. The non-receiver should set up in front of the receiver and block the most dangerous opponent.

KICKOFFS

The average kickoff return is between eighteen and twenty yards. With this in mind, it is important that our kicker put the ball into the end zone. We must be able to keep our opponents inside their thirty-yard line and force them to punt on fourth down.

On our coverage, all men will be turned inside with hands on knees facing the kicker. They line up splitting the forward foot of the man next to them. Our line will have a slight curve to it. (See Fig. 10–4.)

THE KICKING GAME

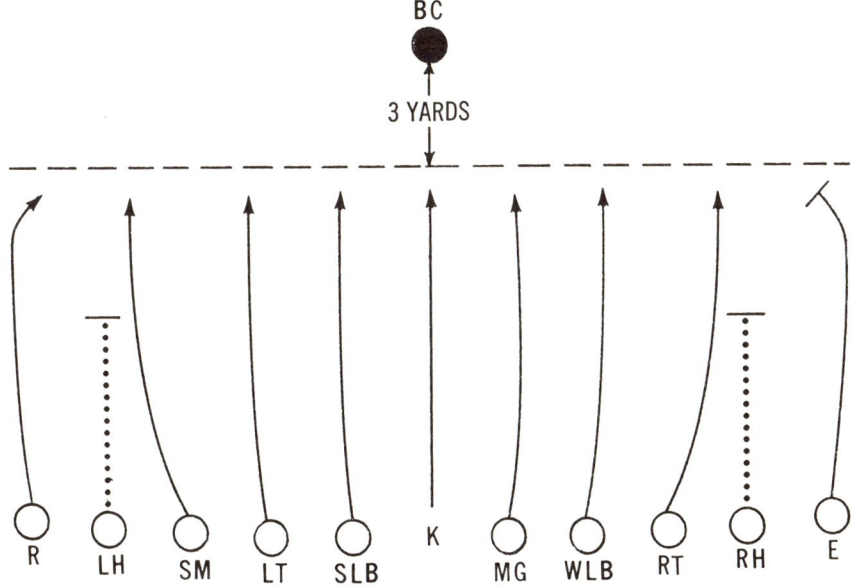

Fig. 10-4. Kickoff coverage.

Responsibilities

R and **RE:** They have outside containment. They cannot let the ball outside of them and cannot ever overrun the ball carrier and get knocked outside.

LH and **RH:** They are safetymen on their respective sides. They stay head up on the ball about eight to ten yards from our initial coverage. If the ball carrier breaks free, they tackle high. They hold the ball carrier or a blocker up until pursuit can come from behind. They never commit themselves to a blocker.

SM and **RT:** After the ball is kicked, they must fan to their outside so as to pick up the safetyman's lane on their side.

LT and **WLB:** They sprint down in their respective lanes.

SLB, MG, and **K:** They sprint down in their respective lanes.

In general we must never feel that the kick won't be returned even if it goes deep in the end zone. This causes 105-yard returns. We go hard all the way picking up our proper lane, approximately six yards from the man on either side of us. We avoid blockers. We fake around them and get back in our rushing lanes. We do not give ourselves up. We get under control when we are about three yards from the ball carrier. We get a wide base and do not cross over with our feet. We do not wait for someone else to make the tackle. We must be aggressive.

Onside Kickoff

We will line up the same way as on our normal kickoff, but our kicker will try to kick the ball on the right side so that it will go to our left side. *After* the ball has traveled ten yards, the closest man to the ball will try to make the recovery. The other men near the ball should block our opponents. We *don't try to pick the ball up*, but make recovery as we would on any fumbled ball.

KICKOFF RETURNS

We have three kickoff returns. They are (1) Wedge Return, Right, (2) Wedge Return, Left, and (3) Wedge Return, Middle. The Wedge Return, Left, can be worked out as a mirror-image of the Right assignments.

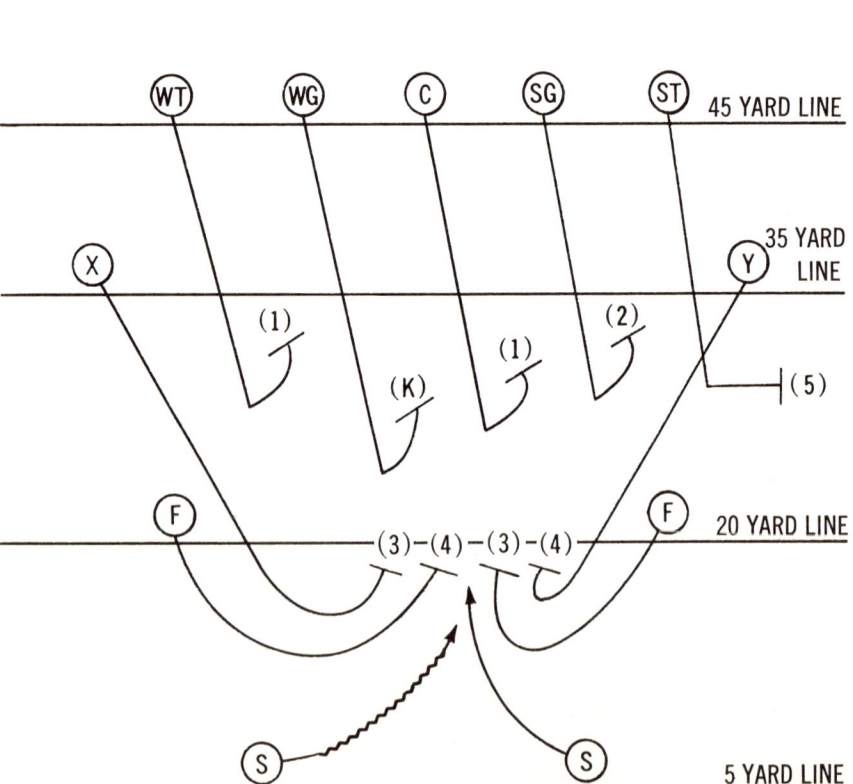

Fig. 10–5. Wedge Return—Right.

THE KICKING GAME

Wedge Return—Right

Our front five line up in front of the forty-five-yard line. When the ball is kicked, they drop back to about the thirty-yard line and form our primary wedge. They then turn and carry out their blocking assignments. (See Fig. 10-5.)

X and Y line up on the thirty-five-yard line. When the ball is kicked, they drop back to about the fifteen-yard line and form a secondary wedge with our two fullbacks, who line up on the twenty-yard line. Our secondary wedge must hustle back and form close together and carry out their blocking assignments when the safety who catches the ball yells GO. The other safety should lead up into the secondary wedge. Whoever fields the football, calls for it.

Assignments

C: Block No. one to right of kicker, in.
SG: Block No. two to right of kicker, in.
ST: Block No. five to right of kicker, out.
WG: Block kicker.
WT: Block No. one to left of kicker, in.
X and Y: Block No. three or four to right of kicker.
FB's: Block No. three or four to right of kicker.
S's: Ball carrier and leader.

Wedge Return—Middle Assignments

(See Fig. 10-6.)

C: Drop back to thirty-yard line and block kicker. Or, go after him (C.P.)
G: Drop back to thirty-yard line and block No. one out.
T: Drop back to thirty-yard line and block No. two out.
E and FB: Drop back and form secondary wedge. When receiver yells GO, turn and block first opponent encountered.
S's: Field ball in the air and whoever takes it call for ball. The other safety should be personal interferer.

DEFENSING THE ONSIDE KICKOFF

Our front five will line up on the forty-eight-yard line. Our two ends and two fullbacks move up to the forty-five-yard line and are ready to field all kicks. Our safety's move up to about our ten-yard line and are ready to go after any balls that get over our second line of defense. (See Fig. 10-7.)

Our front five men should let all balls go through so that our ends and fullbacks can handle the football. After the ball has been kicked, they get over to where the ball is being fielded and block the first

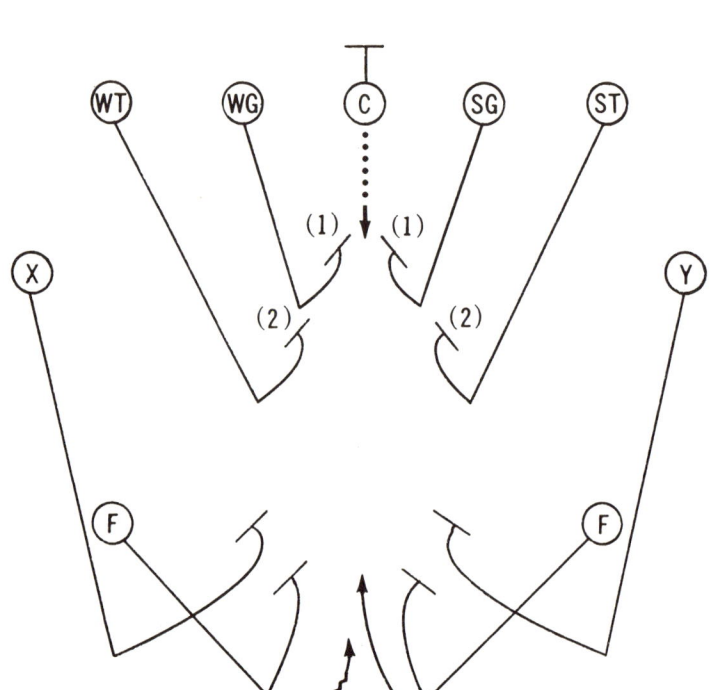

Fig. 10–6. Wedge Return—Middle.

opponent encountered. If the ball goes deep, we form the wedge return up the middle.

Most onside kicks are successful because the defending team panics and loses the ball. We must remember not to try to return the ball, but merely get control of it and stay on the ground.

P.A.T. AND FIELD GOAL

If we are proficient in this phase of the kicking game, we can win many close games. (See Fig. 10–8.)

Our kicker lines up eight and one-half yards from the ball, his kicking foot slightly in front of his other foot with his kicking foot head on the ball. He takes a short step with his kicking foot, then

THE KICKING GAME

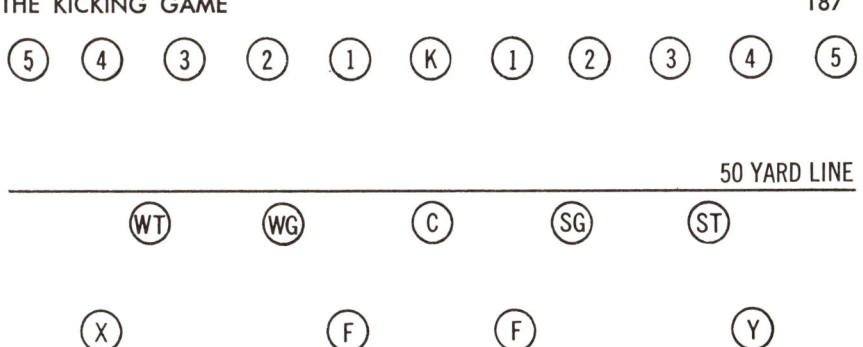

Fig. 10-7. Defensing the onside kickoff.

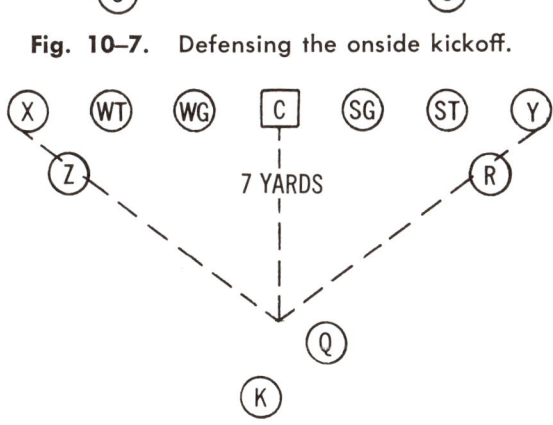

Fig. 10-8. Field goal protection.

a hop with the other foot. He must develop a 1-2-kick rhythm. He keeps his eyes on the spot where the holder is to put the ball. He kicks the ball just below center. In meeting the ball, the ankle joint should be locked back and the kicking leg should work like a pendulum with *good follow through*. He must be sure to keep on a straight line perpendicular to the cross-bar throughout the kick.

Our holder lines up seven yards from ball in a kneeling position with the knee nearest the LOS in an upright position. He extends his hands to receive the ball. It is important that he gets the ball in position as quickly as possible. He should *remind kicker to keep head down.*

Our linemen line up with their hands on their knees and take a six-inch split between men. Their inside foot is well back. All linemen except our center will take a short step with their inside foot and place their head against the hip of the next man to their inside. The center will brace himself so that he cannot be bowled over. Our backs line up with their hands on their knees, splitting the end and tackle and facing out at a ninety degree angle. They brace themselves and block out on the first man that shows. They must let no one penetrate the kicking triangle. After a field goal is kicked, our linemen and up-backs fan out for field coverage in case the kick is short. The kicker fans to his left and our holder fans to his right.

SAFETY

There are two instances when we might take a safety, one intentional and one unintentional. An intentional safety might arise in a game, but the decision would come from the bench. An unintentional safety would most likely occur in a fourth-down punting situation where the ball was snapped over the kicker's head. It is important that our kicker realize down, score, and time in game. Also, he must realize that if, when trying to run the ball out, he is tackled on the one yard line, it is the opponent's ball if we are on fourth down. It is much better to take a safety than to attempt to run and give our opposition the ball so close to our goalline. In taking an intentional safety, we merely run the ball out of the back or side of the end zone. We do not want to get hit and chance a fumble that might give our opponents a TD.

In putting the ball in play after a safety, we line up on the eighteen-yard line and have our punter punt the ball from our twenty-yard line. Our coverage will be the same as our kickoff coverage. We must hustle and prevent a good return.

In receiving the kick after a safety, we line up the same way as on our kickoff return. Our front five will line up inside the opponent's thirty-five-yard line. Our ends will line up on the opponent's forty-five-yard line. Our FB and QB will line up on our own forty-five-yard line. Our R and Z will line up on our own thirty-five-yard line. We *return* the same way as on our regular kickoff returns.

Part IV

ORGANIZATION AND COACHING PROBLEMS

11

Practice and Training

PRACTICE SCHEDULES

All football coaches face a similar problem when it comes to planning practice schedules, and that is the problem of time, especially when preparing for an actual game. There are two types of practice schedules, those that involve game plans, etc., for a specific opponent, and those that involve teaching of techniques in the early fall or spring. I shall discuss the practice schedule for a game week, first.

Game-Week Schedule

To prepare for a game, we have only three full practice days, and it is imperative that we utilize the time to the fullest extent. Our practice schedule for each week follows the same basic pattern, but the work involved in each period varies according to the tendencies of our opponents of the week.

A typical practice plan for game week at USC is:

Sunday
    Players report to trainer for treatment of injuries.
Monday
    4:00– 5:00   Film of USC game of previous week
    5:00– 6:00   Practice (sweat clothes)
    6:30   Dinner
    7:15– 8:00   Film of upcoming opponent
Tuesday
    1:00– 1:30   Offensive and defensive QB meeting
    3:15– 3:45   Team Meeting—Game plans
    4:00– 6:00   Practice (full gear)
    6:30   Dinner

Wednesday
Noon	Offensive and defensive QB meeting
3:15– 3:45	Team meeting—goalline offense and defense
4:00– 6:00	Practice (full gear)
6:30	Dinner
7:15– 8:00	Scout report and short film on opponent

Thursday
1:00– 1:30	Offensive and defensive QB meeting
3:15– 3:45	Team meeting—review of game plan
4:00– 5:30	Practice (full gear)
6:00	Dinner

Friday
4:00– 5:00	Team meeting—film and game plan
5:00– 5:30	Practice (sweat clothes)
6:00	Dinner
7:00– 9:00	Movie
10:00	Lights out

Saturday
9:30	Pre-game meal
10:15–10:45	Team meeting—review
10:45–11:00	Offensive and defensive QB meetings—review
1:30	Game time—The moment of truth

Sunday

The one thing we ask of our players on Sunday is that they report to our trainer for treatment of an injury, no matter how slight. Often a player will come out of a tough game feeling bruised, but not feeling a specific injury, and then the next day an acute soreness will develop. A day of rest and treatment may mean the difference between playing and watching to a player and they are more than willing to take an hour or two out of their Sunday for treatment.

Monday

We allot two hours for actual practice each day, and one hour on Monday is spent showing the film of the previous week's game to our squad. We then take the field in sweat clothes and the main order of business is get the kinks out by running. We also spend a little time acquainting our squad with the basic features of our upcoming opponent. Following the evening meal we spend an hour showing our squad a film of our opponent, again emphasizing the basic features of their offense and defense.

PRACTICE AND TRAINING

Tuesday

We feel Tuesday is a key work day, because it sets the tempo for the entire week. We meet with our offensive quarterbacks and defensive signal callers after lunch on Tuesday and discuss our plans for the week. We want our leaders to have a first-hand idea of how we plan to move the ball and how we plan to stop our opponents. We sometimes have to adjust this time schedule as classes naturally come first for our players. The quarterbacks are given a copy of the game plan of the plays we plan to use and when we want them called. The linebackers are given a copy of our defenses and are told when we want them called. We do not emphasize our opponent's tendencies too thoroughly on Tuesday as we want our callers to absorb our plans, first.

Tuesday practice follows this schedule.

4:00	(5)	Calisthenics
4:05	(20)	Pass offense and defense
4:25	(25)	Group A—offense; Group B—defense
4:50	(20)	Group B—offense; Group A—defense
5:10	(25)	Group A—offense; Group B—defense
5:35	(15)	Group B—offense; Group A—defense
5:50	(10)	Kicking game

Group A consists of our offensive starters, plus those players who will be used primarily as back-up men on offense. Group B consists of our defensive starters, plus those players who are primarily defensive back-up men. Very few of our starters switch groups to practice both offense and defense, but most of our back-up men do. It is very difficult to form a traveling squad if the back-up men are not capable of filling in on both offense and defense. Group A works longer on offense than Group B, and Group B works longer on defense.

We have found the best way to practice our offense is to place the defensive team in aprons, and have them go full speed with no tackling. The defenders are well protected, so that they do not receive the punishment that an un-padded player would receive.

We feel that, to execute our offense properly, we must go full speed. This is especially important for ball-carriers and quarterback. Our ball-carriers must master the option running that is the basis of our running attack, and it is impossible for a player to become a proficient option-runner if he runs against defenders holding dummies rather than giving a game-like reaction. Our quarterback must work against a defense that shows him a true picture of what he will face on Saturday, and again this is impossible if the defenders are holding dummies.

So, we put all defenders except the secondary in the padded aprons and they give a full reaction on each play. The secondary gives a full reaction vs. passes, but do not tackle. Our offense works against a player who is carrying out the same assignment as the opponent will on Saturday, yet the force of contact is lessened considerably by the presence of the padded aprons.

We attempt to prepare a squad of about forty-four men for each game and this leaves approximately twenty-six men to execute the defense and offense of our opposition. An injury to any player on our squad seriously hampers our preparation for that particular week. The aprons have proven to be the answer to preparing our offense with the least possible chance of injury to a team member.

We do not use aprons in practicing our defense, but rather emphasize recognition and reaction rather than scrimmage. The players executing the opponent's offense run pass and running routes full speed, but the blockers do not follow through after their initial blow, and they block high in the open field.

Our full-speed contact work comes in the twenty days of spring practice and in the twice-a-day drills of the early fall. Once a player has proven he will hit, we feel he will do so in a Saturday game if he knows exactly what he is supposed to do on each play. That is, once a coach has performed one of the essential tasks of the profession, that is the teaching of a player to have physical confidence in himself, he must then prepare that player for all the situations he will face on the field during the actual game. The teaching of physical confidence, that is, the love of contact and the knowledge that it is great fun, comes in the spring and early fall. After that, it is a race against time to attempt to teach the assignments and reactions necessary to win the game.

During the pass-offense period, our entire offense executes against the apron-clad defense. At times we will split forces, with the backs and ends executing against a defense without guards and tackles while our line works on pass protection against a defensive line. This is done when we need individual work because of special pass protection rules against stunting defenses.

For pass defense, we split our defensive forces with our backers, ends, and secondary working against an offensive team running pass plays, and our defensive line working against an offensive line executing the run and pass blocking we expect to face.

Once we go into the team periods for offense and defense, we start our actual game preparation. It is important that our offensive QB's run the plays we plan to use and that the correct amount of time is allotted. For example, if we plan to run the power play a lot, we should practice it a great deal. We do not practice every play an equal amount of time. We keep a check list on a big card on the field with a list of the plays we plan to use that week, and each time a play is run we put a check by that play. We keep our QB's constantly aware of this list as it not only advises him to run the plays we want, but also consolidates his mind so that he will know exactly what our plan is for game day.

It is also important for the defenders facing our offense to hustle on each play and give us the correct reaction. We continually try to encourage these men and keep them hustling at all times. They must take pride in the fact that they are helping us prepare for the game.

In practicing defense it is important to check alignment, first, and then reaction to the play. We cannot work against all our opponent's plays, so we concentrate on the plays they like to run the most. The players executing the opponent's offense must run the plays as near to perfection as possible for our defense to get a true picture. The plays must be drawn large and clear on big cards.

Wednesday

Our QB meetings now place emphasis on the opponent and his tendencies, what to expect and when. We give our QB's a copy of the scout report at this time.

Our team meeting is concerned with our goalline plans. During practice we practice our goalline offense and defense during the last ten minutes of the 5:00 and 5:35 periods; and, on occasion we spend more time on goalline situations. Offensively, we practice the plays we plan to use, placing special emphasis on cutting down our line splits to prevent penetration. Defensively we work on our opponent's favorite goalline plays, adhering to the theory that we cannot stop every play, but concentrating on what we expect to see.

Wednesday evening we hand out our scout report to the squad, and show a film of our opponent. We now have our QB's call plays (or defenses) and try to "play a game" as the film is being shown. We often stop the film to question players on their assignments vs. certain defenses or offensive sets. We feel our team should have a better knowledge of the opponent after two practice days and, thus, we are more specific at this time than on Monday night.

Thursday

Thursday is polish day and our aim is to make certain our squad knows what they are to do. This is the dress rehearsal, and our final review of our plans for Saturday.

The QB meetings are mainly a review of our plans with emphasis on questions to the players to check their familiarity with our plans.

The team meeting is held along the same vein, with emphasis on a review of any mistakes we may be making during the practice session.

Practice is cut down a half hour, and there is less contact on Thursday. The emphasis is on speed, quickness and hustle, and if we have prepared well there should be fewer mistakes during the session.

Friday

During the team meeting Friday, we first have our offensive QB's explain our plans to the squad. One describes our general game plan, another describes the defense we expect to face, and a third diagrams the pass plays we plan to use.

During the film our QB's point out plays we expect to call in the various situations. Our defensive signal callers call out the defense they would call in the huddle, and then make the Left or Right call as the offense aligns itself on the ball.

Friday's practice consists of a short review of our key plays and defenses, and then a spirited execution of plays around the field by our various units.

Following dinner, we take our squad to a movie prior to retiring to a hotel for the night.

Saturday

Following our pre-game meal four hours prior to the kickoff, we hold a short meeting to review the key points for the day's game. Following this meeting our QB's meet for a final review on the calls we expect that day. We do not like to arrive at the dressing quarters too early, and we usually allow our players about forty minutes to dress. Much of our taping is done after breakfast and only the "heavy" taping of knees, shoulders, etc. is done at the stadium. We do not feel a long time sitting idly before the game is beneficial to obtaining the mental attitude we want.

We send the specialists out ten minutes before the rest of our team. The kickers and return men loosen up and perform their

PRACTICE AND TRAINING

specialties and then join the balance of the squad for calisthentics, agility, passing and receiving, etc. We do not believe in long-drawn-out warm-ups. The hotter the day, the sooner we return to the dressing room.

When we take the field for the kickoff, we believe in coming on the field exactly as we expect to play. That is, with great speed. At this stage, the preparation of the preceding week goes on display before thousands of fans and it does not take long to find out if your preparation was sound and successful.

Early-Season Practice Schedule

In the early fall, we usually have about ten days of double practice sessions. We practice one hour and forty minutes in the morning and two hours in the afternoon. The daily schedule for a typical day during early fall is listed below:

    7:05 AM   RISE-AND-SHINE
    7:20 AM   Breakfast
    7:45 AM   Taping and dress
    8:45 AM   Group meetings in specified areas, dressed and ready for practice
    9:15 AM   End of meeting
    9:30 AM   Morning practice
  11:10 AM   End of morning practice
  12:10 PM   Lunch
  12:40 PM   Rest period
    3:05 PM   Group meetings in specified areas (fully dressed)
    3:40 PM   End of meetings
    3:45 PM   Specialists
    4:00 PM   Afternoon practice
    6:00 PM   End of afternoon practice
    6:30 PM   Dinner
    7:30 PM   Squad meeting
  10:30 PM   Doors locked and LIGHTS OUT

A typical morning practice on the fourth or fifth day might be as follows:

    9:30 (5)   Calisthentics
    9:35 (5)   Agility
    9:40 (20) Blocking and defensive fundamentals (A and B groups switch at 10)
        F, R: Junction Block
        X, Z: Crackback Block
        Y, ST, WT: Double-team Block
        G, C: Trap Blocking

LB, Ends: Machine Gun (5) and Skate Drill (5)
Def. Line: Machine Gun (5) and Skate Drill (5)
Secondary: To-Zone Drill
10:00   (30)   Technique (A and B groups switch at 15)
QB, X, Z, R: Pass-Pattern Review
C, SG, WG, FB: Sweep and Power Blocking
Y, ST, WT: Far-Shoulder and Cut-Off Blocking
LB, Ends: Plug Drill
Def. Line: One-on-One—Rip and Shiver
Secondary: Shield Drill (5), Hub Drill (10)
10:30   (30)   Group Work (A and B groups switch at 15)
Team Offense vs. Aprons
LB, Ends: Shield Drill (5), Patterns Drill (10)
Def. Line: Slant Technique
Secondary: Patterns Drill—Cover Four
11:00   (10)   Kicking Game
Group A: Punt
Group B: Punt Return

An afternoon practice might follow this schedule:

4:00   (5)   Calisthentics
4:05   (5)   Agility
4:10   (20)   Blocking and defensive fundamentals (A and B groups switch at 10)
Backs: Drive and Power series
Y, ST, WT: Trojan Block, Cut-off Block, Reverse Block
C, SG, WG: Option Block, Cut-off Block, Onside Block
LB, Ends: Shield Drill (5), Hub Drill (5)
Def. Line: Three-on-One, Read technique
Secondary: Shield Drill (5), Hub Drill (5)
4:30   (30)   Technique (A and B groups switch at 15)
Backs: Patterns (add 89 pass)
C, SG, WG: Trap Blocking
Y, ST, WT: Option Block, Trap Blocking
LB, Ends: Rip and Plug Drill, Read defense
Def. Line: Slant Drills and Reaction to blocks
Secondary: Patterns Drills, Cover Three
5:00   (30)   Group Work (A and B groups switch at 15)
Backs, Ends: Pass offense
Off. Line: Review of plays, vs. aprons
Def. Lines; ½ LB, Ends: Run defense
Secondary; ½ LB, Ends: Pass defense
5:30   (30)   Team Work (A and B groups switch at 15)
Offense: Team offense
Defense: 50-slant, Cover Three (scrum last 5)

PRACTICE AND TRAINING

One of the key factors in planning practice schedules is to allow enough flexibility to adjust your plans according to the development of your team. We feel it is extremely important that our staff meet after each workout to discuss our progress. We do not want to move on to another phase of our teaching if we have not adequately taught the previous phase. However, it is also true that there is a certain pace that must be kept to prepare for the first game. Perhaps the most difficult aspect of planning early practice schedules is to keep the pace going while still teaching the rudiments of your game so that they will be solidly absorbed for the entire season.

CONDITIONING AND TRAINING

The game of football seems to become faster each year, and the players seem to become endowed with the greater physical attributes needed to play the ever bigger game—speed, size, and strength. To keep up with the increased tempo of the game, we try to emphasize the need for excellent conditioning year-round.

Summer Conditioning Program

We believe football is primarily a game of the legs, and in this vein we feel the primary exercise needed is running. We stress running in our actual practices, and we want our players to stress running when preparing themselves for the coming season. Seven weeks prior to the start of the season, we send a summer conditioning program to each of our players and we expect them to follow it to the letter (or exceed the prescribed number). (See Fig. 11–1.)

USC Weight-training Program

During the off-season we encourage our athletes to either participate in other sports, such as basketball, track, or baseball, or participate in our weight program. There are several schools of thought regarding weight training, isometric exercises, etc. We do not profess to be experts in these matters, but we have studied the situation quite thoroughly and have made it a point to discuss it with some of the leading authorities.

We feel a weight training program that develops strength in the muscles used in playing the game and at the same time does not slow down the player's reflexes or speed can be a tremendous help in building the confidence of squad members. We feel the key

SUMMER CONDITIONING PROGRAM

Six Week Course, July 19 to August 28.

Workout

  A. Begin each day's workout with the following exercises:
    1. Cross-toe touch—10 each side.
    2. Toe touch and way-back—10
    3. Jumping jack—20
    4. Push-ups—15
    5. Sit-ups—15
    6. Neck bridge—roll each way, stomach and back
    7. One lap (trot) around track

  B. Engage in running exercises including:
    1. Catching passes
    2. Running and dodging bags, etc.
    3. Touch football games
    4. Punting ball and running after it

  C. Agility workouts:
    1. Sprinting backwards, turning hips right and left—20 yard sprint, increase 1 each week
    2. Carioca (side-ways run)—50 yards each way
    3. Forward rolls—10 rolls a day
    4. Cover each other man-for-man on pass defense

  D. Sprints and laps; *must be followed exactly*
    1. 1st week   3 50 yd. sprints; 1 lap; 1 100 yd., 4 days a week
    2. 2nd week 4 50 yd. sprints; 2 laps; 1 100 yd., 4 ″ ″ ″
    3. 3rd week 6 50 yd. sprints; 2 laps; 2 100 yd., 5 ″ ″ ″
    4. 4th week 8 50 yd. sprints; 3 laps; 2 100 yd., 5 ″ ″ ″
    5. 5th week 10 50 yd. sprints; 3 laps; 3 100 yd., 6 ″ ″ ″
    6. 6th week 12 50 yd. sprints; 4 laps; 4 100 yd., 7 ″ ″ ″

Additional Exercises

  1. 100 Push-ups—morning and evening, 50 each
  2. 300 Sit-ups—morning and evening, 150 each
  3. Note: On opening day each team member will be required to do 50 push-ups and 50 sit-ups (without gear).

Fig. 11–1. Summer conditioning program.

areas needing muscular development are the calf and thigh muscles of the legs, the lower back for explosion, and the neck, shoulder and tricep muscles. Our weight-training program is designed to develop these areas of the body. (See Fig. 11–2.)

As you can see, we do not use heavy weight in our program except for the Dead Lift and Bench Press. We want the program to be executed with quickness and as closely similar to an actual practice session as possible. We want the players to participate in

USC WEIGHT-TRAINING PROGRAM

Warm-Up: 1. One-two-way back, 15
2. Cross-toe touch, 10
3. Push-ups, 25
4. Sit-ups, 25

1. Two hands continuous clean and press overhead: 1 set, 12 reps. Start with 75 lb., increase 5 lb. per week.
   Bar on ground. Grab bar and lift to chest and then over head. Place bar to ground and start again.
2. Combination dead hang clean and high pull up to top of head: 1 set, 12 reps. Start 100 lb., increase 5 lb. per week.
   Bar on ground. Grab bar, hands shoulder width apart, and pull to top of head. Palms remain down.
3. Bouncing split squat: 1 set, 20 reps. Start with bar only, increase 5 lb. per week.
   Bar on shoulders, back of head. Jump and thrust one foot forward and one back.
4. Wheelbarrow walk on hands. Start 20 yd., increase 5 yd. every week. Do 10 floor dips end of each 20 yd. After reaching 50 yd., try to increase speed.
   Partner grabs your ankles, places them on his shoulders and walks you 20 yd.
5. Neck exercise, 2 persons: 1 set, 20 reps; back and front of neck.
   Partner applies pressure and lets you barely move your neck.
6. Chins. 1 × 10; heavier fellows, 1 × 5; increase 1 rep per week.
   Palms down on bar.
7. Straddle hop: 1 set, 15 reps. Start 50 lb., increase 5 lb. per week.
   Bar on shoulders, back of head. Jump and thrust feet to side (Jumping Jack).
8. Side bend with bar bell: 1 set, 12 reps. Start with 50 lb., increase 5 lb. per week.
   Bar on shoulders, back of head. Bend sideways about 45°.
9. Dead lift: 4 sets, 3 reps each set. Start 175 lb., increase 10 lb. per week.
   Bar on ground. Grab bar-one up, elbows stiff. Straighten up, keeping back straight. Arms should not bend.
10. Bench Press: 4 sets, 3 reps each set. Start at your body weight, increase 10 lbs. per week.

Fig. 11-2. USC weight-training program.

the weight program three days a week, and to run two days a week.

The one factor that has caused us concern is the desire of some of our players to put on weight. We have found that added weight tends to slow down a player who is either short in height, six feet or under or does not have the leg base to carry the added weight. We have found that the effectiveness and endurance of the player has been lessened by the added weight. We are very conscious of speed and agility, and this is the area where we want our players to show improvement. If a young man's frame is not suited to carrying more weight and at the same time increasing his speed and agility, we discourage him from gaining weight.

PLAYER PERSONNEL POLICY

GENERAL—OFF FIELD

1. You are to make yourself responsible in maintaining a 2-point average and to pass 24 semester hours per year.

    See your coach *immediately* if you have any indication that you may be approaching substandard performance.
2. You must carry at least 12 hours per semester in order to be eligible for competition.
3. Each term, you are required to place on record with your coach your class schedule for the semester. *No drops without permission of your coach.*
4. Off season you are required to check with your coach once every two weeks.
5. Sleeping hours commence at 10:30 P.M. during the season.

    Night life and football don't mix—Give up one!
6. Use of stimulants or depressants is frowned upon.
7. There is to be no stealing, lying, or alibis.
8. You will conduct yourselves as gentlemen at all times.
9. If you have a problem, see your coach *Now*.

Fig. 11–3. Player personnel policy.

GENERAL RULES AND POLICIES

It is your responsibility to be on time for all practices, meetings, and any other appointments. Do not rely on someone else. Excuses will not be accepted.

Never discuss the team, physical condition of the members of the team, planned strategy, etc., with anyone. You may give information that would be extremely helpful to the opposition or to gamblers.

Keep yourself neat and clean-shaven at all times.

Be extremely careful of your language. Swearing, obscene words, etc., will not be tolerated at any time.

Leave all newspaper quotes to the staff.

DRESSING ROOM

If you have equipment problems, you must report to the dressing room early, as the equipment manger will not have time to assist you when the rest of the team reports at the normal time.

Under no circumstances will you be permitted to cut or alter equipment. These problems should be discussed with the equipment manager.

Hang up all equipment after practice.

Be sure to check all money and valuables with the equipment manager before practice.

INJURIES AND THE TRAINING ROOM

Everyone will suit up for practice unless prior permission has been received from a member of the coaching staff. If you are injured and are not able to suit up, or will be available only for limited duty, you will, nevertheless, be required to be at practice and observe the group you would normally be working with.

Treatment will not be given during the practice period except by specific permission of a member of the coaching staff. Be sure every injury, regardless of how minor it may seem, is reported to the trainer.

Fig. 11–4. General rules and policies.

PRACTICE AND TRAINING 203

Player Personnel Policy

As stated previously, each coach has his own ideas on training rules and regulations. We have two sets of player policies we expect our men to follow. Our "Player Personnel Policy" applies to off the field activities (Fig. 11–3).

General Rules and Policies

In addition, we have a set of general rules and policies we give each man that pertains to our total football program (Fig. 11–4).

Conditioning and training play a large part in the success of a football team. The coach must be prepared to enforce his rules and policies if need be; but if a squad has the proper mental attitude to begin with, training rules take care of themselves. If each member of the squad is pulling together to win, then there may not be need for the coaching staff to enforce training rules.

12

Scouting and Analysis

SCOUTING

Scouting an opponent to gather advance information on him is an extremely important phase of coaching the game of football. It is imperative to find out all the information you can, as one seemingly insignificant item may change the course of a game. The coach should plan his strategy around the information gathered and this information must be accurate.

Most coaches use movies to a great extent nowadays, and these films provide an accurate report of exactly how a team deploys its men. Movies provide the most accurate scout report, but the scout is still vitally needed at an opponent's game to report on tempo, injuries, attitude, etc. It is sometimes very difficult to get the feel of a team and its coaching staff from viewing movies. A scout in the stadium can better judge the tempo and contact of the game; and, of course, many teams do not enjoy the opportunity to exchange films.

At the high school level, the coach should take the time and effort to organize a scouting staff. There are two sources available, and both should be utilized if possible. One group that must be utilized is the members of the coaching staff. Most schools have a junior varsity or lightweight program in addition to the varsity squad, and these teams usually play the day preceding the varsity game. The coaches of these teams should serve as scouts for the varsity. In return, varsity coaches can help scout for the JV coaches. An example of how this can be accomplished would be to schedule varsity games for Friday night and JV games for Thursday afternoon. The varsity could hold their final workout Thursday night, enabling the varsity coaches to scout for the JV's on Thursday afternoon.

The other group that can be utilized is one of friends of the coaching staff who are ex-players who still like to keep their hand in the game. These men, if trained properly, can greatly assist your regular scouts.

One method of training scouts is to attend professional exhibitions and split your corps of scouts into two man groups, seat them separately, and then meet and compare reports at a later date. If you are not in an area accessible to pre-season games, your scouts can chart a scrimmage or intra-squad game you are planning to film and then you can compare the reports to the films.

A good scout must be a hard worker and quite quick with the pencil. He must be able to write down his observations and not trust them to memory. He must be up on the game and be aware of various formations, maneuvers, and strategy. If he misses something, he must never guess. It is better to omit a play than to give false information.

The coach should plan his scouting schedule during the summer and try to schedule two scouts to each game. These scouts should be supplied any and all pertinent data on the teams to be scouted so as to be as well prepared as possible. During the off season it is usually possible to obtain films on games of the previous year, and these films should be scouted and analyzed to the last detail.

The scouts should make certain they arrive at the stadium early, and should be thoroughly familiar with the names, numbers, and positions of the first two teams and specialists. The scouts should be well supplied, and make certain their forms are organized, for once the game starts there is no time to sort out material. It is a frantic task just to keep up with the play-by-play.

Some important information can be checked and noted during the warm-up period. Kickers, passers, receivers, and return specialists should all be given attention. Especially important are such items as the time the punter takes, his distance from the center, and the number of steps he takes. Does he punt low or high? The scouts should note any halfback kicking (quick kick possibility) or passing (run-pass option play). One scout should pick up the snap count and the time it takes the QB to approach the center and get set.

During the play-by-play, one scout should observe while the other writes. The writer should observe as much as possible, of course. Our form for charting the offensive plays is shown in Fig. 12-1.

We list the down and distance first, then the territory and yard line. If the offensive team is on its own 20-yard line, we put a minus (−) sign before the 20. If the offensive team is on the opponent's 20-yard line, we put a (+) sign before the 20. We

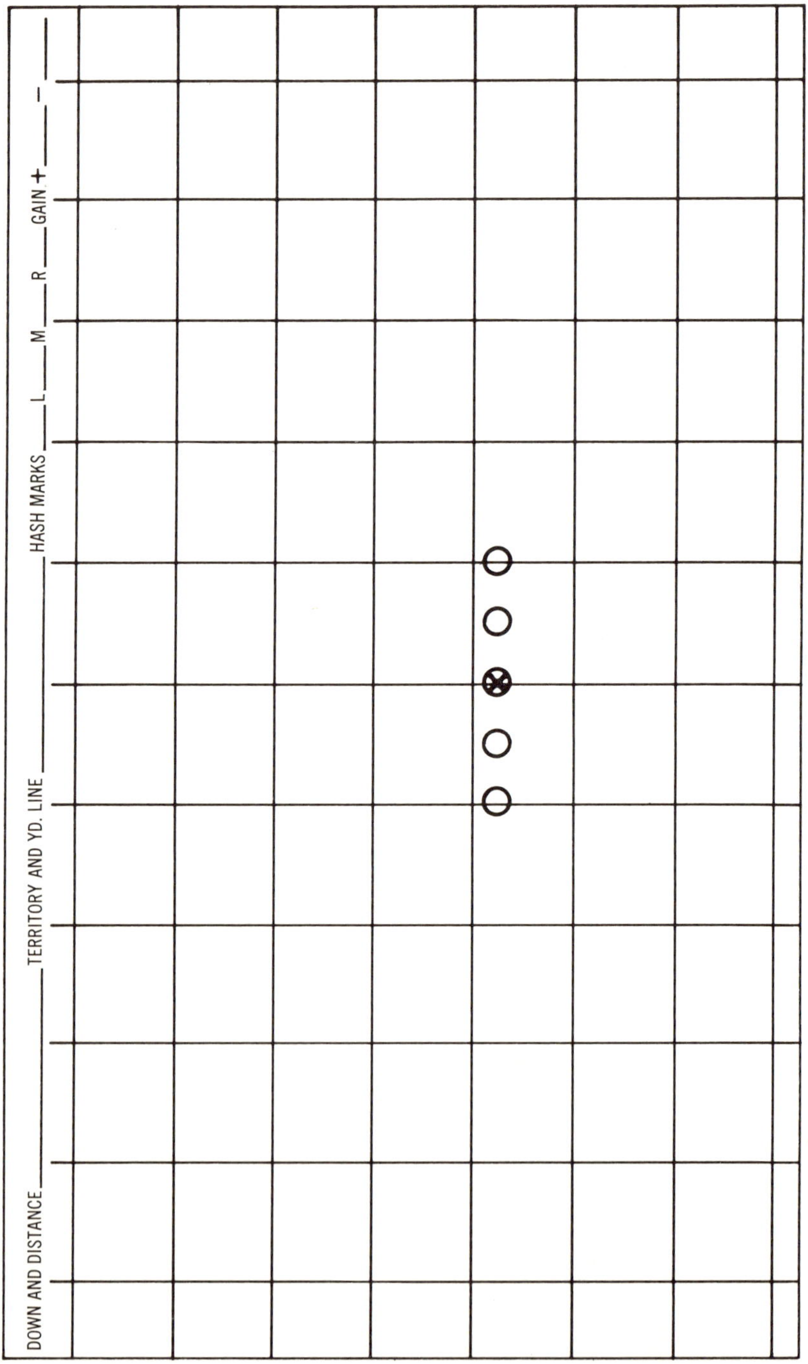

Fig. 12-1. Offense-Play Scouting Form.

SCOUTING AND ANALYSIS

next circle L-M-R for hash mark, always remembering we are in an imaginary position *behind* the offense. We then diagram the play to the best of our ability, which means every player's exact move if scouting a film, or mainly backfield action if scouting an actual game. Following the play, we list the gain or loss. If a pass is incomplete, we put *inc* and if it is intercepted we put *int*. We attempt to list the formation and play, but sometimes this is tough during the game. The scouts should use half-time to catch up on these.

We use cards for these forms as they are easier to work with than paper. Some important points the scouts should remember include a listing of the depth of each pass pattern and depth the ball is caught or dropped, the distance men are split or flanked out. Each square represents five yards on the card. The pivot direction of the QB (reverse or open), any line splits by the guards and tackles, and the intended receiver on a pass play that develops into a run are also important. When scouting a movie, we chart the defense in red, to better distinguish between offensive and defensive moves. We draw the ball carrier with a wavy line, all other offensive men, with straight lines. The ball carrier is designated by having his circle blacked-in. Defensive slants, stunts, etc., are drawn with straight lines, while defensive reactions to the play are drawn with wavy lines. This is important when determining pre-determined reactions (such as pass patterns) as compared to reactions after the play begins. We use the same form to chart defenses, and we still chart the hash mark according to the offensive position.

Our card is large enough to allow the scouts to jot down any comments they wish on individual players, especially any tips as to pulling out, etc. We diagram the kicking game on the back of the card. Below is a check list for our scouts:

Items Which Must Be Written on Card as Play Develops

1. Down and distance
2. Territory and yd. line: own territory is a —, opponent's territory is a +
3. Hash
4. Gain
5. Play number, circled in upper right corner
6. How the team got the ball (received punt, intercepted pass, etc.), upper left corner
7. Time left in quarter when this is a factor
8. Draw in the defense
   a. Linemen in a 3- or 4-point stance, V

b. Backers or ends upright, △
   c. Secondary men (3 or 4 deep), X
   d. Circle the tackler(s), only man (or men) who actually stop(s) play
   e. Show stunts by dark line
9. Diagram the offensive play
   a. Show each man's assignment
   b. List jersey number of each back on each play, list jersey number of lineman when sub enters game
   c. Darken the back who carries the ball
      (1) Darken his path as a runner
      (2) If two men handle ball (reverse, option), darken half of first man
   d. Show wavy line for motion; be sure to draw wavy line as far as back ran until snap
   e. Dot any linemen who pull
   f. One short line for QB exchange to back
   g. Two lines for QB fake
   h. Draw pass routes of all receivers
      (1) Write depth (number of yards) at end of pattern
      (2) Short wavy line shows to which receiver pass was thrown
   i. Line between linemen indicates abnormal split
10. List name of offensive play above diagram and *hole hit*
    a. Abbreviations O.K.
    b. For pass thrown, darken P not thrown, but pass play, P not darkened
    c. For fumble, lost, circle F
    d. For fumble, not lost, plain F

Following the game the scouts should organize and compile their notes. They also answer a set of questions while the game is still fresh in their mind. These are general questions, not requiring specific knowledge. What we want is their reaction immediately following the games. These questions are listed below:

Offense Notes

What is their best running play?
What is their best passing play?
Who is their best ball carrier?
Who is their best receiver?
What is their best short yardage play?
What is their best goalline play?
Who do they substitute for special running or pass plays?
Is their tempo fast or slow?

SCOUTING AND ANALYSIS

What do they do when they get behind?
What do they do when they get ahead?
What do they do when behind late in the half or game?
What plays must we stop to defeat them?

Defense Notes

What is their favorite set?
What is their next favorite set?
Do they stunt much?
Do they shift defenses?
Do they force aggressively, or contain and pursue?
Do they shoot linebackers?
Do they play zone or man-for-man pass defense?
What is their goalline defense?
What is their short-yardage defense?
Where can we move on them?

Kicking Game

Who is their punter?
What is their punt formation?
How many steps does the punter take?
Is the punt high or low?   Distance:
What type punt return do they use?
Who returns the punt?
Who kicks-off?   Distance:
Do they cross men on the kick-off?
What type kick-off return do they use?
Who is their P.A.T. and field-goal kicker?
What is the effective distance of their place kicker?
Do they ever run or pass from punt formation?
Do they ever run or pass from field-goal formation?

Personnel

List the changes from the program starting line-ups.
Any injuries during the game?

Depending on the time they can spend, plus their knowledge of the program, the scouts may or may not analyze their reports; but, their main function is to present an accurate, detailed report to the coaching staff. Once this is accomplished, we advance to the tedious task of analyzing the material.

ANALYZING THE OPPONENT

In analyzing our opponents, we attempt to find out when they will execute a particular play or defense, and also how they will block a play against a certain defense, or stunt the defense against a particular offensive formation.

The first thing we analyze on the opponent's offense is their execution of plays. This includes their blocking, running routes, and pass patterns against our type of defense. One of our coaches diagrams their favorite plays and the way they block them, and another coach diagrams their favorite pass plays. We try to have this material absorbed by Monday, in preparation for an upcoming Saturday game.

We then try to analyze when they will run their plays. We have a rather complicated form we use for this phase of our analysis. We have two sheets, headed Formation Analysis. One is for running plays (Fig. 12–2), the other for passes (Fig. 12–3).

For run analysis we draw in the completed formation, and then list the plays according to the hole hit. In charting the play in the designated hole, we list the following things: Play number (our numbering system as much as possible), the down situation, the gain, the hash mark, the field position, and the score.

The down situation we classify as normal, long, or short. Normal downs are 1st and 10, 2nd and 3 to 7, and 3rd or 4th and 3 to 5. Long-yardage situations are 1st and over 10, 2nd and over 7, 3rd and 4th and over 5. Short-yardage situations are 3rd and 4th and one or two, plus 1st and 5 and 1 or 2. If a play is run in a normal situation we list it in pencil. If a play is run in a long situation, we list it in ink. If a play is run in a short situation, we list it in red. Any play run in a goalline situation, is listed in green.

The gain is listed with a plus or a minus sign, with the hash mark listed as W (wideside), S (short side), or M (if run in the middle of the field).

A column for the 4-hole might list three plays that look like this:

1. 24^1 $+4^W$ (in pencil)
2. 44^2 F $+6^M$ (in ink)
3. 34^3 -1^S (in red)

The figure 24 in pencil would mean 24 was run on 1st and 10, gained four yards and was run to the wide side of the field. The figure 44 in ink was run on 2nd down with over 7 yards to go, gained 6 yards in the middle of the field. The F means the ball was fumble and lost. An F without a circle would mean fumbled, but

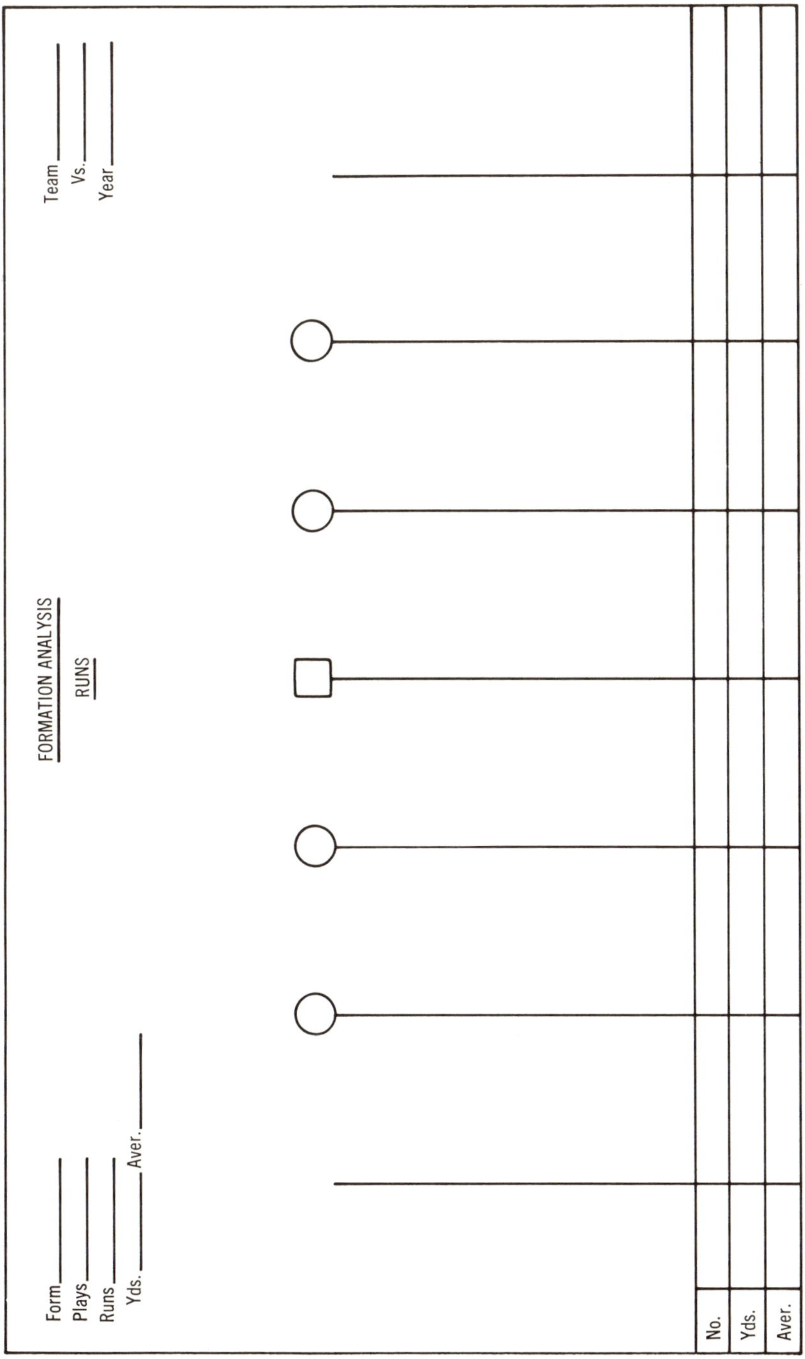

SCOUTING AND ANALYSIS 211

Fig. 12-2. Formation Analysis—Runs.

not lost. Red 34 was run on 3rd and short, lost a yard to the short side of the field.

In addition, we place a colored dot after each play, to indicate field position. If a team is inside its own 15, we place a red dot. If a team is in their 3-down zone (punt on 4th down) we place a pencil dot, and if in the 4-down zone (no punt on 4th down) we place an ink dot. Goalline plays are listed in green, so need no dot.

Also, we list plays used at a time when the team is desperate to score (end of half or game) in orange so that they stand out.

Thus, by looking at the formation analysis, the key goalline and short-yardage plays stand out, as do the long-yardage plays. By combining the various formations we can quickly come up with their favorites in the above situations.

For pass analysis we use the same color scheme, and list each pass in the zone of the intended receiver. We want to find out which zones they like to hit in their various formations. At the bottom of the sheet we total the passes in each zone. (See Fig. 12–3.) The abbreviations used are as follows:

PA, Passes attempted
PC, Passes completed
PI, Passes intercepted
%, Percent completions
YDS, Yards gained passing
RAN, Times the QB wanted to throw to that zone, but ran instead
YDS, Yards gained running on a pass play.

Once we have completed the formation analysis, which also gives us the down and distance and hash-mark analysis, we attempt to plot our defenses according to what we expect them to do against us. We make it a point to separate the plays run against different opponents so that we can tell what they did in each game. We do this by drawing a line under the group of plays run against opponent No. 1, and listing that team's name, as follows.

$$24^1 \qquad\qquad +4^W$$
$$44^2 \quad F \quad +6^M$$
$$34^3 \qquad\qquad -1^S$$
$$\text{UCLA}$$

We do not expect our players to absorb this detailed account of our opponent's offense, but we do diagram their favorite plays plus their basic formations and the holes and pass zones they like to hit. Our defensive signal callers do study this material as thoroughly as possible to be able to carry out our adjustments on game day.

SCOUTING AND ANALYSIS

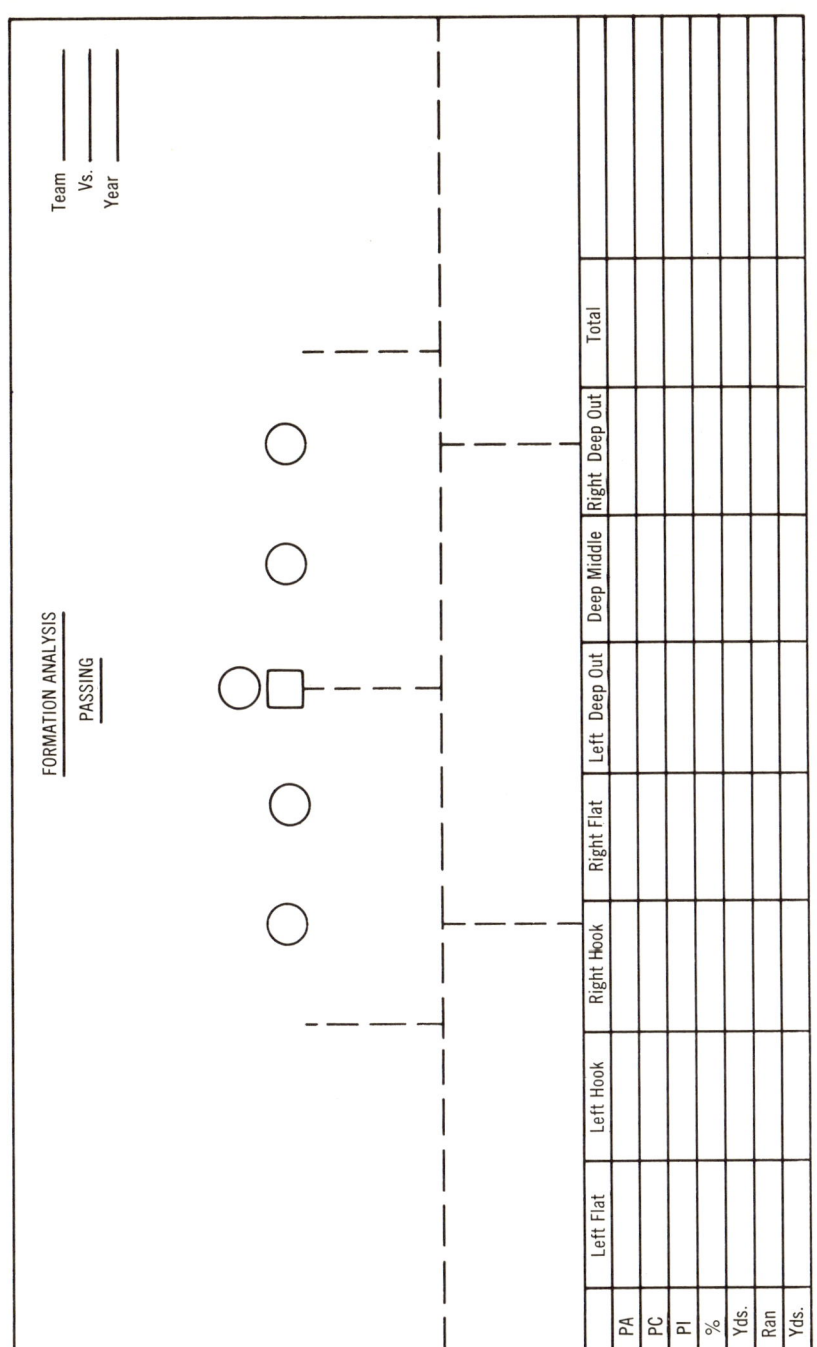

Fig. 12-3. Formation Analysis—Passing.

	DEFENSIVE ANALYSIS SHEET _____ VS. _____							
	Down-Distance and Zone	Hash	Formation	Alignment	Stunt	Pass Coverage	Play	Gain
1								
2								
3								
4								
5								
6								
7								
8								
9								
10								
11								
12								
13								
14								
15								
16								
17								
18								
19								
20								

Fig. 12–4. Defensive Analysis Sheet.

SCOUTING AND ANALYSIS

In analyzing our opponent's defenses we pursue the same line of thinking as in analyzing their offense. We first try to find out just how they are aligning and charging up front, where their linebackers and ends are aligning and who they are keying, and the type of secondary alignment (3 or 4 deep) and the pass coverages used.

Once we have determined what the defensive structure entails, we then try to analyze when they will use the various sets. We use a Defensive Analysis Sheet (see Fig. 12-4) where we make a play-by-play study of their defenses. We list the defenses according to the plays and then transfer them to our Individual Game Down & Distance form (see Fig. 12-5). On this sheet we list the defenses used on 1st and 10 and on down the line and try to come up with a pattern of some sort.

The analysis of an opponent's offense and defense is a time-consuming task, and sometimes goes for naught once the game begins and an opponent springs new formations and plays at us. However, we believe in leaving no stone unturned in our game preparation. We want our players to be sure in the knowledge that we know all our opponent *has* done so that any new wrinkles will also be new to them; but, coaches must never become over-absorbed in the analysis of an opponent as there may be a tendency to miss the over-all feel of the team. Knowledge of tendencies, plus a feel of the opponent, will enable the coach to be best prepared for any changes that may occur.

ANALYZING YOUR OWN TEAM

In analyzing our offense, we use the same forms used in analyzing our opponent's defense, but switch the columns to list our plays.

The Offensive Analysis Sheet (Fig. 12-6) is a play-by-play of the game. Much of the information can be gathered from the press play-by-play which can be obtained immediately following the game. Thus, when the movies are viewed the next day much time is saved, because the down and distance, gain, etc., have already been plotted. Under comments we add the key mistakes that caused the play to break down.

We then transfer the plays to the Individual Game Down and Distance form (Fig. 12-5), and list our plays in the columns under *1st and 10*, etc.

INDIVIDUAL GAME DOWN AND DISTANCE

USC vs. 63

	1 & 10	1 & Long	2nd & Normal	2nd & Long	2nd & Short	3rd & Long	3rd & Normal	3rd & Short	Goal line	Danger
1										
2										
3										
4										
5										
6										
7										
8										
9										
10										
11										
12										
13										
14										

Fig. 12–5. Individual Game Down and Distance Form.

SCOUTING AND ANALYSIS 217

OFFENSIVE ANALYSIS SHEET
_____ USC _____ vs. _____

	Down-Distance and Zone	Hash	Formation	Play	Gain	Ball Carrier	Comment
1							
2							
3							
4							
5							
6							
7							
8							
9							
10							
11							
12							
13							
14							
15							
16							
17							
18							
19							
20							

Fig. 12–6. Offensive Analysis Sheet.

FORMATION SHEET   USC VS. _____ 196 _____

FORMATION _____

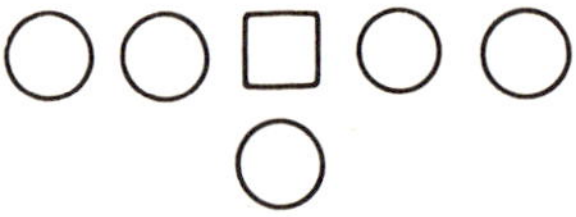

○ ○ □ ○ ○
○

RUNS—NUMBER _____   PASSES—NUMBER _____

TOTAL YARDS _____   COMPLETE _____

AVER. PER CARRY _____   PERCENT _____

MINUS YARDS _____   MINUS YARDS _____

TOTAL PLAYS _____

TOTAL YARDS _____

TOTAL AVER. _____

Fig. 12–7. Formation Sheet.

SCOUTING AND ANALYSIS

We then compile a Formation Sheet (Fig. 12–7) where we chart all the plays run from each formation the previous week. We list the runs opposite each hole and use a second sheet to list the pass plays.

Thus, following each game we have a study of ourselves to contemplate. We can easily see what we have done offensively so that we will know what the opponent is studying. One point that may be well to remember is that a good offensive team should have tendencies at certain points of attack. If a team has success moving the ball, they will naturally repeat the successful plays, and this is as it should be. We do not change or alter plays just to be changing.

In analyzing our defense we chart the play-by-play first, once again utilizing the press play-by-play for down and distance and gain. We then analyze our movie, and chart it on our Offensive Play Analysis sheet (Fig. 12–8). In the Mistake column we list the key mistakes that caused our defense to falter. We use the player's number and then an abbreviation for his mistake.

We then plot each defense onto the previously discussed Formation Analysis sheets (Figs. 12–2 and 12–3). We draw our defense in red and then list the runs against us in the holes they hit, and the passes in the zones they hit (Fig. 12–9).

This chart shows clearly that in this particular defense we were hurt most by the trap play to our left side. We then must analyze whether this was caused by a defensive structure mistake, or because we played a weak man at the hole.

We keep an up-to-date chart on our defenses to see how well they are stopping our opponents. An example of what a chart shows following a game follows:

Defense	Runs	Yds.	Aver.	Long Gain	Play	Aver. Without Long Gain
50	11	29	2.6	+ 9	48 Sweep	2.0
50 Read	7	25	3.6	+13	39 Sweep	2.0
61	12	14	1.2	+ 4	48 Sweep	0.7
61 Inside	3	5	1.7	+ 2	34 Drive	1.5
50 Bingo	8	28	3.5	+10	33 Drive	2.6
50 Crash	1	9	9.0	+ 9	Broken Pass	—
	42	110	2.6	+13	39 Sweep	

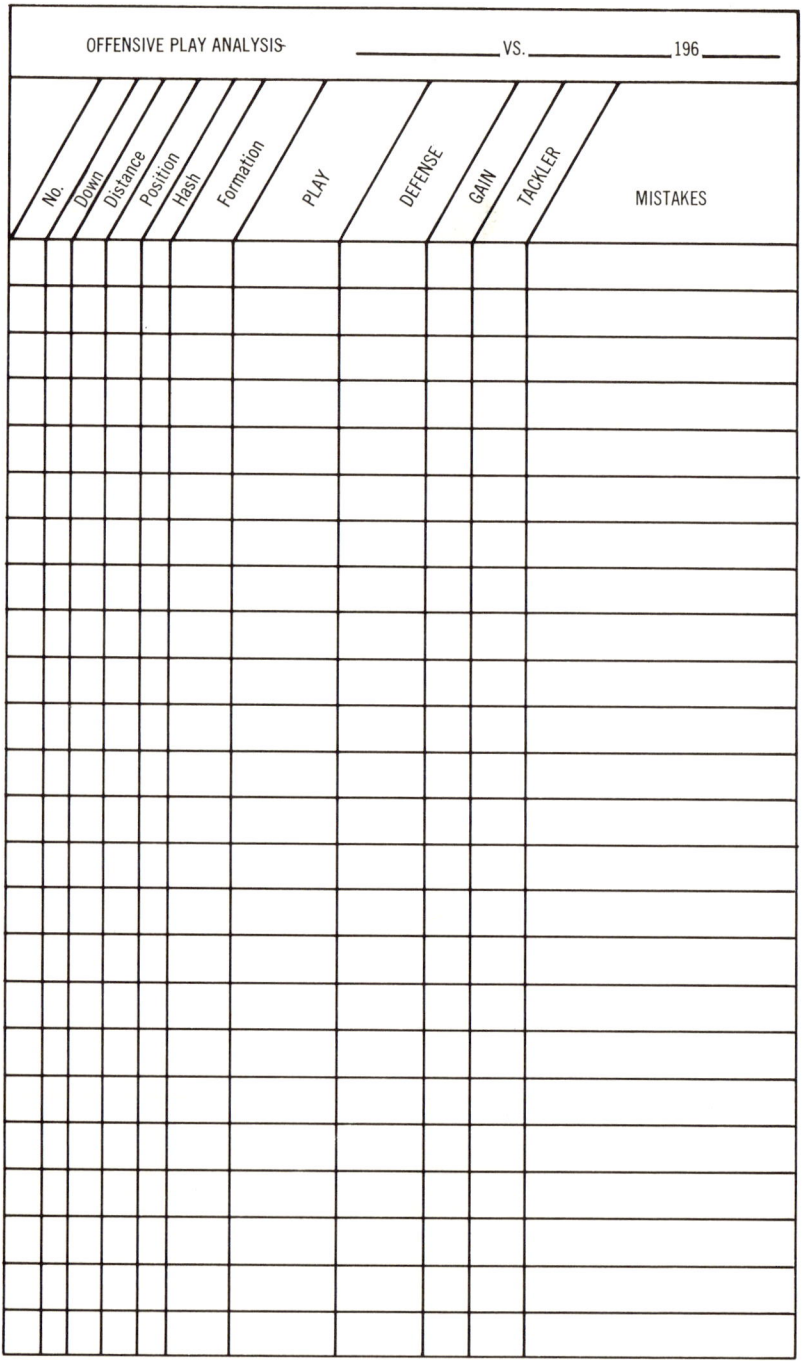

Fig. 12-8. Offensive Play Analysis.

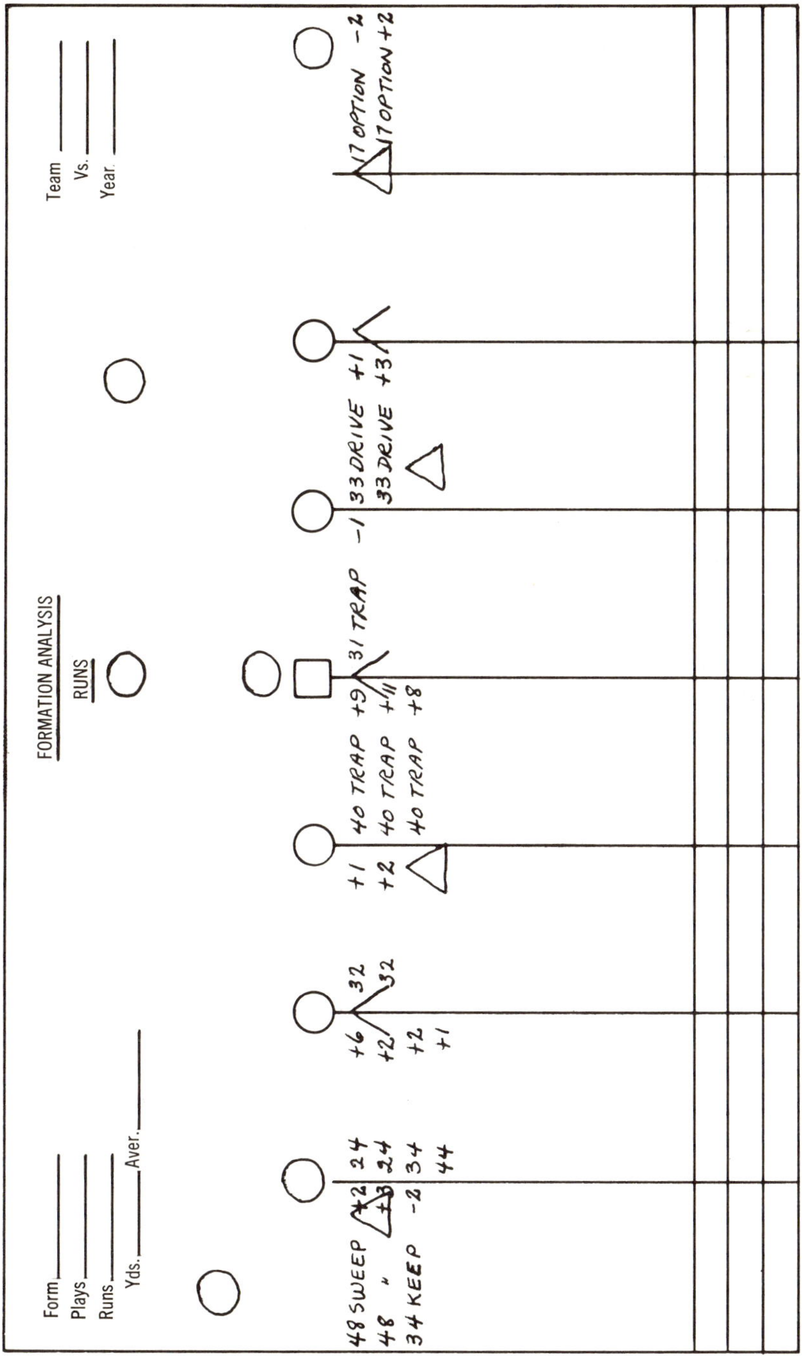

SCOUTING AND ANALYSIS

Fig. 12-9. Formation Analysis—Runs.

This chart shows our defenses and how they fared against running plays. We make the same analysis against pass plays. In addition we list each play run against a defense and how it fared, as follows:

Defense	Call	Play	To Our Side	Gain
50	Left	48 Sweep	Strong	+ 0
50	Left	31 Counter	Weak	+ 3
50	Right	13 Keep	Weak	+ 12 (Fumbled for 8 yds.)
50	Left	24 Power	Strong	+ 4
50	Right	84 Pass—Z check	Strong	Inc.

(This list would be as long as the number of plays run against us.)

GRADING AND ANALYZING INDIVIDUALS

We constantly strive to find better and quicker ways to evaluate our personnel from the game films. The most thorough process is to grade each player on each play, and we try to do this early in the season, but it is a time-consuming process. Once our personnel is pretty well set we try to evaluate each play and why it gained or was stopped and also evaluate the personnel and their mistakes.

When we grade our personnel on each play, we use a simple plus and minus system. If the player does his job he receives a plus, if he fails to carry out his assignment he receives a minus. If he is far removed from the point of attack we do not grade him. We arrive at a grade by dividing the total pluses and minuses into the pluses. We feel we must have a 70% performance to play consistently good football. However, we have won games with less, and lost games when we averaged more.

Besides the plus and minus grade, we have two extra grades that we consider perhaps more important than the plus or minus. We have borrowed the terms *RBI* and *Error* from baseball and each time a player performs an extra function he receives an RBI and each time he makes a mental mistake he receives an Error. We know of quite a few teams who use this system and it certainly did not originate with us. Examples of RBI's on offense include: second effort in blocking, a tremendous run or catch under pressure, recovery of a teammate's fumble, a devastating block. On defense, we give RBI's for the following things: intercepted pass, knocked down pass, pass rush causing an incompletion or interception, causing or recovering a fumble, a key stop on a crucial down.

SCOUTING AND ANALYSIS

Offensively we coaches choose a Blocker of the Week following each game and post the player's picture on our bulletin board. This becomes a real contest each week and I believe our players strive quite hard to earn the award.

Defensively we choose a Hitter of the Week and he receives similar accolades. A Hit is scored when one of our defenders records a hard enough blow with his shoulder to jolt an offensive man hard enough for it to show in our film. We do not count blows delivered with the forearm or helmet, and we forbid this type of play. In addition, we keep a record of the number of individual and assisted tackles each player executes. An Individual tackle is one made alone, and an Assist occurs when a defender gets his shoulder on the ball carrier before he hits the ground. We forbid shoulder hits once the ball carrier is down. We also keep a record of Vicinity of the Tackle which we count when a defender is in position to tackle the ball carrier if he had continued on. We feel this encourages pursuit. Our goals are 10 RBI and 50 hits a game.

In summation, we feel the players look forward to some form of grading system as long as it emphasizes achievement and does not involve our staff in a multitude of paper work.

13

The Coach's Personal and Public Relations

A coach's work isn't confined just to the athletic field. He has many obligations other than that of turning out an athletic team. He has off-the-field responsibilities to his players and assistants, fellow coaches, his school, the alumni, the press, and the general public. He is likely to be an important person in his community, which makes it very important that he live up to his responsibilities as a citizen. He has an obligation to himself to live cleanly, deal fairly, work faithfully at his job, uphold the traditions of clean, hard play and good sportsmanship—and maintain his self-respect. He has a tremendous responsibility to the game itself.

Relations with Assistant Coaches

A coach should work hard to gain the respect and confidence of his own staff. Loyalty is a two-way street and begins with the head coach.

He should encourage suggestions from staff members and should treat all suggestions or ideas with respect; and if the idea is rejected, the originator should be told why it will not fit in with the plans; but he should not allow long-winded discussions to cause time to be wasted.

He should hire men who are willing to work as hard as he is and who are dedicated to the game of football. An assistant who does not place the team first, above all else will weaken the program. Assistant coaches must be selected with this in mind and they must be willing to work around the clock if need be.

In return, the head coach must back his assistants in the matter of dealings with personnel. Once he sets his policies, the head coach must have confidence in his assistants' ability to handle problems.

The assistants should be allowed to coach on the field. The head coach should designate how he wants the various techniques of play taught, make certain his staff fully understands what he wants taught, and then let them teach on the field, making corrections on the field in private or off the field in meetings. It is very important that the players have confidence in the assistant coaches' teaching ability.

The head coach should clearly define the duties of each assistant and make certain each coach understands his functions. Some of the categories designated on the field should be: offensive coach (usually coaching the backfield), offensive line coach (blocking), offensive passing game (receivers mainly), defensive coach (usually coaching linebackers and ends), defensive line coach, defensive backfield coach, and a coach in charge of setting up and handling opponent's offense and defense. Naturally, the size of the staff will determine how many of these categories overlap.

Off the field, certain coaches should be in charge of equipment, injuries, off-season training, movie exchange, and filling, off-season employment, scouting, and, in college or junior college, recruiting.

In addition, each assistant coach should be responsible for the non-football activities of a group of players. This can be divided by positions or any other way, but the key is personal contact with each player at least once a week. The main concern, of course, is the player's academic progress, plus, of course, any personal problems the player may want to discuss.

Relations with the Players

The relationship between a coach and his players should be one of closeness both on and off the field. Most coaches are interested in their players not only as athletes but also as students. It is natural for a player to feel free to bring any of his problems to some member of the coaching staff whenever he feels the need of help or advice, and the coach should be ready to help on any problem that comes up. One of the rewards of coaching is the opportunity of getting to know, and occasionally to help, a fine group of young men year after year.

The coach must sell his program to his players. This is especially true at the high school level, where many underclassmen are hesitant to turn out for the team because of lack of exposure to the game. One of the best methods I know is to show a genuine interest in the boy's future. At times we at the collegiate level find a boy who appears to possess the mental and physical capabilities to become a fine collegiate player, but who has not taken the required course of study in high school to qualify for college entrance. The high-school coach can aid his players by making certain they progress scholastically if they are so inclined.

The high-school and the junior-college coach can also further his program by informing collegiate coaches of his top prospects. Many high-school coaches have a detailed roster of their squad, which lists size, speed, honors, etc. Some leagues meet and formulate a list of the top players in the league and send these to the four-year institution. If the high-school coach takes the time to sit down and discuss the future with his players, he not only promotes his program, but greatly enhances the chance of his players to receive a college scholarship.

In dealing with his players on the field, the coach must be himself, and never attempt to emulate someone else. The coach must find the delicate balance between closeness and familiarity. The coach should expect loyalty and respect from his players, but he must earn it. Perhaps the best way is to be firm, but fair. He must never let personal likes or dislikes influence his judgment of an individual as a player. He should never make promises he cannot keep and, above all, should never administer threats he does not intend to keep.

Training rules vary from coach to coach, but three things a coach should never tolerate are lying, cheating, and alibying. Training rules must be honored, because if a player cannot make a sacrifice off the field, he is very likely to find it infinitely more difficult on the field, especially in the fourth quarter of a tight game.

The coach should show no favoritism to an individual or group. Special privileges should not be granted. Each player must feel the coach is as interested in him as in the next fellow; but, he must remember that each player is a separate individual and must be dealt with in a different manner. *Individual differences* is a canned phrase, but it especially holds true for football players. Part of the coach's job is to ascertain who performs best with a pat on the back and who with a verbal admonishing. Each player wants to perform to the best of his ability, and it is up to the coach to bring this out. All other factors being equal, the coach that can bring out the best in his players will win with regularity.

Players at the high school and collegiate levels are in school to obtain an education, and the coach should remember this. He

THE COACH'S PERSONAL AND PUBLIC RELATIONS

should not require a player's presence if it means missing a class. Road trips are an exception to this, of course.

In attempting to aid our players in their pursuit of an education, we maintain a counseling contact once a week and also keep a comprehensive record of their academic progress. Each coach keeps a card on each of the players in his group (Fig. 13-1).

NAME				YEAR		
Last	First	Middle		DORM ___ FRAT ___ APT ___		
USC ADDRESS				PHONE		
HOME ADDRESS				PHONE		
PARENTS or GUARDIAN						
USC ACADEMIC RECORD: UNITS ___ UP/DOWN ___ GPA ___						
MAJOR						
COURSE	TIME		INSTRUCTOR	5 WEEKS	10 WEEK	FINAL
1						
2						
3						
4						
5						
6						

Fig. 13-1. Academic Progress Card.

Each coach also has in his file the Cumulative Scholastic Record of his players, and it is his job to keep this up to date (Fig. 13-2).

In addition, at the five-week and ten-week period of our semester we send a Progress Report to each instructor to check on the grades, attitude, and attendance of each man (Fig. 13-3).

We do not attempt to run our players' life off the field, but we do feel that any help we can render that will aid the athlete to better himself academically will benefit him directly and, in return, indirectly help our program. We take pride in the knowledge that a high percentage of our players graduate from our university, and we try to help all we can along this line. One of the great services a coach can perform is to encourage his players to excel in the classroom.

NAME...
　　　　First　　　　　　　　　　　　　　　　　　　　　　　　　　　　　　　　　Last

FRESHMAN
FALL

Course No.	Instructor	Units	Grade	Gr. Pts.	Abs.

SPRING

Units Attempted.............................　　Gr. Pts..............................

　　　Passed...............................　　IE.......................................

　　　Failed................................　　IW......................................

JUNIOR
FALL

Course No.	Instructor	Units	Grade	Gr. Pts.	Abs.

SPRING

Units Attempted.............................　　Gr. Pts..............................

　　　Passed...............................　　IE.......................................

　　　Failed................................　　IW......................................

Fig. 13–2. Cumulative Scholastic Record.

CUMULATIVE SCHOLASTIC RECORD

SOPHOMORE
FALL

Course No.	Instructor	Units	Grade	Gr. Pts.	Abs.

SPRING

Units Attempted............................ Gr. Pts..

Passed............................... IE..

Failed............................... IW...

SENIOR
FALL

Course No.	Instructor	Units	Grade	Gr. Pts.	Abs.

SPRING

Units Attempted............................ Gr. Pts..

Passed............................... IE..

Failed............................... IW...

PROGRESS REPORT FALL ☐ 5th ☐ 10th ☐
SPRING ☐ 5th ☐ 10th ☐

Student	Course	Hour	Day	Units	Professor

Grade					Attitude			
A	B	C	D	F	Excellent	Good	Poor	Absences

Remarks: (Any comments which might better enable us to help this student help himself would be appreciated):

(Please return to the Department of Athletics)

Signature (Professor)

10-63—5M—C 4

Fig. 13–3. Progress Report.

Relations with School Officials

The coach owes a great deal of loyalty to the school that he is serving and also to the faculty and administrative officers with whom he is associated. If a coach cannot give his loyalty to all concerned, then he should seek another job, because the coach and player alike need to believe in their institution. More important than anything else, a coach must carry on his sport in such a way that it may rightfully be called a part of the educational process.

The American Football Coaches Association approved a code of ethics, and Article II, on the coach's responsibility, states:

THE COACH'S RESPONSIBILITY TO THE INSTITUTION

Section 1: The Coach as an Educator. The function of the coach is to educate students through participation in the game of football. This primary and basic function must never be disregarded.

Section 2: The Coach and the Administration. Because of the unique niche which the football coach holds in the educational organization, it is highly important that he support the administration in all policies, rules and regulations which may from time to time be activated. Where differences of opinion develop, these should be discussed behind closed doors, and not aired through public press and radio.

THE COACH'S PERSONAL AND PUBLIC RELATIONS

Section 3: The Coach and the Athletic Council. By whatever name the governing body of the school athletic program may be known, the coach should lend his training and experience to this body in the solution of football problems. He should constantly be alert to see that the game for which he is responsible is being properly conducted and promoted. Where differences of opinion arise, and the Council over-rides a coach's judgment discretion should be exercised in airing or discussing such differences outside of Council meetings.

Section 4: The Coach and the Athletic Director. Where the coach is not the Athletic Director, it is important that a harmonious relationship exist between the two. The coach should feel free to suggest and initiate any action which has to do with the conduct or improvement of the football program. Controversial matters should be discussed on a friendly basis, but once final decisions have been reached they should be accepted and given complete support by the coach.

Section 5: The Coach and the Admissions Office. Every coach should have the right and privilege of recommending qualified students for admission. Official student records and transcripts should never pass through the coach's office, nor should a coach ever attempt to bring pressure to bear upon an admissions officer to admit an applicant merely because he possesses exceptional athletic ability.

Section 6: The Coach and Eligibility Requirements. Participation in interschool athletics is generally predicated upon the individual student's fulfillment of established rules and regulations. Every coach should be thoroughly acquainted with these rules and regulations. He should assume responsibility for their observance and enforcement in co-operation with the school official who has been delegated this responsibility. Any attempt by a coach to circumvent eligibility rules, or to use ineligible players, shall be considered unethical conduct. Nor shall a coach be a party to exerting pressure of any sort on members of the faculty for the purpose of influencing player grades in academic work.

Section 7: The Coach and Scholarship. One of the coach's fundamental responsibilities must be to inspire his players to achieve academic success; not only to make good grades but secure professional training and graduate with honors.

The coach must maintain cordial and cooperative relations with the school administration and with the faculty. These groups are running the school and their authority is to be respected. However, he should insist that they show him the same consideration. The school board, the athletic council, and the president set the policies, and these policies should be followed.

It is not difficult to develop cordial relations with the administration and faculty, as they generally are as interested as you in seeing their school well represented. By talking with them at lunch and school functions and sharing ideas, the coach can promote friendship and understanding between school officials and himself.

Relations with Booster Groups

Booster organizations can be of value to athletics if they have proper objectives. It would be unethical for coaches to use such groups to attempt to defeat or obstruct administrative or institutional athletic controls, or to encourage violation of established rules and regulations in order to strengthen existing athletic programs. It is likewise unethical for coaches to make demands, financial or otherwise, upon such organizations, that are not in keeping with the letter and spirit of existing controls, or in any other manner to misuse such strength and power in violation of accepted rules and regulations.

Booster clubs are of tremendous value if properly handled. The reason many schools do not have booster clubs is because the administrators are afraid it may enter into the operation of the school plant. The only place where this happens is in the case of weak leadership in the school in the first place. Where there is strong school leadership, it is generally recognized and appreciated by a booster club because of the club's closeness to the school.

Here is a brief organizational plan for high-school booster groups. The group should be for adults; men alone; or men and women. It should meet once a week, usually as soon after a game as possible, which makes Monday night the best meeting night. The club should have a president, vice president, secretary and treasurer, and executive board. All past presidents should become members of the executive board. Each past president or executive should have a certain function to perform yearly for the club. The president is selected so that it is possible to be sure the man who will lead the club is familiar with the organization and is willing to work. The secretary and treasurer hold their jobs as long as the executive board desires. The presidents should be as representative a group as possible, from various clubs and industries and jobs around the city. In this manner they can get other men interested from the same clubs and industries and jobs around the city. In this manner they can get other men interested from the same clubs and industries as members in the organization; and, of course, they should be loyal to the school and coaching staff.

The coach has basic responsibilities in the development of a booster group. The coach plays an important role in creating enthusiasm which is needed for the success of the club. Since this booster club is to help the coach, it is necessary for him to do everything possible to keep the club alive. The program itself should be short and as interesting as possible concerning the last game and the game coming up. The coach should diagram and explain different situations involved in the game. Probably the most interesting points to talk about concern the players themselves and some of the interesting events that went on during the week.

At the collegiate level booster clubs are usually controlled and run by alumni groups, but the coach still has a responsibility to show an enthusiastic interest in the groups. Some of our most enjoyable social outings are spent with loyal alumni and friends of the university.

Relations with Men of the News Media

The responsibility of coaches to accredited writers and radio and television commentators is to give them news about their team and players. They should be treated with courtesy, honesty, and respect. Derogatory and misleading statements should be avoided. Direct questions should be answered honestly in a straight-forward manner. Coaches should take responsibility for and stress the importance of ethical procedures in teaching their players how to act in player-interviews, in the best interests of all sports. Coaches shouldn't stress the negative aspects of their sport with the press, radio, or television. No good purpose can be gained by emphasizing such matters.

A coach must reach the public in order to be completely successful, and the best method of doing this is through newspapers, radio, and television. First a coach must keep these people informed of his players and sport. High-school coaches should find someone interested in sports to keep the news media informed of what is going on in the athletic department. If the coach can't find a person to do this job, then it is up to him to do it himself. Collegiate institutions employ an athletic publicity man, but the coach must still be available at any time to discuss his team with members of the news media. In order to help the press, it is good to have a publicity folder giving pertinent facts about the team, the coaches, and the athletic program in general.

The coach should consider the news media as a very important factor in his favor and not a necessary evil. Good news releases will create player, parent, and fan interest, sell tickets, and be of help to the coach. It is very true that good publicity may not win any games, but it will certainly make it more pleasant if he happens to lose one.

Relations with the General Public

When a person accepts a coaching job, he becomes a public figure, for many spectators follow his fortunes and his name will be often mentioned in the newspapers. His actions are of public interest, and, similar to other members in the teaching profession, he must maintain certain standards of conduct.

The coach should live with, and associate with, respectable people. He should join service clubs and keep his downtown contacts. Speech-making is one of his big obligations, and he should always be ready to deliver one on any occasion.

The coach owes a direct and considerable obligation to the public. The public pays part of the coach's salary and keeps the athletic program alive. In return for this, they have a right to see a well played, hard fought, and honest athletic contest. The coach is obligated to field a team that will realize its maximum possibilities, whether they be great or small. Also every coach holds a sacred trust to stamp out crookedness, bribery, and commercial exploitation wherever they may be found.

Above all, the coach is a direct representative of the institution he serves, and at times he will be the only representative that will be judged by the public. He owes it to his school to keep his conduct above reproach at all times.

Index

Academic Progress Card, 227
Administration, coaches relations with, 230–31
Alumni groups, 233
American Football Coaches Association, 230–31
Awards and prizes, 222–23
   Blocker of the Week, 223
   Hitter of the Week, 223

B-Star formation, 12, 13
Backs
   F-back (F), 6
   numbering, 16
   R-back (R), 6
   Z-back (A), 7
Banana Pattern, passing attack, 76–77
Belly play, 31
Belly Strongside—34 Belly, 48–49
   assignments, 48
   coaching points, 48–49
Belly Weakside—35 Belly, 50–51
   assignments, 50
   coaching points, 50–51
Blast play, 31
Blast Strongside—22 Blast, 55–57
   assignments, 55
   coaching points, 55–56
Blast Weakside—23 Blast, 57–58
   assignments, 57–58
   coaching points, 58
Blocker of the Week, 223
Blockers, meeting, 124–25, 139–40
Blocking, 20–30
   area block, 27
   assignments, 20–21
   bump block, 26
   calls, 28–30
      eagle blocking, 29
      gap blocking, 30
      George blocking, 30
      pigeon blocking, 29
      Roman blocking, 29
      solid blocking, 30
      Trojan blocking, 29
      X blocking, 20
   chop block, 26
   close block, 24–25
   crackback block, 26–27
   cut-off block, 23
   double-team, 28
   drills, 106–107
   drive blocks, 22–23
   far-shoulder block, 24
   fill block, 28
   influence block, 26
   junction block, 27–28
   numbering, 20
      5-3 defense, 22
      6-1 defense, 21
      50 defense, 21
      60 defense, 21
   option block, 23–24
   over block, 25
   pin block, 24
   punts, 178–79
   reverse block, 24–25
   rules, 16
   seal block, 23
   types of, 22–28
   wall-off block, 25–26
Booster groups
   development of, 232
   organization plan, 232
   relation with, 232–33
Boot Strong Pass, 99–100
   assignments, 99
   coaching points, 99–100
Bounce on Flow Away, linebacker play, 150–52

C-Gee formation, 10
Cadence, 12–15
Calling plays
   cadence, 12–14
   hole numbering, 15–19
   method of, 14–15

Calls
  blocking, 28–30
  defensive play, 113
Center (C), 5–6
  requirements, 5–6
Check Pattern, passing attack, 79
"Close" positions, 11
Coaches and coaching, 224–34
  Academic Progress Card, 227
  academic record of players, 226–27
  assistant, 224–25
  Cumulative Scholastic Record, 227–28
  interest in academic progress of players, 226–27
  loyalty and respect, 226
  obligations to the public, 234
  off-the-field responsibilities, 224
  personal and public relations, 224–34
  relations with alumni groups, 233
  relations with assistant coaches, 224–25
  relations with booster groups, 232–33
  relations with news men, 233
  relations with players, 225–30
  relations with school officials, 230–31
  responsibility to the institution, 230–31
  rewards of coaching, 225
  selling program to players, 225
  speech-making by, 234
Conditioning and training, 199–201
  general rules and policies, 202–203
  player personnel policy, 202
  summer program, 199, 200
  weight-training program, 199–201
Corner Pattern, passing attack, 75
Counter play, 31
Cover Blue, 167–68
Cover Four, 163–65
Cover One, 156–58
Cover Prevent, 166
Cover Red, 167
Cover Three, 160–63
Cover Two, 158–59
Coverage
  kickoffs, 183
  man-for-man, 167–68
    Cover Blue, 167–68
    Cover Red, 167
  punts, 179–80
  zone, 156–66
Crash Charge, 118, 122
  middle guard, 115, 121–24
  tackles, 115–21
Crashing to the Near Back, 137
Crease Pattern, passing attack, 74
Cross Pattern, passing attack, 72
Cumulative Scholastic Record, 227–28

Defense, 113–88
  alignments, 113–14
  basic techniques, 124–29
    rushing the passer, 126–27
    Shiver and Pursuit, 125–26
    tackling, 127–28
  calls, 113
  Crash Charge, 118
  drills, 124–29; see also Drills
  end, 115
  end play, 130–43
    basic techniques and drills, 139–43
    Crashing to Near Back, 137
    Keying the End, 130–33
    Keying the QB, 133–35
    meeting blocker, 139–40
    pass defense—man-for-man, 143
    pass defense—zone, 141
    rushing the passer, 140
    shiver and pursuit, 140
    Shooting for the QB, 135–36
    Slanting Outside, 136–37
    tackling, 140
    technique vs. split end, 138–39
  fundamentals, 113–29
Defense
  linebacker plays, 144–55; see also Linebacker play
  meeting a blocker, 124–25, 139–40
  middle guard, 115, 121–24
    Crash Charge, 122
    Gap Charge, 124
    Read Charge, 121–22
    Slant Charge, 123
  objectives, 113
  onside kickoff, 185–87
  personnel, 114–15
  Read Charge, 115–17
  rover, 114
  scouting notes, 208, 219, 222
  secondary play, 115, 156–74
    basic techniques and drills, 169–74
    man-for-man coverages, 167–68
    zone coverages, 156–66
  strong backer, 115
  swing man, 114–15
  tackles, 115–21
    Crash Charge, 118
    Gap Charge, 121
    Slant Charge and Loop Charge, 118–20
    Strong Tackle—Slanting Inside, 118–19
    Weak Tackle—Looping Outside, 119–20
  weak backer, 115
Delay Pattern, passing attack, 71

INDEX

Draw (special running play), 65–67
  assignments, 65–66
  coaching points, 66–67
Drills
  defense, 124–29
    Machine-gun drill, 125, 140, 153
    McKay Drill, 128–29
    one-on-one, 125
    one-on-one drill—cut-off block, 125
    one-on-one pass-rush drill, 126
    Skate drill, 126, 153
    square drill for tackling, 128
    stance and get-off drill, 105
    three-on-one pass-rush drill, 127
  for ends, 140–43
    Machine-gun drill, 140
    Man drill, 142–43
    Patterns drill, 142
    Shield drill, 141–42
    Spot drill, 141–42
    To-Zone drill, 141
  linebackers, 152–55
    Machine-gun drill, 153
    pass defense—man-for-man, 155
    pass defense—zone, 155
    Plug and Rip drill, 154
    Plug drill, 154
    Skate drill, 153
    tackling drills, 155
  Machine-gun, 125, 140, 153
  offense, 105–9
    Bag-Blocking drill, 106
    Bag drill, 106
    Blocking drill, 106–7
    Double-Team drill, 109
    Half-line Drill—Strongside, 107–8
    Individual Pass Cut drill, 107–8
    Option and Keep drill, 107
    Stance and Get-off drill, 105
  secondary, 169–74
    Fill drill, 169, 171
    Hub Drill, 171–72
    Patterns Drill, 172–73
    Shield drill, 171
    Shuffle drill, 169–70
    Skate drill, 126, 153
    Spot Drill, 171
    tackling, 170
    To-Zone Drill, 141, 171
Drive play, 31
Drive Strongside—32 Drive, 51–53
  assignments, 51
  coaching points, 53
Drive Weakside—33 Drive, 53–55
  assignments, 53
  coaching points, 53–54

East formation, 12
80 Series Passes, 86–93
  assignments, 86
  coaching points, 87–93
83 Pass, 94–95
  assignments, 94
  coaching points, 94–95
88 Pass, 96–97
  assignments, 96
  coaching points, 96–97
89 Pass, 97–98
  assignments, 97
  coaching points, 97–98
End play, defensive, 130–43
  basic techniques and drills, 139–43
    meeting a blocker, 139–40
    pass defense—man-for-man, 143
    pass defense—zone, 141–43
    rushing the passer, 140
    shiver and pursuit, 140
    tackling, 140
  Crashing to the Near Back, 137
  Keying the End, 130–33
  Keying the QB, 133–35
  meeting a blocker, 139–40
  shooting for the QB, 135–36
  Slanting Outside, 136–37
  technique vs. split end, 138–39
Ends
  drills
    Machine-gun, 140
    Man drill, 142–43
    Patterns drill, 142
    Shield drill, 141–42
    Spot drill, 141–42
    To-Zone drill, 141
  split end (X), 4
  tight end (Y), 4

F-Back (F), 6
Faculty, coaches relations with, 230–31
Fan Pattern, passing attack, 78
"Far" positions, 11
Field goals, 186–88
  protection, 187
  technique, 186–88
Flag Pattern, passing attack, 76
"Fly" motion by T-back, 16, 19
Formations, 8–12
  B-Star, 12, 13
  C-Gee, 10–11
  calls, 8–15
  East, 12
  Gee formation, 8
  hole numbering, 15–19
  huddle procedure, 12–13, 14
  learning, 14–15

Formations—*Continued*
  Pro-Gee formation, 9
  Pro-Star, 12–13
  Right, 11
  Split-Gee, 9–10
  split positions, 10
  Star, 12
  Strong-Gee, 9–10
  Strong-Right, 11
  strongside to left, 8–9
    haw formation, 9
  strongside to right, 8
44 Power, 16
  from Split-Star formation, 18

Gap Charge, 121
  middle guard, 124
Gee formation
  hole numbering, 15
  strongside to the right, 8
  24 Power from, 16
Green 24, play-action passes, 79–83
  assignments, 79
  coaching points, 79–83
Green 25, play-action passes, 83–86
  assignments, 83
  coaching points, 83–86
Guards
  strong guard (SG), 5
  weak guard (WG), 5

Haw formation, Strongside to the left, 9
Hitch Pattern, passing attack, 70
Hitter of the Week, 223
Hole numbering, 15–19
Huddle procedure, 12–13, 14

Interceptions, 69
Isometric exercises, 199

Keep play, 31
Keep Strongside—34 Belly Keep, 40–42
  assignments, 40–41
  coaching points, 42
Keep Weakside—35 Belly Keep, 42–44
  assignments, 42
  coaching points, 43–44
Keying the End, end play, 130–33
Keying the QB, end play, 133–35
Kicking, 177–88
  defensing the onside kickoff, 185–86
  kickoff returns, 184–85
    Wedge Return—Middle, 185–86
    Wedge Return—Right, 184–85
  kickoffs, 182–84
    coverage, 183
    onside kickoff, 184
    responsibilities, 183

P.A.T. and field goal, 186–88
punt returns, 180–82
  responsibilities, 181–82
punts, 177–80
  blocking assignments, 178–79
  coverage, 179–80
  safety, 188
  scouting notes, 209
Kickoff return, 184–85
  Wedge Return—Left, 184
  Wedge Return—Middle, 184–86
  Wedge Return—Right, 184–85
Kickoffs, 182–84
  coverage, 183
  onside, 184
    defensing, 185–87
  responsibilities, 183

Left formation, hole numbering, 15
Linebacker play, 144–55
  basic techniques and drills, 152–55
    Machine-gun drill, 153
    meeting a blocker, 153
    pass defense—man-for-man, 155
    pass defense—zone, 155
    Patterns drill, 155
    Plug and Rip drill, 154
    Plug drill, 154
    plugging and bouncing, 154
    shiver and pursuit, 153
    tackling drills, 155
  Bounce on Flow Away, 150–52
  importance of, 144
  Plugging on Flow, 144–47
  Ripping the Guard, 148–49
  Scraping Off on Flow, 148
  Shooting the Gap, 150
Look Pattern, passing attack, 71

Machine-gun drill, 125, 140, 153
McKay drill, 128–29
Man-for-man coverages, 167–68
  Cover Blue, 167–68
  Cover Red, 167
Man-for-man pass defense
  defensive end plays, 141–43
  linebacker drills, 155
  secondary play, 172–74

"Near" positions, 11
Newspapers, coach's relations with, 233
90 Series Passes, 104
Numbering
  backs, 16
  holes, 15–19

Offense
  blocking, 20–31

INDEX

assignments, 20–21
calls, 28–30
types of blocks, 22–28
cadence, 13–15
drills, 105–9; see also Drills
formations, 8–12
hole numbering, 15–19
huddle procedure, 12–13
passing attack, 69–104
    pass patterns, 70–79
    pass plays, 70
    play-action passes, 79–98
    roll-out passes off inside fakes, 99–104
personnel, 3–8
philosophy, 3
running attack, 31–68; see also Running attack
running plays, 31–68
scouting notes, 208–9
Option play, 31
Option Strongside—16 Option, 37–39
assignments, 38
coaching points, 38–39
Option Weakside—17 Option, 39–40
Out and Up Pattern, passing attack, 76
Out Pattern, passing attack, 72

Pass defense
  man-for-man
    defensive end plays, 141–43
    linebacker drills, 155
    secondary play, 172–74
  zone
    defensive end plays, 141–43
    linebacker drills, 155
    secondary play, 171–72
Passers, rushing, 140
Passing attack, 69–104
  calls, 70
  dropback passes, 104
  patterns, 70–79
    Banana Pattern, 76–77
    Check Pattern, 79
    Corner Pattern, 25
    Crease Pattern, 74
    Cross Pattern, 72–73
    Delay Pattern, 71
    Fan Pattern, 78
    Flag Pattern, 76
    Flare Pattern, 78
    Hitch Pattern, 70
    Look Pattern, 71
    Out and Up Pattern, 76

    Out Pattern, 72
    Post Pattern, 75
    Quick Pattern, 71
    Recon Pattern, 72
    Seam Pattern, 74
    Snake Patterns, 73
    Squirrel Pattern, 73
    Swing Pattern, 77–78
    Up Pattern, 74
    Wheel Pattern, 77
  play-action passes, 70, 79–98
    80 Series Passes, 86–93
    83 Pass, 94–95
    88 Pass, 96–97
    89 Pass, 97–98
    Green 24, 79–83
    Green 25, 83–86
  pass plays, 70
  roll-out passes off inside fakes, 70, 99–104
    Boot Strong, 99–100
    90 Series Passes, 104
    79 Pass, 101–2
    Waggle Strong, 100–101
    Waggle Weak, 103–4
  sprint-out series, 70
  standard dropback pass, 70
  statistics on, 69
  threat of interception, 69
Philosophy, offensive, 3
"Pickle" positions, 11
Pitch Strongside—28 Pitch, 64–65
  assignments, 64
  coaching points, 64–65
Players
  academic progress, 226–27
  coach's relations with, 225–30
  general rules and policies, 202–3
  grading and analyzing, 222–23
  personnel policy, 202
  Progress Report, 227, 230
Plays, naming, 16
Plugging on Flow, 144–47
Point-after-touchdown, 186–88
Port formation, 12
Post Pattern, passing attack, 75
Power play, 31
Power Strongside—24 Power, 31–34
  assignments, 33
  coaching point, 33–34
Power Weakside—25 Power, 34–36
  assignments, 34
  coaching points, 36–37
Practice and training, 191–203
  conditioning and training, 199–201
    summer program, 199, 200
    weight-training program, 199–201

Practice and training—*Continued*
  rules and policies, 202–3
  schedules, 191–99
    early-season, 197–99
    game-week, 191–97
Pro-Gee formation, 9
Pro-Star formation, 12–13
Pro-Star 44 Power, 16
Progress Report, 227, 230
Public, coach's relations with, 234
Publicity, need for good, 233
Punts, 177–80
  blocking assignments, 178–79
  coverage, 179–80
    lineman, 179
    personal protector and kicker, 179
    up-back, 179
  returns, 180–82

Quarterbacks (QB), 7–8
  basic moves, 7–8
  defensive, 144
  requirements, 7
Quick Pattern, passing attack, 71

R-back (R), 6
Radio and television, coach's relations with, 233
Read Charge, 115–17
  middle guard, 121–22
Recon Pattern, passing attack, 72
Right formation, 11
  24 Power from, 17
Right 44 Power, 16
Ripping the Guard, 148–49
Road trips, 227
Roll-out passes off inside fakes, 99–104
Running attacks, 31–68
  belly play, 31
  Belly Strongside—34 Belly, 48–49
    assignments, 48
    coaching points, 48–49
  Belly Weakside—35 Belly, 50–51
    assignments, 50
    coaching points, 50–51
  blast play, 31
  Blast Strongside—22 Blast, 55–57
    assignments, 55
    coaching points, 55–56
  Blast Weakside—23 Blast, 57–58
    assignments, 57–58
    coaching points, 58
  Counter Strongside—44 Counter, 46–48
    assignments, 46–47
    coaching points, 48
  drive play, 31

Drive Strongside—32 Drive, 51–53
  assignments, 51
  coaching points, 53
Drive Weakside—33 Drive, 53–55
  assignments, 53
  coaching points, 53–54
keep play, 31
Keep Strongside—34 Belly Keep, 40–42
  assignments, 40–41
  coaching points, 42
Keep Weakside—35 Belly Keep, 42–44
  assignments, 42
  coaching points, 43
option play, 31
Option Strongside—16 Option, 37–39
Option Weakside—17 Option, 39–40
  assignments, 40
  coaching points, 40
power play, 31
Power Strongside—24 Power, 31–34
  assignments, 33
  coaching points, 33–34
Power Weakside—25 Power, 34–38
  assignments, 34
  coaching points, 36–37
running plays, 31–61
special plays, 62–68
  Draw, 65–67
  Pitch Strongside—28 Pitch, 64–65
  Toss Weakside—39 Toss, 63–64
  Weak-Tackle Trap, 67–68
sweep play, 31
Sweep Strongside—48 Sweep, 44–46
  assignments, 44
  coaching points, 45–46
trap play, 31
Traps Strongside—30 and 40 Trap, 58–61
  assignments, 58–59
  coaching points, 60–61
Trap Weakside—31 Trap, 61
  assignments, 61
  coaching points, 61

Safety, 188
  intentional, 188
  unintentional, 188
Scouting, 204–23
  analyzing opponent, 210–14
  analyzing own team, 214–22
  chart on defenses, 219, 222
  cards for, 207
    items to be written on, 207–8
  defensive analysis sheet, 214–15
  during warm-up period, 205
  formation analysis
    passing, 213

INDEX 241

runs, 210–11
forms, 205
  on cards, 207–8
  Formation Analysis sheets, 211, 213, 218–19
  Individual Game Down and Distance, 214–16
  Offensive Analysis Sheet, 215, 217
  Offensive Play Analysis sheet, 218, 220
  grading and analyzing individuals, 222–23
  importance, 204
  notes, 208
    defense, 208
    kicking game, 209
    offense, 208–9
  personnel, 209
  schedule, 205
  staff, 204
  training scouts, 205
  two scouts for each game, 205
  use of motion pictures, 204, 207
Seam Pattern, passing attack, 74
Secondary play, defensive, 156–74
  basic techniques and drills, 169–74
    Fill Drill, 169, 171
    Hub drill, 171–72
    initial move, 169
    pass defense—man-for-man, 172–74
    pass defense—zone, 171–72
    Patterns drill, 172–73
    run defense, 169–70
    Shuffle drill, 169–70
    tackling, 170
  man-for-man coverages, 167–68
    Cover Blue, 167–68
    Cover Red, 167
  zone coverages, 156–66
    Cover Four, 163 65
    Cover One, 156–58
    Cover Prevent, 166
    Cover Three, 160–63
    Cover Two, 158–59
Schedules, practice, 191–99
  early-season, 197–99
  game-week, 191–92
    Sunday, 192
    Monday, 192
    Tuesday, 193–95
    Wednesday, 195
    Thursday, 196
    Friday, 196
    Saturday, 196–97
Scraping Off on Flow, 148
79 Pass, roll-out pass, 101–2

Shiver and pursuit, 125–26, 140
  linebacker play, 153
Shooting for the QB, end play, 135–36
Shooting the Gap, linebacker play, 150
Signal calling, 144
Slant Charge, 123
Slant Charge and Loop Charge, 118–20
Slanting Outside, end play, 136–37
Snake Pattern, passing attack, 73
Split end (X), 4
  requirements, 4
  technique vs., 138–39
Split-Gee formation, 9–10
Split positions, 10
Split-Star formation, 44 Power from, 18
Squirrel Pattern, passing attack, 72
Stance, 14
Star formation, 12
  24 Power from, 17
Strong-Gee formation, 9–102
Strong guard (SG), 5
Strong-Right formation, 11
Strong Tackle—Slanting Inside, 118–19
Strong tackles (ST), 5
Sweep play, 31
Sweep Strongside—48 Sweep, 44–46
  assignments, 44
  coaching points, 45–46
Swing Pattern, passing attack, 77–78

T-back
  "Fly" motion by, 16, 19
  normal motion by, 18
Tackles
  Crash Charge, 118
  Read Charge, 115–17
  Slant Charge and Loop Charge, 118–20
  strong tackles (ST), 5
  weak tackles (WT), 4–5
Tackling, 127–28
  defensive end plays, 140
Tight end (Y), 4
  requirements, 4
Toss Weakside—39 Toss, 63–64
  assignments, 63
  coaching points, 63–64
Training program, 199–201
  rules, 226
Trap play, 31
Trap Strongside—30 and 40 Trap, 58–61
  assignments, 58–59
  coaching points, 60–61
Trap Weakside—30 Trap, 61
  assignments, 61
  coaching points, 61

24 Power, 16
  Power Strongside, 31–32

Up Pattern, passing attack, 74

Waggle Strong, roll-out pass, 100–101
Waggle Weak, roll-out pass, 103–4
Weak guard (WG), 5
Weak tackle (WT), 4–5
Weak Tackle–Looping Outside, 119–20
Weak-Tackle Trap, 67–68
  assignments, 67
  coaching points, 67–68
Wedge Return–Left, 184
Wedge Return–Middle, 184–86

Wedge Return–Right, 184–85
Weight-training program, 199–201
West formation, 12
Wheel Pattern, passing attack, 76–77

Z-back (Z), 7
Zone coverages, 156–66
  Cover Four, 163–65
  Cover One, 156–58
  Cover Prevent, 166
  Cover Three, 160–63
  Cover Two, 158–59
Zone pass defense
  defensive end plays, 141–43
  linebacker drills, 155
  secondary play, 171–72